"Wilhelm Röpke was one of the pivotal figures in the twentieth-century intellectual fight against totalitarianism. At a time when the tide had turned in philosophy, social science, and practical politics toward technocratic social engineering by unchecked government planners, Röpke stood tall and defended not only the free economy, but the free society. He championed Western civilization in its ethical and moral foundations as well as its legal and political institutions. As the outstanding introduction to this volume by Professor Stefan Kolev details, not all of his positions were fully consistent nor was his behavior with regard to others always impeccable. Röpke was a man, and like all of us imperfect, but his curiosity and intellectual courage are worthy of our study, and his writings have much to teach us today as we find ourselves grappling once again with challenges to the liberal order both from within and without. This volume is a great place for students of society to start to learn about the humane economy and its relevance for the twenty-first century."

PETER BOETTKE
University Professor of Economics & Philosophy
George Mason University

"Wilhelm Röpke was one of the most important economists and social philosophers of the twentieth century. This new anthology brings together selections from some of his most important books and essays, spanning the many decades of his productive professional career. It offers not just an excellent overview of Röpke's views on a wide variety of economic, social, and political themes, but also serves as a guide-book to better understand the public policy issues of our own times, because of the timeless qualities to be found in Ropke's analysis of the human condition, and his vision of a humane society that assures freedom and prosperity for all. If you've never read Röpke before, you are in for a wonderful intellectual treat. If you have read him before, you will find that in rereading through these selections, his original and fresh insights on every page will again make it all worthwhile."

RICHARD EBELING
BB&T Professor of Ethics and Free Enterprise Leadership
The Citadel

"Wilhelm Röpke not only produced the outlines of a humane economy, but he was also the embodiment of a humane economist. In these useful selections from his works, one encounters the elements of what is called fusionism: an understanding of free markets and a sturdy devotion to Western civilization. Where else does one find Ludwig von Mises, F. A. Hayek, and even Murray Rothbard, juxtaposed with G. K. Chesterton, Hilaire Belloc, and Christopher Dawson? Röpke is truly the complete American-style conservative."

William F. Campbell
Emeritus Professor of Economics
Louisiana State University

"Dan Hugger has compiled a captivating Röpke reader with carefully selected and annotated texts and an excellent introduction by Stefan Kolev. The selections and introduction reveal an economist who was not only one of the formative figures of the German economic order after the dictatorship of National Socialism, but who with his sharp eye for the political, legal, and cultural framework, as well as for the moral and religious foundations of a free economic and social order, was also one of the great social theorists of the twentieth century. This anthology succeeds in presenting Röpke in the tradition of great liberal conservatives such as Edmund Burke, Alexis de Tocqueville, and Lord Acton."

Manfred Spieker
Professor of Christian Social Sciences
Institute of Catholic Theology
University of Osnabrück

"I highly recommend *The Humane Economist: A Wilhelm Röpke Reader*. Röpke's recognition of the necessity of a strong moral and religious framework for a free society needs to be more widely known and understood. This fine anthology brings together extracts from his most important works, and it would work well as an undergraduate text and as an introduction to Röpke's thought for the intelligent reader."

Andrew V. Abela
Dean, Busch School of Business
The Catholic University of America

The Humane Economist

A WILHELM RÖPKE READER

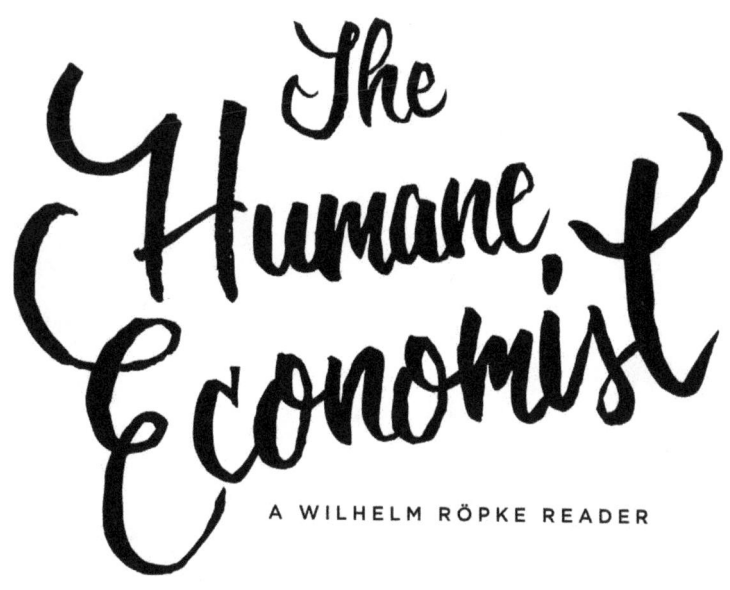

A WILHELM RÖPKE READER

EDITED BY DANIEL J. HUGGER

INTRODUCTION BY STEFAN KOLEV

ACTON INSTITUTE

Copyright © 2019 by Acton Institute

All rights reserved. No part of this publication may be reproduced, stored in a retrieval system, or transmitted in any form or by any means, including electronic, mechanical, photocopying, recording, or otherwise without the prior permission of the publisher.

ISBN 978-1-942503-51-4 (paperback)
ISBN 978-1-942503-53-8 (ebook)

Cover image is a derivative of "Wilhelm Röpke" by Ludwig Von Mises Institute, used under CC BY-SA 3.0.

ACTON INSTITUTE
98 E. Fulton
Grand Rapids, Michigan 49503
616.454.3080
www.acton.org

Interior composition: Judy Schafer
Cover: Scaturro Design

Contents

Preface   *vii*

Introduction: Wilhelm Röpke as a Student and Defender of Western Civilization   *xv*
    STEFAN KOLEV

1. The Economic Necessity of Freedom   1

2. The Problem   19

3. The Basic Data of Economics   37

4. The Conditions and Limits of the Market   61

5. Centrism and Decentrism   137

6. Liberalism and Christianity   187

7. The Place of Economics among the Sciences   201

8. Keynes and the Revolution in Economics: Economics Old, New, and True   225

9. A Value Judgment on Value Judgments   239

Appendix 1: A Glance at Economic History	263
Appendix 2: Marginal Utility: Foundation of Modern Economic Theory	267
Appendix 3: Economics and Ethics	275
Appendix 4: Costs as a Renunciation of Alternative Utilities	277
Subject Index	281

Preface

Nobel laureate Friedrich Hayek once warned "that the economist who is only an economist is likely to become a nuisance if not a positive danger."[1] No economist was so acutely aware of what a dangerous game he was playing as Wilhelm Röpke (1899–1966). It was in the trenches of Europe during World War I, where he and so many men of his generation fought what H. G. Wells ironically called "the war that will end war,"[2] that Röpke dedicated himself to what would become his life's work:

> To understand the reasons for the crisis, to learn what brought it to the stage of war, and to find if war indeed resolved anything, I determined to become an economist and a sociologist. Like all who are young, much of my curiosity must have been for its own sake, but since from the first my studies were directed toward

---

[1] F. A. Hayek, "The Dilemma of Specialization," in *Studies in Philosophy, Politics and Economics* (London: Routledge & Kegan Paul, 1967), 123.

[2] H. G. Wells, *The War That Will End War* (London: F. & C. Palmer, 1914).

the prevention of the thing I studied, a moral imperative lay behind them.[3]

Even at this early stage of inquiry, Röpke saw his project in holistic terms involving intersecting and interdependent spheres or *orden* that to be fully appreciated and understood scientifically must be examined in their economic, social, and moral dimensions. The combined commitments to mainline economic analysis,[4] the importance of social institutions, and the moral and religious framework of what Röpke calls the "classic-Christian heritage"[5] makes him a unique figure in the history of economics. As such he was ideally suited to avoid the dangers of economic reductionism, embodying the maxim: "life is economic; economics is not all of life."[6]

It may be precisely on account of these strengths that Wilhelm Röpke has been neglected in the present mainstream of the economics profession. Increasing specialization, reductionism, and "mathiness"[7] in academic economics is antithetical to Röpke's interdisciplinary and humanistic approach. While he was widely read and influential in his own day in the academy, the public square, and both classical liberal and conservative movements in Europe and the United States, since his death in 1966 Röpke's thought has been neglected until recently. There has been a recent revival of interest in Röpke among scholars

---

[3] Wilhelm Röpke, "The Economic Necessity of Freedom," in *The Humane Economist*, 3.

[4] See Matthew D. Mitchell and Peter J. Boettke, *Applied Mainline Economics: Bridging the Gap between Theory and Public Policy* (Arlington, VA: Mercatus Center at George Mason University, 2017).

[5] Wilhelm Röpke, "The Economic Necessity of Freedom," in *The Humane Economist*, 11.

[6] Ross B. Emmett, "Economics Is Not All of Life," *Econ Journal Watch* 11, no. 2 (May 2014): 148.

[7] Paul Romer, "Mathiness in the Theory of Economic Growth," *American Economic Review* 105, no. 5 (May 2015): 89–93.

of the history of economic thought that could serve as leaven to lift mainstream economics out of its present malaise.[8]

The purpose of this anthology is to introduce the contemporary reader to Wilhelm Röpke and his work exploring the nature of the organic social order in its economic, institutional, moral, and religious dimensions. The first selection, "The Economic Necessity of Freedom" (1959), is autobiographical. Röpke here lays out his personal history from his idyllic childhood to the horrors of World War I, his academic career, exile at the hands of the Nazi regime, and the then present crisis of the Cold War. Woven throughout the narrative is another tale, a tale of how his personal experiences shaped his research program as well as his religious and political commitments. It is a revelation of the man, his convictions, and the major currents of his thought.

The next two selections, "The Problem" and "The Basic Data of Economics," were taken from Röpke's introductory economics textbook, *Economics of the Free Society* (1963). "The Problem" explores the nature of economics as an inquiry into the spontaneous order that emerges from the market process. "The Basic Data of Economics" examines the moral foundation of exchanges we define as "economic," the concept of costs, and alternative institutional frameworks for economic coordination. The appendices included in this anthology, "A Glance at Economic History," "Marginal Utility: Foundation of Modern Economic Theory," "Economics and Ethics," and "Costs as a Renunciation of Alternative Utilities," were originally lengthy footnotes in these two selections from *Economics of the Free Society*. These notes explore the history of economics in general, the marginal revolution in economics in particular, the relationship between ethics and economics, and the nature of costs. "The Problem" and "The Basic Data of Economics" are an excellent introduction to the basic principles and categories

---

[8] See the introduction by Stefan Kolev to this volume.

of economics attentive to the wider institutional and cultural contexts of the market.

While the two selections from *Economics of the Free Society* keep the market order in the foreground, the next two selections from *A Humane Economy* (1960), "The Conditions and Limits of the Market" and "Centrism and Decentrism," bring the cultural, spiritual, moral, institutional, political, and geopolitical contexts of the market order to the fore. Röpke observes that advocates for the market economy,

> in so far as they are at all intellectually fastidious, have always recognized that the sphere of the market, of competition, of the system where supply and demand move prices and thereby govern production, may be regarded and defended only as part of a wider general order encompassing ethics, law, the natural conditions of life and happiness, the state, politics, and power.[9]

A stable, prosperous, and dynamic market economy is only possible when free persons guided by conscience are animated by a transcendent sense of purpose, receive moral formation in family and community, are protected by the rule of law, and enjoy peaceful material and cultural exchange with those of other nations. The conditions of human flourishing are only ever partially fulfilled by bread alone, "Man can wholly fulfill his nature only by freely becoming part of a community and having a sense of solidarity with it. Otherwise he leads a miserable existence and he knows it."[10]

The place of Christianity in rooting and grounding a free and virtuous society is, for Röpke, paramount. In his essay "Liberalism and Christianity" (1957), he relates a story of how

---

[9] Wilhelm Röpke, "The Conditions and Limits of the Market," in *The Humane Economist*, 62.

[10] Wilhelm Röpke, "The Conditions and Limits of the Market," in *The Humane Economist*, 62.

at an early meeting of the Mont Pèlerin Society the discussion took a turn toward the subject of Christianity:

> In this circle of technicians, the discussion turned upon the increasing conviction that if we intend to win the battle for freedom, we must pay attention not primarily to supply and demand, but to quite different things; and once the ice was broken, we "hardened liberals" spoke of what Christianity means for freedom—and, inversely, of what freedom means for Christianity. We were conscious that in speaking in the first place as Christians *or* liberals concerned for freedom and human dignity, we were on common ground: ground we did not share with the enemy.[11]

Röpke then, like Lord Acton,[12] posits that the ur-text of classical liberalism is the admonition of Jesus Christ to "render to Caesar the things that are Caesar's, and to God the things that are God's" (Mark 12:17). He turns to Pope Pius XI's encyclical *Quadragesimo Anno* as both an inspiration and model for social thought in the modern world, concluding that "what matters is that we recognize our entry into the decisive phase of the battle for freedom and the dignity of man; and, or in this battle, the patrimony of Christian social philosophy which, increasingly, merges with all that is essential and enduring in liberalism."[13]

The final three selections, "The Place of Economics among the Sciences," "Keynes and the Revolution in Economics: Old, New, and True," and "A Value Judgement on Value Judgements," all touch on questions of methodology in economics. These

---

[11] Wilhelm Röpke, "Liberalism and Christianity," in *The Humane Economist*, 188.

[12] Lord Acton, "The History of Freedom in Antiquity," in *Lord Acton: Historical and Moral Essays*, ed. Daniel J. Hugger (Grand Rapids, MI: Acton Institute, 2017), 27.

[13] Wilhelm Röpke, "Liberalism and Christianity," in *The Humane Economist*, 199.

questions, although seemingly tedious and obscure, are of great importance:

> The fact that our science has attained such a high rank in public esteem at the very moment when it is less sure of itself than ever before must appear striking to anyone who concerns himself with economics—a science which may truly lay claim, by reason of its maturity, experience, and methods, to a place second to none among the sciences which seek to establish the essential laws that govern society itself.[14]

The fact that many people, and especially those with political power and influence, turn to economists for solutions to the problems of modern life makes an understanding and appraisal of the methodological assumptions of economics necessary for politicians and citizens alike. While earlier selections focused on the nature and limits of the market economy, these selections center on the nature and limits of economic analysis itself. The unique promise and challenge of economics as a "border science" is explored; the ever-present threat of the ideological capture of economic science is assessed; and the role of ultimate ends and human values in economics is affirmed.

Röpke was a man of immense erudition whose interests and reading were both broad and deep. To assist the reader's understanding, editorial footnotes have been added to explain references that Röpke makes to various concepts, places, events, and persons, many of which may be obscure to the contemporary reader. English translations of many words, phrases, and passages which Röpke used or cited in their original languages have also been provided in the footnotes. These editorial notes are all indicated with "Ed. note." Röpke's original footnotes have been preserved, though as discussed above, a few of the longer

---

[14] Wilhelm Röpke, "The Place of Economics Among the Sciences," in *The Humane Economist*, 203.

notes have been moved to appendices. In some instances editorial explanations or translations of foreign language terms have been inserted into Röpke's original notes and enclosed in brackets. These insertions are marked accordingly with the notation "—Ed."

My own appreciation of Wilhelm Röpke's social thought has been shaped and sharpened by Samuel Gregg's concise and comprehensive book *Wilhelm Röpke's Political Economy* (2010), which I would commend to any reader interested in diving deeper into Röpke's life and work. The recently published *Wilhelm Röpke (1899–1966): A Liberal Political Economist and Conservative Social Philosopher* (2018), edited by Patricia Commun and Stefan Kolev, contains many excellent essays by a wide range of scholars that are the fruit of the recent revival of interest in Röpke and his many contributions to economics and social thought. It is my hope that the present anthology will contribute further to this revival of interest in this most humane economist and theorist of the free and virtuous society.

—Daniel J. Hugger
Acton Institute

INTRODUCTION

Wilhelm Röpke as a Student and Defender of Western Civilization

Stefan Kolev *

ORDOLIBERALISM'S RENAISSANCE

The times of oblivion for ordoliberal political economy and Wilhelm Röpke's legacy seem to be coming to an end. For decades ordoliberalism has been disregarded by Anglo-Saxon academia and successively displaced at German universities, but a renewed interest has occurred in recent years, with a sizable and multifaceted literature emerging to reflect this. Different factors constitute this ordoliberal renaissance. First, Germany's widely debated stance in the eurozone crisis regarding fiscal and monetary policy and the possibility that this stance is attributable to the legacy of ordoliberalism have motivated the publication of a large number of books and articles.[1] Second, historians of the social sciences have developed

---

* Deputy Director of the Wilhelm Röpke Institute, Erfurt, Germany and Professor of Political Economy at the University of Applied Sciences, Zwickau, Germany.

[1] For example, see Lars P. Feld, Ekkehard A. Köhler, and Daniel Nientedt, "Ordoliberalism, Pragmatism and the Eurozone Crisis: How the German Tradition Shaped Economic Policy in Europe," *European Review of International Studies* 2, no. 3 (2015): 48–61; Markus K. Brunnermeier, Harold James, and Jean-Pierre Landau, *The Euro and the*

INTRODUCTION

a resurging interest in ordoliberalism as a historical artefact.[2] Third, the potential of revitalizing ordoliberalism as a progressive research program has also been explored.[3]

Battle of Ideas (Princeton: Princeton University Press, 2016); Thorsten Beck and Hans-Helmut Kotz, eds., *Ordoliberalism: A German Oddity?* (London: CEPR Press, 2017); Josef Hien and Christian Joerges, eds., *Ordoliberalism, Law and the Rule of Economics* (Oxford: Hart, 2017); and Malte Dold and Tim Krieger, eds., *Ordoliberalism and European Economic Policy: Between Realpolitik and Economic Utopia* (London: Routledge, 2020).

[2] For example, see Jean Solchany, *Wilhelm Röpke, l'autre Hayek: Aux origines du néolibéralisme* (Paris: Éditions de la Sorbonne, 2015); Tim Petersen, *Theologische Einflüsse auf die deutsche Nationalökonomie im 19. und 20. Jahrhundert—drei Fallbeispiele* (Hamburg: Staats- und Universitätsbibliothek Hamburg, 2016); Daniel Nientiedt and Ekkehard A. Köhler, "Liberalism and Democracy—A Comparative Reading of Eucken and Hayek," *Cambridge Journal of Economics* 40, no. 6 (2016): 1743–60; Werner Bonefeld, *The Strong State and the Free Economy* (London: Rowman & Littlefield, 2017); Thomas Biebricher and Frieder Vogelmann, eds., *The Birth of Austerity: German Ordoliberalism and Contemporary Neoliberalism* (London: Rowman & Littlefield, 2017); Ekkehard A. Köhler and Daniel Nientiedt, "The Muthesius Controversy: A Tale of Two Liberalisms," *History of Political Economy* 49, no. 4 (2017): 607–30; Stefan Kolev, *Neoliberale Staatsverständnisse im Vergleich* (Berlin: De Gruyter, 2017); Raphaël Fèvre, "Denazifying the Economy: Ordoliberals on the Economic Policy Battlefield (1946–50)," *History of Political Economy* 50, no. 4 (2018): 679–707; Quinn Slobodian, *Globalists: The End of Empire and the Birth of Neoliberalism* (Cambridge, MA: Harvard University Press, 2018); Thomas Biebricher, *The Political Theory of Neoliberalism* (Stanford: Stanford University Press, 2019); and Stefan Kolev, Nils Goldschmidt, and Jan-Otmar Hesse, "Debating Liberalism: Walter Eucken, F. A. Hayek and the Early History of the Mont Pèlerin Society," *Review of Austrian Economics*, forthcoming 2019.

[3] For example, see Joachim Zweynert, Stefan Kolev, and Nils Goldschmidt, eds., *Neue Ordnungsökonomik* (Tübingen: Mohr Siebeck, 2016); Lars P. Feld and Ekkehard A. Köhler, "Ist die Ordnungsökonomik zukunftsfähig?," in Zweynert et al., *Neue Ordnungsökonomik*, 69–95; and Stefan Kolev, "James Buchanan and the 'New Economics of Order' Research

Introduction

Wilhelm Röpke (1899–1966) was one of the most prominent representatives of ordoliberalism. Even though ordoliberalism is sometimes too narrowly equated with the Freiburg School, to which Röpke did not belong, his political economy and social philosophy represent key pillars of the ordoliberal legacy.[4] This introduction to the current volume on Röpke's thought pursues three aims. First, it reconstructs Röpke's biography, which can be read as a paradigmatic tour through the intricacies of the Central European twentieth century. Second, it depicts Röpke as a political economist who, as one of the shining stars in the generation experiencing the demise of the German Historical School, played a crucial role in the debates during the Great Depression. Third, it distills in a nutshell Röpke's social philosophy, showing his specific approach as a student of Western civilization—and as its defender when it was so close to extinction.[5] It is important to emphasize at the outset that Röpke will not be portrayed as a saint or hero; instead, the non-hagiographical perspective of this introduction depicts him as a curious thinker whose thought involved multiple tensions, and as someone who often asked challenging questions while

---

Program," in *James M. Buchanan: A Theorist of Political Economy and Social Philosophy*, ed. Richard E. Wagner (London: Palgrave Macmillan, 2018), 85–108.

[4] Nils Goldschmidt, "Walter Eucken's Place in the History of Ideas," *Review of Austrian Economics* 26, no. 2 (2013): 127–47; Joachim Zweynert, "How German Is German Neo-Liberalism?," *Review of Austrian Economics* 26, no. 2 (2013): 109–25; Stefan Kolev, "Ordoliberalism and the Austrian School," in *The Oxford Handbook of Austrian Economics*, ed. Christopher J. Coyne and Peter J. Boettke (New York: Oxford University Press, 2015), 419–44; and Patricia Commun and Stefan Kolev, eds., *Wilhelm Röpke (1899–1966): A Liberal Political Economist and Conservative Social Philosopher* (Cham: Springer, 2018).

[5] Erwin Dekker, *The Viennese Students of Civilization: The Meaning and Context of Austrian Economics Reconsidered* (New York: Cambridge University Press, 2016).

leaving their solutions for posterity.[6] Seen in this light, Röpke is one of those thinkers who can be particularly stimulating for today's students, challenging them to wrestle with the numerous intellectual riddles he left behind.

A BRIEF BIOGRAPHY OF WILHELM RÖPKE

Wilhelm Röpke was born on October 10, 1899, in Schwarmstedt, a small town not far from Hanover in northwest Germany. Röpke's passionate defense of small organizations and towns, a cornerstone of his anthropology and sociology and usually related to his affection for his later home Switzerland, had its roots in the geographical setting of his youth. After serving in World War I, he studied *Staatswissenschaften*: literally translated as "sciences of the state," it was the traditional program for economists and included a broad array of subjects in the areas of economics, sociology, and law. Röpke attended the universities of Göttingen, Tübingen, and Marburg and received his first degree in 1922 for his dissertation.[7] At this point he was already given the title "doctor" because until 1923 there was no lower degree to graduate with. In the same year he published his second thesis, the habilitation,[8] and thus became eligible for a professorship. At this early point in his career, he dedicated his habilitation to the business cycle phenomenon, something quite uncommon for young economists in Germany at the time. The German Historical School was already in decline but was

---

[6] Patricia Commun and Stefan Kolev, "Wilhelm Röpke as a Pragmatic Political Economist and Eclectic Social Philosopher: An Introduction," in Commun and Kolev, *Wilhelm Röpke*, 1–8.

[7] Wilhelm Röpke, *Die Arbeitsleistung im deutschen Kalibergbau, unter besonderer Berücksichtigung des hannoverschen Kalibergbaues* (Berlin: De Gruyter, 1922).

[8] Wilhelm Röpke, *Die Konjunktur. Ein systematischer Versuch als Beitrag zur Morphologie der Verkehrswirtschaft* (Jena: Gustav Fischer, 1922).

nevertheless still quite powerful and formative, so theoretical treatises were fairly rare.[9]

Despite choosing this unusual track, Röpke had a truly stellar early career: at the age of twenty-four he became extraordinary professor at Jena in 1924, moved briefly to Graz in 1928, and settled down in Marburg in 1929, where he would remain until 1933. Already in the late 1920s, Röpke was among the relatively few professors openly supporting the Weimar Republic and was also an outspoken opponent of National Socialism as an ideology that threatened the very foundations of Western civilization. In early 1933, amid the tumultuous years of the Great Depression, during which Röpke was among the most prominent public policy discussants, he had to leave Marburg following conflicts with the new authorities, and after a brief detour in Amsterdam and London, where he met J. M. Keynes, in October 1933 he and his family settled down in Istanbul.[10] The city at the Bosporus became one of the centers of German academic emigration since Mustafa Kemal Atatürk actively pursued the policy of hosting German refugees. Röpke was among the few who left without being of Jewish origin or having socialist beliefs. Even though the Turkish modernization process was of scholarly interest to him, and although he showed commitment by publishing in Turkish, he did not feel at home in the foreign culture and with the limited academic infrastructure there.[11] At the end of his time in Istanbul, he published in Vienna a textbook that went through several editions in postwar

---

[9] Helge Peukert, "Walter Eucken (1891–1950) and the Historical School," in *The Theory of Capitalism in the German Economic Tradition: Historism, Ordo-Liberalism, Critical Theory, Solidarism*, ed. Peter Koslowski (Berlin: Springer, 2000), 93–146.

[10] Hans Jörg Hennecke, *Wilhelm Röpke: Ein Leben in der Brandung* (Stuttgart: Schäffer Poeschel, 2005), 93–94.

[11] Antonio Masala and Özge Kama, "Between Two Continents: Wilhelm Röpke's Years in Istanbul," in Commun and Kolev, *Wilhelm Röpke*, 11–29.

Germany and contained, earlier than Hayek's works, the concept of "spontaneous order."[12] But when it became possible to move to Geneva and join the faculty of the Institut Universitaire de Hautes Études Internationales (Graduate Institute for International Studies, HEI), he was more than happy to come back to Central Europe.

Geneva became Röpke's home in October 1937, and despite numerous offers from other universities, he never left the HEI until his death in 1966. In 1938 he was one of the most active participants of the Colloque Walter Lippmann in Paris, one of the founding conferences to promote what some attendants called "neoliberalism."[13] After the outbreak of World War II, several Genevan refugees left, notable examples being Ludwig von Mises and his fellow Austrian, law professor Hans Kelsen, who both left for the United States in 1940.[14] Röpke decided to persevere in Geneva, although he and his family had to live with the dire threat of being deported to Germany until the end of the war.[15] Like many academics in his generation, most notably F. A. Hayek,[16] Röpke shifted his research and publication focus in those years: he moved away from technical economics and turned toward political economy and social philosophy. Along

---

[12] Wilhelm Röpke, *Die Lehre von der Wirtschaft* (Vienna: Julius Springer, 1937); translated as *Economics of the Free Society* (Chicago: Henry Regnery, 1963).

[13] Jurgen Reinhoudt and Serge Audier, *The Walter Lippmann Colloquium: The Birth of Neo-Liberalism* (London: Palgrave Macmillan, 2018).

[14] Jörg Guido Hülsmann, *Mises: The Last Knight of Liberalism* (Auburn: Ludwig von Mises Institute, 2007), 752–54.

[15] Hennecke, *Wilhelm Röpke: Ein Leben in der Brandung*, 127.

[16] Gerold Blümle and Nils Goldschmidt, "From Economic Stability to Social Order: The Debate about Business Cycle Theory in the 1920s and Its Relevance for the Development of Theories of Social Order by Lowe, Hayek and Eucken," *European Journal of the History of Economic Thought* 13, no. 4 (2006): 543–70.

Introduction

with *International Economic Disintegration*,[17] released in London in 1942 as the result of the research project that helped him obtain the Genevan position, he published during the war years his famous trilogy: *Die Gesellschaftskrisis der Gegenwart* (*The Social Crisis of Our Time*); *Civitas Humana* (*Civitas Humana: A Humane Order of Society*); and *Internationale Ordnung* (*International Order and Economic Integration*).[18] These books, although personally banned by Heinrich Himmler and Joseph Goebbels in the National Socialist press,[19] nevertheless trickled into Germany and had some impact, most notably on Ludwig Erhard, who read the books during the war and received from them decisive inspiration in his journey toward liberalism.[20] At the end of the war, Röpke published another book, *Die deutsche Frage* (*The German Question*),[21] hoping to shape Allied plans for how to treat occupied Germany. In the same year, a German translation of Hayek's *Road to Serfdom* was published in Zurich by Eugen Rentsch, the publishing house which contracted most of Röpke's books starting in 1942. Hayek's book was translated by Röpke's wife, Eva, and contained a preface by Röpke.[22]

---

[17] Wilhelm Röpke, *International Economic Disintegration: With an Appendix by Alexander Rüstow* (London: William Hodge, 1942).

[18] Wilhelm Röpke, *Die Gesellschaftskrisis der Gegenwart* (Erlenbach-Zurich: Eugen Rentsch, 1942); Wilhelm Röpke, *Civitas Humana: Grundfragen der Gesellschafts- und Wirtschaftsreform* (Erlenbach-Zurich: Eugen Rentsch, 1944); and Wilhelm Röpke, *Internationale Ordnung* (Erlenbach-Zurich: Eugen Rentsch, 1945).

[19] Hennecke, *Wilhelm Röpke: Ein Leben in der Brandung*, 138–39.

[20] Ludwig Erhard, "Gedenkrede," in *In Memoriam Wilhelm Röpke*, ed. Erich Hoppmann (Marburg: N. G. Elwert, 1968), 9–21; and Alfred C. Mierzejewski, *Ludwig Erhard: A Biography* (Chapel Hill: University of North Carolina Press, 2004), 27–42.

[21] Wilhelm Röpke, *Die deutsche Frage* (Erlenbach-Zurich: Eugen Rentsch, 1945).

[22] Friedrich A. von Hayek, *Der Weg zur Knechtschaft*, ed. and with a preface by Wilhelm Röpke, trans. Eva Röpke (Erlenbach-Zurich: Eugen Rentsch, 1945).

xxi

Röpke was not only a widely recognized scholar and well-received public intellectual but also a talented networker. The most notable example for his networking was the founding of the Mont Pèlerin Society, which owes its name to the venue of its first meeting in April 1947, Mont Pèlerin on the shore of Lake Geneva. This location was not a coincidence: Röpke and a Swiss business representative, Albert Hunold, were the originators of the society, raising funds and setting up the logistics of the meeting.[23] Röpke was among the formative members of the Mont Pèlerin Society during its first fifteen years, a period when other ordoliberals, such as Walter Eucken, Franz Böhm, and Alexander Rüstow, also shaped the spirit of the society.[24] During those years, Röpke became a preeminent public intellectual in the young Federal Republic, even though—unlike Rüstow, who returned to Heidelberg—he never came back permanently. Two of Röpke's roles are especially worth mentioning here: defending the Social Market Economy and accompanying the early process of European integration. The concept of a "Social Market Economy" was developed by economist and sociologist Alfred Müller-Armack, and it has experienced a truly ecumenical spread ever since.[25] It became visible to the

---

[23] Ronald M. Hartwell, *A History of the Mont Pelerin Society* (Indianapolis: Liberty Fund, 1995), 29–33; Philip Plickert, *Wandlungen des Neoliberalismus: Eine Studie zur Entwicklung und Ausstrahlung der "Mont Pèlerin Society"* (Stuttgart: Lucius & Lucius, 2008), 127–32; and Angus Burgin, *The Great Persuasion: Reinventing Free Markets since the Depression* (Cambridge, MA: Harvard University Press, 2012), 82–86.

[24] Ralf Ptak, "Neoliberalism in Germany: Revisiting the Ordoliberal Foundations of the Social Market Economy," in *The Road from Mont Pèlerin: The Making of the Neoliberal Thought Collective*, ed. Philip Mirowski and Dieter Plehwe (Cambridge, MA: Harvard University Press, 2009), 98–138; and Kolev et al., "Debating Liberalism."

[25] Nils Goldschmidt and Michael Wohlgemuth, "Social Market Economy: Origins, Meanings, and Interpretations," *Constitutional Political Economy* 19, no. 3 (2008): 261–76; and Samuel Gregg, *Wilhelm Röpke's Political Economy* (Cheltenham: Edward Elgar, 2010), 39–42.

public in June 1948 when, parallel to the introduction of the new D-Mark currency in the three Western occupation zones, Ludwig Erhard—the soon-to-be minister of the economy in the Federal Republic—abolished a large number of price controls introduced by the National Socialists and initially preserved by the Allies.[26] Even though the years to follow were anything but easy, the June 1948 reforms have been commonly portrayed as the initiation of the so-called German economic miracle. At the same time, in 1949 to 1950, at the initiative of French foreign minister Robert Schuman, the first steps were taken toward integration of the war-plagued continent, first with the European Coal and Steel Community and then, after the Treaties of Rome in 1957, the European Communities.[27] Röpke supported both processes intensively, defending the Social Market Economy and the principle of integration against critics from both the left and the right, but always remaining critical, which led to times of estrangement even from his close intellectual ally Erhard.[28] Regarding the evolution of Europe, Röpke proposed two possible trajectories: it could evolve into a "large France," economically integrated, politically centralized, and potentially protectionist; or into a "large Switzerland," economically integrated, politically decentralized, and ideally free-trade inspired, the latter clearly being his preference.[29]

---

[26] Anthony J. Nicholls, *Freedom with Responsibility: The Social Market Economy in Germany (1918–1963)* (Oxford: Clarendon Press, 2000), 178–205.

[27] Dalibor Rohac, *Towards an Imperfect Union: A Conservative Case for the EU* (Lanham: Rowman & Littlefield, 2016), 31–52.

[28] Nicholls, *Freedom with Responsibility*, 323–24; Hennecke, *Wilhelm Röpke: Ein Leben in der Brandung*, 202–6; and Sara Warneke, *Die europäische Wirtschaftsintegration aus der Perspektive Wilhelm Röpkes* (Stuttgart: Lucius & Lucius, 2013), 168–80.

[29] Warneke, *Die europäische Wirtschaftsintegration*, 126–41; and Lars P. Feld and Michael Wohlgemuth, "Mehr Schweiz wagen!" *Frankfurter Allgemeine Zeitung*, April 22, 2013.

Introduction

The last decade of Röpke's life was not a happy one. Even though his *Jenseits von Angebot und Nachfrage* (*A Humane Economy: The Social Framework of the Free Market*)[30] was widely received, and although he connected to new networks of conservative thinkers in the United States,[31] Röpke experienced a cumulative estrangement from his fellow liberals in the Mont Pèlerin Society. Although he became its second president in September 1960 after Hayek's long tenure beginning in 1947, during the so-called Hunold Affair he radically broke with Hayek as well as the American liberals headed by Milton Friedman, a process that resulted in a serious deterioration of his health.[32] Because of political developments on both sides of the Atlantic, especially during the presidency of John F. Kennedy,[33] as well as the process of decolonization, Röpke's view of the prospects for Western civilization became increasingly bleak, so that especially in his last years, he "suffered in the face of modernity."[34] On February 12, 1966, he passed away in Geneva.

Wilhelm Röpke's Political Economy

As mentioned, Röpke chose a trajectory in his early career that made him a shining star in many of his contemporaries' eyes. He matured academically among the Younger and Youngest

---

[30] Wilhelm Röpke, *Jenseits von Angebot und Nachfrage* (Erlenbach-Zurich: Eugen Rentsch, 1958).

[31] Alan S. Kahan, "From Basel to Brooklyn: Liberal Cultural Pessimism in Burckhardt, Röpke, and the American Neoconservatives," in Commun and Kolev, *Wilhelm Röpke*, 157–64; Tim Petersen, "Wilhelm Röpke and American Conservatism," in Commun and Kolev, *Wilhelm Röpke*, 175–86; and Jean Solchany, "Wilhelm Röpke: Why He Was a Conservative," in Commun and Kolev, *Wilhelm Röpke*, 165–73.

[32] Hartwell, *A History of the Mont Pelerin Society*, 100–130; and Burgin, *The Great Persuasion*, 133–46.

[33] Warneke, *Die europäische Wirtschaftsintegration*, 141–65.

[34] Karen Horn, "Die rechte Flanke der Liberalen," *Frankfurter Allgemeine Sonntagszeitung*, May 17, 2015.

Historical Schools.[35] His books on business cycles, international trade, money, public finance, and capital accumulation, as well as other topics, soon established him as a respectable theorist always keen to combine theoretical insights with practically relevant questions.[36] With Eucken, Rüstow, and other economists, including some with socialist leanings, Röpke became part of the "German Ricardians" group in the second half of the 1920s, aiming to reestablish economic theorizing to its pre–Historical School importance.[37] A cornerstone of Röpke's incipient political economy was discussing the concept of interventionism, given the increasing state interference in the economy during the Weimar Republic. Along with its practical relevance, this endeavor can be seen as the initiation of Röpke's

---

[35] Heinz Rieter, "Historische Schulen," in *Geschichte der Nationalökonomie*, ed. Otmar Issing (Munich: Vahlen, 2002), 131–68; Erik Grimmer-Solem and Roberto Romani, "The Historical School, 1870–1900: A Cross-National Reassessment," *History of Economic Ideas* 24, no. 4–5 (1998): 267–99; Heath Pearson, "Was There Really a German Historical School of Economics?," *History of Political Economy* 31, no. 3 (1999): 547–62; Bruce Caldwell, "There Really *Was* a German Historical School of Economics: A Comment on Heath Pearson," *History of Political Economy* 33, no. 3 (2001): 649–54; and Geoffrey M. Hodgson, *How Economics Forgot History: The Problem of Historical Specificity in Social Science* (London: Routledge, 2001).

[36] Respectively, Röpke, *Die Konjunktur*; Wilhelm Röpke, *Die internationale Handelspolitik nach dem Kriege* (Jena: Gustav Fischer, 1923); Wilhelm Röpke, *Geld und Außenhandel* (Jena: Gustav Fischer, 1925); Wilhelm Röpke, *Finanzwissenschaft* (Berlin: Spaeth & Linde, 1929); and Wilhelm Röpke, *Die Theorie der Kapitalbildung* (Tübingen: J. C. B. Mohr [Paul Siebeck], 1929).

[37] Hauke Janssen, *Nationalökonomie und Nationalsozialismus. Die deutsche Volkswirtschaftslehre in den dreißiger Jahren des 20. Jahrhunderts* (Marburg: Metropolis, 2009), 34–48; and Roman Köster, *Die Wissenschaft der Außenseiter. Die Krise der akademischen Nationalökonomie in der Weimarer Republik 1918–1933* (Göttingen: Vandenhoeck & Ruprecht, 2011), 222–33.

lifelong process of emancipation from Ludwig von Mises,[38] whose contemporaneous theory of interventionism was challenged by Röpke.[39] Röpke developed a sophisticated typology of interventions, some of which—especially the ones called "market-conformable"—were in line with his idea of a well-ordered market economy.[40] To what extent this more ramified typology when compared to the one proposed by Mises could be abused by politicians and bureaucrats in the democratic process remained an open question.

When the Great Depression hit in, Röpke's expertise along these lines became direly needed: the central question now was in what ways and with which instruments the state should intervene on the macroeconomic level to counteract the gigantic slump. After being incapable of handling the hyperinflation of the early 1920s, the Historical School's representatives failed yet again to provide either a coherent diagnosis or an effective therapy for the depression. For the second time in less than a decade, after having lost large parts of their savings during World War I and in the hyperinflation, German workers and the middle class in general were hit by a severe economic shock—this time skyrocketing unemployment. Röpke positioned himself between the positions of Keynes and the Austrian economists, above all Hayek, and his peculiar approach granted him the label of one of the German "proto-Keynesians."[41] He developed

---

[38] Stefan Kolev, "Paleo- and Neoliberals: Ludwig von Mises and the 'Ordo-Interventionists,'" in Commun and Kolev, *Wilhelm Röpke*, 65–90.

[39] Ludwig von Mises, *Kritik des Interventionismus: Untersuchungen zur Wirtschaftspolitik und Wirtschaftsideologie der Gegenwart* (Jena: Gustav Fischer, 1929); and Wilhelm Röpke, "Staatsinterventionismus," in *Handwörterbuch der Staatswissenschaften*, supplemental vol., ed. Ludwig Elster et al. (Jena: Gustav Fischer, 1929), 861–82.

[40] Helge Peukert, *Das sozialökonomische Werk Wilhelm Röpkes* (Frankfurt: Peter Lang, 1992), 137–38.

[41] Hansjörg Klausinger, "German Anticipations of the Keynesian Revolution? The Case of Lautenbach, Neisser and Röpke," *European Journal of the History of Economic Thought* 6, no. 3 (1999): 378–403.

the concept of the "secondary depression," which helped him distinguish between the allegedly dichotomous positions of an interventionist Keynes and a non-interventionist Hayek. While Röpke agreed with the Austrian business cycle theory that the adequate first reaction after the crisis was to wait for its beneficial effects to purify the malinvestments from the preceding boom, he agreed with Keynes that if the slump reached the phase of secondary depression, the state had to use its macroeconomic tools for an "initial ignition" to boost the economy.[42] He tried to promote this position both to the public and to other experts in 1931 and 1932.[43] But the existing constraints on Germany's fiscal situation and politicians' unwillingness proved insurmountable obstacles, so that Röpke's proposal did not make it into the practical policies of the last Weimar cabinets. Already at this early stage he showed that he was not only a technical economist but also a political economist who fundamentally understood the core ordoliberal notion of "interdependence of orders." As Röpke saw that the political order was about to crash, he advocated measures to preserve the existing economic order, which may not have been extremely valuable in terms of economics but which he assessed as psychologically valuable, proving that the political order of Weimar had not lost all its ability to act. Hayek later admitted that his theory had a blind spot here[44] and acknowledged that Röpke's stance

---

[42] Lachezar Grudev, "The Secondary Depression: An Integral Part of Wilhelm Röpke's Business Cycle Theory," in Commun and Kolev, *Wilhelm Röpke*, 133–54; Patricia Commun, "Wilhelm Röpke's Report on the Brauns Commission: Advocating a Pragmatic Business Cycle Policy," in Commun and Kolev, *Wilhelm Röpke*, 121–31; and Raphaël Fèvre, "Was Wilhelm Röpke Really a Proto-Keynesian?," in Commun and Kolev, *Wilhelm Röpke*, 109–20.

[43] Wilhelm Röpke, *Krise und Konjunktur* (Leipzig: Quelle & Meyer, 1932).

[44] Antonio Magliulo, "Hayek and the Great Depression of 1929: Did He Really Change His Mind?," *European Journal of the History of Economic Thought* 23, no. 1 (2016): 31–58.

embodied his own famous dictum that "an economist who is nothing but an economist cannot be a good economist."[45] In subsequent years, Röpke gradually embraced an ardent anti-Keynesian position. While he added further complexity to his theory of the secondary depression, especially regarding the difficulty of empirically distinguishing the primary from the secondary phase,[46] he accused Keynes of having illegitimately "upgraded" the specific toolbox of fighting one of the most severe crises of capitalism to an allegedly "general theory" for any regular crisis.

WILHELM RÖPKE'S SOCIAL PHILOSOPHY

From the perspective of the Röpke-Hayek-Eucken generation in the mid-1930s, technical economics had failed to save Central Europe from the advent of fascism and National Socialism. Given the new regimes in an increasing number of European countries, Western civilization seemed at the brink of extinction, and other tools were desperately needed to rescue it. Walter Lippmann's *Good Society*, along with the aforementioned Colloque Walter Lippmann in Paris in 1938, provided a manifesto to build on.[47] As aptly shown in portrayals of the Viennese and associated economists as "students of civilization," in the late 1930s and early 1940s these economists split into two camps.[48] The first camp consisted mostly of the older generation with scholars like Mises and Joseph A. Schumpeter, who, out of resignation or deterred by distance as émigrés to the United States, declined to fight for the embattled civilization. The sec-

---

[45] Friedrich A. von Hayek, "Tribute to Röpke" (1959), in *Fortunes of Liberalism: Essays on Austrian Economics and the Ideal of Freedom*, ed. Peter G. Klein (Chicago: University of Chicago Press, 1992), 196.

[46] Wilhelm Röpke, *Crises and Cycles* (London: William Hodge, 1936).

[47] Walter Lippmann, *The Good Society* (Boston: Little, Brown & Co., 1937).

[48] Dekker, *The Viennese Students of Civilization*.

ond camp featured younger protagonists like Röpke, Hayek, and Karl Popper, who saw their responsibility to leave the purity of the ivory tower. In addition to academic writings in economics and philosophy, they wrote popular books aimed to convince citizens that liberty had a future even in those darkest hours. Along with Hayek's *Road to Serfdom* and Popper's *Open Society and Its Enemies*, Röpke's trilogy[49] is an example of a popular publication that was successful well beyond Switzerland and Germany in the immediate postwar years, as English translations were soon published by prominent presses in the United Kingdom and the United States. Röpke was vehemently opposed to an understanding of Max Weber's "value freedom" that required completely withholding value judgments, especially in light of the current age, and he saw "the insistence on fiddling while Rome is burning" as a genuinely untenable stance.[50] The trilogy goes well beyond technical economics or political economy; instead, it can be viewed as Röpke's key contribution to social philosophy, incidentally comparable in substance and rhetoric to the contemporaneous contributions of what would later be called the Frankfurt School, as initiated by Theodor Adorno and Max Horkheimer.[51]

Röpke's famous quotation captures the gist of the trilogy and of his later writings in social philosophy: "Market economy, price mechanism, and competition are fine, but they are not enough."[52] While this is true of Hayek's social philosophy as

---

[49] Röpke, *Die Gesellschaftskrisis der Gegenwart*; Röpke, *Civitas Humana: Grundfragen der Gesellschafts- und Wirtschaftsreform*; and Röpke, *Internationale Ordnung*.

[50] Wilhelm Röpke, *Civitas Humana: A Humane Order of Society* (London: William Hodge, 1948), 79.

[51] Frans Willem Lantink, "Cultural Pessimism and Liberal Regeneration? Wilhelm Röpke as an Ideological In-Between in German Social Philosophy," in Commun and Kolev, *Wilhelm Röpke*, 187–200.

[52] Wilhelm Röpke, *A Humane Economy: The Social Framework of the Free Market* (Chicago: Henry Regnery, 1960), 35.

well, Röpke's perspective differs significantly both from that of Hayek and from that of the Freiburg School that developed around Eucken and Böhm. While both Hayek and the Freiburgians acknowledge that the economy is one of several societal orders among interdependent relationships, they focus on the link between the economic and the legal orders. Röpke is different insofar as he goes beyond the interdependence of the economy to other formal institutions like law, striving to theorize the linkages to informal institutions that can be captured with "culture."[53] But his concept of culture, potentially static and deterministic, also incurs problems when it is used to analyze non-Western parts of the world.[54] Such a formal-and-informal institutions perspective on the economic order's embeddedness has led some to label Röpke's, Rüstow's, and Müller-Armack's contributions to ordoliberalism as "sociological"[55] or "communitarian."[56] Röpke's sociological liberalism is particularly tied to his notion of culture. In *Das Kulturideal des Liberalismus*, one finds two variations of liberalism that must be distinguished carefully: "fleeting liberalism" and "lasting liberalism."[57] The distinction is crucial, as "fleeting liberalism" includes political and social movements from the nineteenth century that, according to him, often earn the criticism of "economism" because of their exaggerated focus

---

[53] Nils Goldschmidt and Julian Dörr, "Wilhelm Röpke on Liberalism, Culture, and Economic Development," in Commun and Kolev, *Wilhelm Röpke*, 203–17.

[54] Quinn Slobodian, "The World Economy and the Color Line: Wilhelm Röpke, Apartheid, and the White Atlantic," *Bulletin of the German Historical Institute*, supplement 10 (2014): 61–87.

[55] Gregg, *Wilhelm Röpke's Political Economy*, 37–42.

[56] Andreas Renner, *Jenseits von Kommunitarismus und Neoliberalismus. Eine Neuinterpretation der Sozialen Marktwirtschaft* (Grafschaft: Vektor, 2002), 217–58.

[57] Wilhelm Röpke, *Das Kulturideal des Liberalismus* (Frankfurt: G. Schulte-Bulmke, 1947).

on economics, while "lasting liberalism" attempts to moderate and balance the different societal orders and thus focuses on Western culture as "a wealth of ideas beyond the despotism of man" that accepts "the inviolability of natural orders prior to and beyond state power as a guiding light."[58] Especially in his late work and in the process of increasing his connection to new networks in the United States, Röpke attempted to merge this "lasting liberalism" with his specific conservatism, resulting in a mélange which has often been frowned on from both the liberal and the conservative side because of the alien ingredients it contains.[59]

This sociological perspective has advantages in the context of the implicit "division of labor" within the Röpke-Hayek-Eucken generation. This generation accepted Mises's challenge regarding interventionism and devoted substantial intellectual energy to the question as to what kind of state activity not only might not be harmful but might be even systemically necessary for a thriving market economy—a question that, in their view, Mises had not answered in a sufficiently elaborate manner. A cornerstone of the systems of Röpke, Hayek, and Eucken is the distinction within the market-process-as-a-game metaphor between rules of the game and moves of the game. Differentiating these two levels of analysis is essential to structure the division of labor between state and market. While safeguarding the rules of the game is agreed to be the proper domain for state activity, the moves of the game should be left to the autonomy of private individuals. Despite this consensus, and despite the common rejection of Mises's "night-watchman" state, some nuance is necessary to keep distinct the roles that Röpke, Hayek, and Eucken attribute to the state. Hayek's state may best be understood by the metaphor of a gardener of an

---

[58] Röpke, *Das Kulturideal des Liberalismus*, 12.

[59] Kahan,"From Basel to Brooklyn"; Petersen,"Wilhelm Röpke and American Conservatism"; and Solchany, "Wilhelm Röpke: Why He Was a Conservative."

English garden, while Eucken's state can be best understood as an impartial arbiter. The advantage of sociological liberalism becomes clear here: along with asking the question about what the adequate rules of the game are, Röpke additionally asks the stability question: What are the foundations of the playing field on which the game is played in the first place? On what pillars is this playing field positioned, and what has to be done to sustainably ensure the statics of those pillars so that phenomena like Russia in 1917 or Germany in 1933 do not recur? Even though such a concept of the state—depictable through the metaphor "state as a structural engineer"—suggests that Röpke puts a heavier burden of activity on the state when compared to his fellow liberals, this is not necessarily true. Within the Röpke-Hayek-Eucken generation, he is unique in explicitly emphasizing that the state is only one of the many necessary actors in the polity to ensure its statics,[60] the others being civil society organizations that share responsibility for leadership in different domains, players captured in Röpke's concept of a "*nobilitas naturalis.*"[61]

Röpke's sociology can be elegantly depicted with what later became famous as the "Small Is Beautiful" program formulated by E. F. Schumacher.[62] Small units, in terms of geographical entities such as towns and organizational entities such as companies, provide in Röpke's view a setting "à la taille de l'homme"[63]—that is, a context of life best suited to human nature.[64] Religion played an important role in the lives of the ordoliberals and in determining their anthropology, the con-

---

[60] Kolev, "Ordoliberalism and the Austrian School," 430–31.

[61] Röpke, *A Humane Economy*, 129–36.

[62] E. F. Schumacher, *Small Is Beautiful: Economics as if People Mattered* (New York: Harper & Row, 1973).

[63] Wilhelm Röpke, *The Social Crisis of Our Time* (Chicago: University of Chicago Press, 1950), 179.

[64] John Zmirak, *Wilhelm Röpke: Swiss Localist, Global Economist* (Wilmington: ISI Books, 2001), 168–85.

cept of "ordo" being one of the immediately obvious considerations in finding connections between one's religiosity and one's economic theorizing.[65] Röpke was a practicing Lutheran, but this did not keep him from diagnosing Lutheranism as one "pathology" that contributed to the German tragedy initiated under Bismarck's Prussia.[66] Röpke had sympathies for the Catholic social teaching and engaged in extended and often controversial exchanges with its German proponents, among them Johannes Messner, Oswald von Nell-Breuning, and Egon Edgar Nawroth, hoping to find common ground. These scholars constituted a discursive antidote to his liberal economist friends, whom he often struggled to convince of the dangers of an "economistic" liberalism. Röpke was especially eager to discuss questions such as the extent to which his concepts of small-units decentralization and of federalism concurred with the notion of subsidiarity in Catholic social teaching, a topic that has gained additional politico-economic prominence during the past decades in the process of European integration as an official term in a number of European Union treaties.[67]

WILHELM RÖPKE IN THE GLOBAL-DIGITAL AGE

This introduction aimed to portray a man who was among the most prominent European economists and public intellectuals of his age. Röpke witnessed both World Wars and the disastrous interwar disintegration of the global economic and political

---

[65] Nils Goldschmidt, *Entstehung und Vermächtnis ordoliberalen Denkens: Walter Eucken und die Notwendigkeit einer kulturellen Ökonomik* (Münster: LIT, 2002), 101–8; and Jakob Friedrich Scherer, *Das Verhältnis von Staat und Ökonomie: Walter Euckens Ordoliberalismus im Angesicht der Schwächung des nationalstaatlichen Regulierungsmonopols* (Berlin: Duncker & Humblot, 2018), 48–52.

[66] Wilhelm Röpke, *The German Question* (London: George Allen, 1946), 158.

[67] Petersen, *Theologische Einflüsse*, 176–91.

order, as well as its painful reconstruction after 1945. While during the Great Depression he was not successful in convincing his colleagues and the public, after 1945 he experienced moments of satisfaction, both regarding the young Federal Republic and the incipient European integration, but also moments of disappointment, both regarding these two projects and regarding his liberal friends. Röpke presciently used terms like "spontaneous order" or "initial ignition" before they became common among Hayekians or Keynesians. And he posed a number of challenging questions, most importantly perhaps the "stability question" about the statics of the playing field on which the game of a free economy and society can sustainably take place. The Röpke Archives reveal that, unlike many of his friends, he was willing to sacrifice time and energy that others would dedicate to scholarly work for conversations with the media and for correspondence with the regular citizen, believing that "the task for the constitutional political economist is to assist individuals, as citizens who ultimately control their own social order."[68] Last but not least, Röpke was a gifted networker, both with primarily European liberals and American conservatives.

To what extent is Röpke relevant today? Regarding his political economy, during the past decades Western democracies fortunately have been spared from a crisis qualitatively and quantitatively comparable to the Great Depression, so that Röpke's cure of a "secondary depression" has not been necessary. Regarding his social philosophy, the importance of informal institutions has been widely recognized in the social sciences, but the decline of religiosity in Western societies seems to proceed unstoppably. In contrast, cultural issues of identity—some of them related to religion—have become prevalent in recent years on both sides of the Atlantic. And is "Small Is Beautiful" still relevant? Röpke's vision has provoked criticism, the most

---

[68] James M. Buchanan, *Economics: Between Predictive Science and Moral Philosophy* (College Station: Texas A & M University Press, 1987), 250.

extreme being the label of "retro-utopia,"[69] but it may be that the global-digital age calls for a reconsideration. Our intensified environmental debates and also discussions about whether democracy functions better in small contexts are at least two reasons to take Röpke seriously. Of course this issue has been with us at least since the beginning of modernity: we are bound to simultaneously live in small communities (*Gemeinschaft*) and in a large society (*Gesellschaft*). In our global-digital age, globalization further reinforces the logic of *Gesellschaft*, while digitalization enables new communities and thus bolsters the logic of *Gemeinschaft*. Röpke and Hayek had diametrically opposed apprehensions in this respect: while Hayek feared that the atavistic logic of *Gemeinschaft* could seriously hinder accepting the logic of *Gesellschaft* in the citizen's life, Röpke feared that the logic of *Gemeinschaft* could be impeded by the ever-expanding logic of *Gesellschaft*. It remains to be seen whether the Hayekian or the Röpkean tension becomes more relevant today and in the future, or if perhaps the conflict may disappear as we live a globalized *and* a digitalized life. Above all, in this respect the ordoliberals left behind as a crucial part of their legacy a dual criterion about judging the properties of a societal order that is equally applicable to the past, present, and future: an order which is "à la taille de l'homme" has to enable not only a materially prosperous life but also a humane life in liberty and justice, a life in which the individual can autonomously find meaning in his or her existence.

---

[69] Solchany, *Wilhelm Röpke, l'autre Hayek*, 570.

REFERENCED PUBLICATIONS BY WILHELM RÖPKE

Die Arbeitsleistung im deutschen Kalibergbau, unter besonderer Berücksichtigung des hannoverschen Kalibergbaues. Berlin: De Gruyter, 1922.

Die Konjunktur. Ein systematischer Versuch als Beitrag zur Morphologie der Verkehrswirtschaft. Jena: Gustav Fischer, 1922.

Die internationale Handelspolitik nach dem Kriege. Jena: Gustav Fischer, 1923.

Geld und Außenhandel. Jena: Gustav Fischer, 1925.

Finanzwissenschaft. Berlin: Spaeth & Linde, 1929.

Die Theorie der Kapitalbildung. Tübingen: J. C. B. Mohr (Paul Siebeck), 1929.

"Staatsinterventionismus." In *Handwörterbuch der Staatswissenschaften*, supplemental volume, edited by Ludwig Elster, Adolf Weber, and Friedrich von Wieser, 861–82. Jena: Gustav Fischer, 1929.

Krise und Konjunktur. Leipzig: Quelle & Meyer, 1932.

Crises and Cycles. London: William Hodge, 1936.

Die Lehre von der Wirtschaft. Vienna: Julius Springer, 1937. Translated as *Economics of the Free Society.* Chicago: Henry Regnery, 1963.

Die Gesellschaftskrisis der Gegenwart. Erlenbach-Zurich: Eugen Rentsch, 1942. Translated as *The Social Crisis of Our Time.* Chicago: University of Chicago Press, 1950.

International Economic Disintegration: With an Appendix by Alexander Rüstow. London: William Hodge, 1942.

Civitas Humana: Grundfragen der Gesellschafts- und Wirtschaftsreform. Erlenbach-Zurich: Eugen Rentsch, 1944. Translated as *Civitas Humana: A Humane Order of Society.* London: William Hodge, 1948.

Die deutsche Frage. Erlenbach-Zurich: Eugen Rentsch, 1945. Translated as *The German Question.* London: George Allen, 1946.

Internationale Ordnung. Erlenbach-Zurich: Eugen Rentsch, 1945. Translated as *International Order and Economic Integration.* Dordrecht: D. Reidel, 1959.

Das Kulturideal des Liberalismus. Frankfurt: G. Schulte-Bulmke, 1947.

Jenseits von Angebot und Nachfrage. Erlenbach-Zurich: Eugen Rentsch, 1958. Translated as *A Humane Economy: The Social Framework of the Free Market.* Chicago: Henry Regnery, 1960.

OTHER WORKS REFERENCED

Beck, Thorsten, and Hans-Helmut Kotz, eds. *Ordoliberalism: A German Oddity?* London: CEPR Press, 2017.

Biebricher, Thomas. *The Political Theory of Neoliberalism.* Stanford: Stanford University Press, 2019.

Biebricher, Thomas, and Frieder Vogelmann, eds. *The Birth of Austerity: German Ordoliberalism and Contemporary Neoliberalism.* London: Rowman & Littlefield, 2017.

Blümle, Gerold, and Nils Goldschmidt. "From Economic Stability to Social Order: The Debate about Business Cycle Theory in the 1920s and Its Relevance for the Development of Theories of Social Order by Lowe, Hayek and Eucken." *European Journal of the History of Economic Thought* 13, no. 4 (2006): 543–70.

Bonefeld, Werner. *The Strong State and the Free Economy.* London: Rowman & Littlefield, 2017.

Brunnermeier, Markus K., Harold James, and Jean-Pierre Landau. *The Euro and the Battle of Ideas.* Princeton: Princeton University Press, 2016.

Buchanan, James M. *Economics: Between Predictive Science and Moral Philosophy.* College Station: Texas A & M University Press, 1987.

Burgin, Angus. *The Great Persuasion: Reinventing Free Markets since the Depression.* Cambridge, MA: Harvard University Press, 2012.

Caldwell, Bruce. "There Really *Was* a German Historical School of Economics: A Comment on Heath Pearson." *History of Political Economy* 33, no. 3 (2001): 649–54.

Commun, Patricia. "Wilhelm Röpke's Report on the Brauns Commission: Advocating a Pragmatic Business Cycle Policy." In Commun and Kolev, *Wilhelm Röpke,* 121–31.

Commun, Patricia, and Stefan Kolev, eds. *Wilhelm Röpke (1899–1966): A Liberal Political Economist and Conservative Social Philosopher.* Cham: Springer, 2018.

Commun, Patricia, and Stefan Kolev. "Wilhelm Röpke as a Pragmatic Political Economist and Eclectic Social Philosopher: An Introduction." In Commun and Kolev, *Wilhelm Röpke*, 1–8.

Dekker, Erwin. *The Viennese Students of Civilization: The Meaning and Context of Austrian Economics Reconsidered.* New York: Cambridge University Press, 2016.

Dold, Malte, and Tim Krieger, eds. *Ordoliberalism and European Economic Policy: Between Realpolitik and Economic Utopia.* London: Routledge, 2020.

Erhard, Ludwig. "Gedenkrede." In *In Memoriam Wilhelm Röpke*, edited by Erich Hoppmann, 9–21. Marburg: N. G. Elwert, 1968.

Feld, Lars P., and Ekkehard A. Köhler. "Ist die Ordnungsökonomik zukunftsfähig?" In *Neue Ordnungsökonomik*, edited by Joachim Zweynert, Stefan Kolev, and Nils Goldschmidt, 69–95. Tübingen: Mohr Siebeck, 2016.

Feld, Lars P., Ekkehard A. Köhler, and Daniel Nientiedt. "Ordoliberalism, Pragmatism and the Eurozone Crisis: How the German Tradition Shaped Economic Policy in Europe." *European Review of International Studies* 2, no. 3 (2015): 48–61.

Feld, Lars P., and Michael Wohlgemuth. "Mehr Schweiz wagen!" *Frankfurter Allgemeine Zeitung*, April 22, 2013.

Fèvre, Raphaël. "Denazifying the Economy: Ordoliberals on the Economic Policy Battlefield (1946–50)." *History of Political Economy* 50, no. 4 (2018): 679–707.

———. "Was Wilhelm Röpke Really a Proto-Keynesian?" In Commun and Kolev, *Wilhelm Röpke*, 109–20.

Goldschmidt, Nils. *Entstehung und Vermächtnis ordoliberalen Denkens: Walter Eucken und die Notwendigkeit einer kulturellen Ökonomik.* Münster: LIT, 2002.

———. "Walter Eucken's Place in the History of Ideas." *Review of Austrian Economics* 26, no. 2 (2013): 127–47.

Goldschmidt, Nils, and Julian Dörr. "Wilhelm Röpke on Liberalism, Culture, and Economic Development." In Commun and Kolev, *Wilhelm Röpke*, 203–17.

Goldschmidt, Nils, and Michael Wohlgemuth. "Social Market Economy: Origins, Meanings, and Interpretations." *Constitutional Political Economy* 19, no. 3 (2008): 261–76.

Gregg, Samuel. *Wilhelm Röpke's Political Economy.* Cheltenham: Edward Elgar, 2010.

Grimmer-Solem, Erik, and Roberto Romani. "The Historical School, 1870–1900: A Cross-National Reassessment." *History of Economic Ideas* 24, no. 4–5 (1998): 267–99.

Grudev, Lachezar. "The Secondary Depression: An Integral Part of Wilhelm Röpke's Business Cycle Theory." In Commun and Kolev, *Wilhelm Röpke*, 133–54.

Hartwell, Ronald M. *A History of the Mont Pelerin Society.* Indianapolis: Liberty Fund, 1995.

Hayek, Friedrich A. von. *Der Weg zur Knechtschaft.* Edited and with a Preface by Wilhelm Röpke. Translated by Eva Röpke. Erlenbach-Zurich: Eugen Rentsch, 1945.

———. "Tribute to Röpke." 1959. In Fortunes of Liberalism: Essays on Austrian Economics and the Ideal of Freedom, edited by Peter G. Klein, 195–97. Chicago: University of Chicago Press, 1992.

Hennecke, Hans Jörg. *Wilhelm Röpke: Ein Leben in der Brandung.* Stuttgart: Schäffer Poeschel, 2005.

Hien, Josef, and Christian Joerges, eds. *Ordoliberalism, Law and the Rule of Economics.* Oxford: Hart Publishing, 2017.

Hodgson, Geoffrey M. *How Economics Forgot History: The Problem of Historical Specificity in Social Science.* London: Routledge, 2001.

Horn, Karen. "Die rechte Flanke der Liberalen." *Frankfurter Allgemeine Sonntagszeitung*, May 17, 2015.

Hülsmann, Jörg Guido. *Mises: The Last Knight of Liberalism.* Auburn: Ludwig von Mises Institute, 2007.

Janssen, Hauke. *Nationalökonomie und Nationalsozialismus. Die deutsche Volkswirtschaftslehre in den dreißiger Jahren des 20. Jahrhunderts.* Marburg: Metropolis, 2009.

Kahan, Alan S. "From Basel to Brooklyn: Liberal Cultural Pessimism in Burckhardt, Röpke, and the American Neoconservatives." In Commun and Kolev, *Wilhelm Röpke*, 157–64.

Klausinger, Hansjörg. "German Anticipations of the Keynesian Revolution? The Case of Lautenbach, Neisser and Röpke." *European Journal of the History of Economic Thought* 6, no. 3 (1999): 378–403.

Köhler, Ekkehard A., and Daniel Nientiedt. "The Muthesius Controversy: A Tale of Two Liberalisms." *History of Political Economy* 49, no. 4 (2017): 607–30.

Kolev, Stefan. "Ordoliberalism and the Austrian School." In *The Oxford Handbook of Austrian Economics*, edited by Peter J. Boettke and Christopher J. Coyne, 419–44. New York: Oxford University Press, 2015.

———. *Neoliberale Staatsverständnisse im Vergleich*. Berlin: De Gruyter, 2017.

———. "Paleo- and Neoliberals: Ludwig von Mises and the 'Ordo-Interventionists.'" In Commun and Kolev, *Wilhelm Röpke*, 65–90.

———. "James Buchanan and the 'New Economics of Order' Research Program." In *James M. Buchanan: A Theorist of Political Economy and Social Philosophy*, edited by Richard E. Wagner, 85–108. London: Palgrave Macmillan, 2018.

Kolev, Stefan, Nils Goldschmidt, and Jan-Otmar Hesse. "Debating Liberalism: Walter Eucken, F. A. Hayek and the Early History of the Mont Pèlerin Society." *Review of Austrian Economics*, forthcoming 2019.

Köster, Roman. *Die Wissenschaft der Außenseiter. Die Krise der akademischen Nationalökonomie in der Weimarer Republik 1918–1933*. Göttingen: Vandenhoeck & Ruprecht, 2011.

Lantink, Frans Willem. "Cultural Pessimism and Liberal Regeneration? Wilhelm Röpke as an Ideological In-Between in German Social Philosophy." In Commun and Kolev, *Wilhelm Röpke*, 187–200.

Lippmann, Walter. *The Good Society*. Boston: Little, Brown & Co., 1937.

Magliulo, Antonio. "Hayek and the Great Depression of 1929: Did He Really Change His Mind?" *European Journal of the History of Economic Thought* 23, no. 1 (2016): 31–58.

Masala, Antonio, and Özge Kama. "Between Two Continents: Wilhelm Röpke's Years in Istanbul." In Commun and Kolev, *Wilhelm Röpke*, 11–29.

Mierzejewski, Alfred C. *Ludwig Erhard: A Biography*. Chapel Hill: University of North Carolina Press, 2004.

Mises, Ludwig von. *Kritik des Interventionismus: Untersuchungen zur Wirtschaftspolitik und Wirtschaftsideologie der Gegenwart*. Jena: Gustav Fischer, 1929.

Nicholls, Anthony J. *Freedom with Responsibility: The Social Market Economy in Germany (1918–1963)*. Oxford: Clarendon Press, 2000.

Nientiedt, Daniel, and Ekkehard A. Köhler. "Liberalism and Democracy—A Comparative Reading of Eucken and Hayek." *Cambridge Journal of Economics* 40, no. 6 (2016): 1743–60.

Pearson, Heath. "Was There Really a German Historical School of Economics?" *History of Political Economy* 31, no. 3 (1999): 547–62.

Petersen, Tim. *Theologische Einflüsse auf die deutsche Nationalökonomie im 19. und 20. Jahrhundert—drei Fallbeispiele*. Hamburg: Staats- und Universitätsbibliothek Hamburg, 2016.

———. "Wilhelm Röpke and American Conservatism." In Commun and Kolev, *Wilhelm Röpke*, 175–86.

Peukert, Helge. *Das sozialökonomische Werk Wilhelm Röpkes*. Frankfurt: Peter Lang, 1992.

———. "Walter Eucken (1891–1950) and the Historical School." In *The Theory of Capitalism in the German Economic Tradition: Historism, Ordo-Liberalism, Critical Theory, Solidarism*, edited by Peter Koslowski, 93–146. Berlin: Springer, 2000.

Plickert, Philip. *Wandlungen des Neoliberalismus: Eine Studie zur Entwicklung und Ausstrahlung der "Mont Pèlerin Society."* Stuttgart: Lucius & Lucius, 2008.

Ptak, Ralf. "Neoliberalism in Germany: Revisiting the Ordoliberal Foundations of the Social Market Economy." In *The Road from Mont Pèlerin: The Making of the Neoliberal Thought Collective*, edited by Philip Mirowski and Dieter Plehwe, 98–138. Cambridge, MA: Harvard University Press, 2009.

Reinhoudt, Jurgen, and Serge Audier. *The Walter Lippmann Colloquium: The Birth of Neo-Liberalism*. London: Palgrave Macmillan, 2018.

Renner, Andreas. *Jenseits von Kommunitarismus und Neoliberalismus. Eine Neuinterpretation der Sozialen Marktwirtschaft*. Grafschaft: Vektor, 2002.

Rieter, Heinz. "Historische Schulen." In *Geschichte der Nationalökonomie*, edited by Otmar Issing, 131–68. Munich: Vahlen, 2002.

Rohac, Dalibor. *Towards an Imperfect Union: A Conservative Case for the EU*. Lanham: Rowman & Littlefield, 2016.

Scherer, Jakob Friedrich. *Das Verhältnis von Staat und Ökonomie: Walter Euckens Ordoliberalismus im Angesicht der Schwächung des nationalstaatlichen Regulierungsmonopols*. Berlin: Duncker & Humblot, 2018.

Schumacher, E. F. *Small Is Beautiful: Economics as if People Mattered*. New York: Harper & Row, 1973.

Slobodian, Quinn. "The World Economy and the Color Line: Wilhelm Röpke, Apartheid, and the White Atlantic." *Bulletin of the German Historical Institute* supplement 10 (2014): 61–87.

———. *Globalists: The End of Empire and the Birth of Neo-liberalism*. Cambridge, MA: Harvard University Press, 2018.

Solchany, Jean. *Wilhelm Röpke, l'autre Hayek: Aux origines du néolibéralisme*. Paris: Éditions de la Sorbonne, 2015.

———. "Wilhelm Röpke: Why He Was a Conservative." In Commun and Kolev, *Wilhelm Röpke*, 165–73.

Warneke, Sara. *Die europäische Wirtschaftsintegration aus der Perspektive Wilhelm Röpkes*. Stuttgart: Lucius & Lucius, 2013.

Zmirak, John. *Wilhelm Röpke: Swiss Localist, Global Economist*. Wilmington: ISI Books, 2001.

Zweynert, Joachim. "How German Is German Neo-Liberalism?" *Review of Austrian Economics* 26, no. 2 (2013): 109–25.

Zweynert, Joachim, Stefan Kolev, and Nils Goldschmidt, eds. *Neue Ordnungsökonomik*. Tübingen: Mohr Siebeck, 2016.

1

THE ECONOMIC NECESSITY
OF FREEDOM[*]

Born in the last days of 1899 on the Lüneburger Heide, where my father was a country doctor, I had the good luck to pass my childhood and earliest youth in the sunset of the long, rosy European day lasting from the Congress of Vienna to 1914.[1] Those whose lives began in our present Arctic night can have no just conception of those times, and to try to summon up their atmosphere makes one feel rather like an Adam telling his sons about the life that had existed before they could have been. That figure is not, of course, applicable to the whole world of my youth, which was hardly everywhere a Paradise, but it is true enough of what I knew or could understand of the world before I became a soldier. The beginnings of 1914 were laid long before my birth, but history does not advance by the orderly route that the notion of "progress" implies; study and

---

[*] From *Modern Age* 3, no. 3 (Summer 1959): 227–36. Used by permission.

[1] Ed. note: The Congress of Vienna (1814–1815) was a meeting of ambassadors of European states that sought to secure a lasting peace in Europe after the Napoleonic Wars (1803–1815). The work of the congress contributed to the prevention of another widespread European war until the outbreak of World War I (1914).

reflection may find the present's furthest source, but through the years the stream from it runs a random way, accepting now one tributary and now another, so that many far uplands remained untouched before the gathering waters burst into flood with the First World War.

A man's own life meanders in a similar way, and I know I shall find it hard to indicate all the currents that, hindering or sustaining me, have brought me to the point at which I presently rest. The names on the way are numerous—Hanover, the neighborhood of Hamburg, the universities of Goettingen, Tuebingen and Marburg, Berlin, Jena, the United States, an Austrian provincial capital, Istanbul, and now Geneva—and the chances that led me to each, though I cannot scrutinize the providence that intended them, seem to me to have some pattern of logic directed toward my own deeper education and understanding of the world in which I have lived. The immeasurably greater flow of history has its logic, too, and my task as an economist has been to explore a delimited portion of it, to decide why it had gone the ways it had, and to apply whatever rules were there discovered to surmising its future course, depending upon whether or not men acknowledged these rules. The smaller region I am now attempting to explore is where my own life and history have been confluent, so I think I can properly begin with the cataclysm by which the next forty years of history were to be determined—the war of 1914.

I belong, then, to the generation of Germans, Englishmen, Frenchmen, and Belgians who in their youth and young manhood went through the horrors of gigantic battles on the plains of France and whose subsequent lives have been shaped by this common experience. At an early and receptive age, there was brutally revealed to me much that in the quiet pre-War dusk had been obscured, and the sights of these times were ever to remain in my mind's eye, the constantly renewed starting points of the thoughts that confirmed in me a violent hatred of war. War I came to see as the expression of a brutal and stupid national pride that fostered the craving for domination and set its approval on collective immorality. Shortly in the course of this revelation, I vowed that if I were to escape from the hell in which it was given to me, I would make my remaining life meaningful by devoting it to the task of preventing the recurrence of this abomination, and I resolved to extend my hand beyond the confines of my nation to any who might be my collaborators in the task. In this I was only typical of many thousands of my contemporaries, who, facing each other on the battle lines, were determined that no one should again find himself forced into their positions.

My adult life began with a crisis of international society, passed into the stage of revolution we call war. To understand the reasons for the crisis, to learn what brought it to the stage of war, and to find if war indeed resolved anything, I determined to become an economist and a sociologist. Like all who are young, much of my curiosity must have been for its own sake, but since from the first my studies were directed toward the prevention of the thing I studied, a moral imperative lay behind them. Looking back on the third of a century that had passed since then—a third of a century that has taken me through two revolutions, the biggest inflation of any time, the spiritual ferment and social confusion of my country, and my own exile—I see that the determining background of my scientific studies has been far less those quiet halls of learning I have known in the Old and the New Worlds than it has been the battlefields of Picardy. The tendency of my thought, I can see from a later vantage-point, has always been *international*, seeking to examine the larger relationship between countries, for it was in a crisis of this relationship that my thought began.

If I was typical of those who went through the War in my wish to make sure that it should not happen again, I think I was also typical in the analysis I made of it. We who were under a common obligation to kill one another had a great deal more in common too, and, since all of us on either side were roughly trained along the same lines, our revulsion with war brought us pretty much to a single conclusion. Our personal experience told us that a society capable of such monstrous depravity must be thoroughly rotten. We had been educated just enough to call this society "capitalism." Dumping everything into this concept that seemed to us rightly damnable, we became socialists.

Particularly for a young German of those days, this seemed the obvious path to take, for the political system of which Prussia was the exponent had been supported by every political group except the socialists. Those who wished to make a radical protest against the Prussian system became socialists almost as a matter of course. No one can understand modern socialism as a mass movement who does not see it as a product of the political development that took place in the nineteenth century in Germany after Bismarck had deprived of all influence the liberal and democratic forces that made their appearance on the surface during the unfortunate Revolution of 1848.[2] To the extent that the German bourgeoisie made its peace with Bismarck and his state, social democracy became the gathering point, and the only one, not alone of social revolutionaries but also of those for whom the social was quite secondary to the political revolution. Very few guessed how much Prussian mentality lay hidden in this same socialism, for so long as it was merely a persecuted opposition, kept away from all responsibility, its leaders managed to conceal its inner contradictions.

So, as I have said, the explanation of things we formed in the trenches of the First World War was quite simple. This means war, we told ourselves, the bankruptcy of the entire "system." Our protest against imperialism, militarism, and nationalism was a protest against the prevailing economic and political system, which was a feudal and capitalistic one. The protest and its attendant denial made, the affirmation followed of itself:

---

[2] Ed. note: In 1848 there was tremendous political upheaval in many parts of Europe that was primarily liberal and democratic in nature. Otto von Bismarck (1815–1898), who would later become chancellor of the German Empire (1871–1890), opposed the forces of revolution as a young Prussian politician in 1848.

socialism. None of us was quite clear about the concrete content of our affirmation, and those of whom we expected enlightenment seemed, at bottom, no more certain than we; but this, rather than a discouragement, was a challenge to search further.

And, in fact, we searched; I know that I did. And I think that many of us, after years of confusion, arrived at a point we had hardly expected. We learned that we had gone astray with our very point of departure. In my own case the realization came, as it must have with most others, bit by bit through study and experience. Because the starting point had been the protest against war and nationalism, there followed from it a commitment to liberalism in the sphere of international economic relations; in other words, to free trade. This commitment I myself made, and I have not since departed from it. No more than average insight was needed to see that there was an irreconcilable difference between socialism and international economic liberalism, a difference not to be done away with by the lip-service of individual socialists to free trade.

After all, nobody was immediately working for world socialism. But if socialism could only be achieved within a national framework, state boundaries took on a new and primarily economic significance. Did not the simplest logic make it clear that a socialist state, which directed economic life within the nation, could not grant even so much freedom to foreign trade as had the protective tariffs against which we had protested? The deduction was this: there is only one ultimate form of socialism, the national. With that, my generation wanted nothing to do.

Other reflections followed. With a recognition of the responsibility of one's own government in causing the war, went a great wariness about the powers of the modern state and, along with this, about the powers of the various pressure groups within the nation. That neither state nor pressure group should again attain the evil eminence it had in the War, the power of one would have to be limited and the other would have to be suppressed. At first, these seemed essential points of a socialist program. But in time it became evident that they were liberal notions, expressed by the great liberal thinkers, and they appeared to be socialist only because the socialists, so long as they were not in power, found them useful. Wherever socialism approached power after the War and exerted influence on government, the tendency was all toward acknowledging the omnicompetence of the state, and, looking at the socialists who held office, what slightest guarantee was there that the proposed tyranny would be a rule of the wisest and the best? What proof was there that the new despotism would be for the general good when "nationalization" and "planned economy," those two vaunted socialist weapons against monopoly and vested interest, in actual practice led to the strengthening of the pressure groups? And where socialism had entire control, as in Russia, and power increasingly gathered in a single hand, wasn't the situation worse for the mere individual's liberty than in those countries where many private groupings of wealth and power continued to compete side by side?

Doubts of this kind were not merely the result of an abstract enthusiasm for liberty. Life in the army had shown what it meant for the individual to exist as part of an apparatus whose every function assumed lack of freedom and unconditional obedience. The immoralities and discomforts of army life were obvious enough; to make war means to kill and be killed, the exaltation of lying and the fostering of hatred for these purposes, and the destruction, filth, thirst, hunger, and illness that accompanied large-scale killing; but this physical degradation was also accompanied by a spiritual one that worked to the total debasement of human dignity in mass existence, mass feeding, mass sleep—that frightful soldier's life in which a man was never alone and in which he was without resource or appeal against the might (inhuman but wielded by man) that had robbed him of his privacy. Less well organized than the army, civilian life retained a few crevices where privacy could be enjoyed, but there too the notion worked that the fundamental liberties could be abrogated. Looking back on it today, I can see that this life of constraint had its compensations, which lay in the human contacts its very inhumanity enforced; but at the time I saw only its inhumanity and could not have borne it but for the thought of a higher goal—the elimination of this same thing in the future—and the sense of duty in which I had been raised.

I could not then have extolled for you the peculiar virtues of the soldier, for I was profoundly antimilitarist, so longing for civilian life that every leave was a foretaste of paradise. The fact that I and my fellows who were university graduates did not differ in this from our comrades who were proletarians proves that we did not have a sentimental longing for something that the proletariat had long ago forgotten. Leave—the periodic return to the basic freedom of civilian existence—meant as much to the worker as to us of the "professional classes." It is not class prejudice, anxious for outmoded privileges, that speaks out against the lack of freedom in a collectivized, i.e. militarized, system.

The more I looked into it, the more clearly I saw that my indignation over the war was a protest against the unlimited power of the state. The state—this elusive but all-powerful entity that was outside of moral restraints—had led us into the War, and now continued to make us suffer while it intimidated and deceived us. War was simply the rampant essence of the state, collectivity let loose, so was it not absurd to make one's protest against the dominance of man over man take the form of professing collectivism? Not all the pacifist, antimilitarist, and freedom-demanding statements of even the most honest socialists could obscure the fact that socialism, if it was to mean anything at all, meant accepting the state as Leviathan not only for the emergency of war but also for a long time to come.

Any future increase of state power could only bring about an increase of what was now issuing from the unwarranted, but still limited, power of the state, and only the extremest gullibility could expect deliverance from the evils of militarism by a society that made militarism a permanent institution. Collectivism and war were, in essence, one and the same thing; they both gave endless and irresponsible power to the few and degraded the many. If socialists really were not serious about their collectivism, they were playing a curious and dangerous game in trying to fill their ranks by announcing goals that no one whose final commitment was to freedom could accept.

Thus was marked out a route of inquiry and effort that I continued along for a quarter of a century. The signposts were few and not often clear, and often enough I had to grope my way painstakingly back. Nor was the way itself easy, for at every turn stood the spirit of war, nationalism, Machiavellianism, and international anarchy. As my professional career progressed and I was called to positions of some official importance, I spoke for what reason dictated in the field of political economy, and this meant speaking against most of the groups and policies that prevailed in the field of economics between the wars. It was a struggle against economic nationalism, the groups that supported it, or the particular strategies it employed—a struggle against monopolies, heavy industry, and large-scale farming interests, against the inexcusable inflation, whose engineers obscured what they were doing with fantastic monetary theories, against the aberrations of the policy of protective tariffs, against the final madness of autarky.

To whatever extent my abilities and my office allowed, and wherever I found those with whom to join cause, I sought to mend the torn threads of international trade and to normalize international money and credit relations, to have German reparations considered in their proper aspect and without regard to "patriotism," to aid the re-integration of the vanquished countries into a democratic and peaceful world, and, when the crisis of 1929 broke out, to have adopted an economy that would not end in the blind alley of deflation and autarky. Those of us who spoke thus were a small company, and the degree of our effectiveness is shown in the history of 1918–1939. Forced out of my position by the Nazi regime, I had to emigrate from Germany, and first from Turkey and then from Switzerland could contemplate the flood of political nihilism that swirled over Europe.

It would only be a sort of inverted vanity to say that the Second World War marked the failure of the effort that I had conceived in the trenches of the First World War. I think it more modest to say that in a fashion I succeeded—not, of course, in external accomplishment but in having now learned how the goal may be achieved that my youthful optimism looked toward, though the way there is a far harder one than my youth dreamed. And I think the history of the past thirty-five years proves that my starting-point was a good one. The starting-point was apparently paradoxical: I sided with the socialists in their rejection of capitalism and with the adherents of capitalism in their rejection of socialism. I was to find in time that these two negatives amounted, as two minuses in algebra can be a plus, to a positive. Both rejections were accepted because they were based on certain positive notions about the nature of man and the sort of existence that was fitting to that nature, so that as the inquiry proceeded it always had something concrete and real to refer to and was protected from the tendency of the over-abstract to result in monstrosities when it is brought into the human realm. The third way I have pursued, beginning on it as it were out of the accident of history, has come with good reason to be called "economic humanism."

The accident of history has also required, as I have said, that I should look on economics largely in their international aspect, and in this aspect the operation of economics has again and again shown itself to be a question of order. Order is something continuous; in its true sense, it is a harmony of parts, not a regularity imposed from without. International order can only be a wider projection of the order prevailing within nations, and if today, as in the immediate past, we find ourselves more engaged with the problems of international order, that is because international relations are a screen upon which the internal phenomena of a disintegrating society are thrown and enlarged, making them visible long before they become evident within the various nations. The disturbance of the international order is not only a symptom of the inner malaise; it is also a sort of quack therapy, as is proved by the case of the totalitarian states, which temporarily avert collapse by aggressively diverting the forces of the destruction to the outside.

The years between the wars saw much mistaking of the symptoms for the disease. The international crisis, looked on in isolation, was taken for a regrettable aberration of an otherwise healthy society of nations. So followed the attempts to mend things by improving the charter of the League of Nations, holding world-economy conferences, revising debts, arranging the co-operation of money-issuing banks, repeating the irrefutable arguments for free trade, and the rest of it. August, 1939, was terrible proof that profounder measures were needed. The lessons of it are lost if we assume the present international crisis is simply one of a healthy West besieged by forces from without.[3] There remains an internal crisis and the external, the international, one will not be resolved until the two are grasped as a unity and so dealt with.

I think I have demonstrated how I came to see that socialism did not have the cure for our social ills, that indeed socialism was a heresy which aggravated these ills the more men acted on it. The economic "orthodoxy" according to which I adjudged socialism a heresy was historical liberalism, and with this liberalism I am quite willing to take my stand. What such liberalism advocates in the economic realm can be very simply stated. It holds that economic activities are not the proper sphere of any planning, enforcing, and penalizing authority;

---

[3] Ed. note: The Cold War (1945–1991) was a period of geopolitical tension between communist nations led by the Soviet Union and the Western Bloc led by the United States. At the time of this essay's original publication in 1959, the Hungarian Revolution of 1956 had recently been suppressed by Soviet military intervention and the Soviet premier Nikita Khruschchev had only recently rescinded an ultimatum to the Western Bloc to withdraw their military forces from Berlin.

these activities are better left to the spontaneous co-operation of all individuals through a free market, unregulated prices, and open competition.

But there is more to the matter than the advocacy of a certain economic technique. As an economist, I am supposed to know something about prices, capital interests, costs, and rates of exchange, and all of them supply arguments for free enterprise; but my adherence to free enterprise goes to something deeper than mere technical grounds, and the reason for it lies in those regions where each man's social philosophy is ultimately decided. Socialists and non-socialists are divided by fundamentally different conceptions of life and life's meaning. What we judge man's position in the universe to be will in the end decide whether our highest values are realized in man or in society, and our decision for either the former or the latter will also be the watershed of our political thinking.

Thus my fundamental opposition to socialism is to an ideology that, in spite of all its "liberal" phraseology, gives too little to man, his freedom, and his personality; and too much to society. And my opposition on technical grounds is that socialism, in its enthusiasm for organization, centralization, and efficiency, is committed to means that simply are not compatible with human freedom. Because I have a very definite concept of man derived from the classic-Christian heritage of Europe in which alone the idea of liberty has anywhere appeared, because that concept makes man the image of God whom it is sinful to use as a means, and because I am convinced that each man is of unique value owning to his relationship to God but is not the god declared by the *hubris* of an atheistic humanism—because of these things, I look on any kind of collectivism with the utmost distrust. And, following from these convictions along the lines of reason, experience, and the testimony of history, I arrive at the conclusion that only a free economy is in accordance with man's freedom and with the political and social structure and the rule of law that safeguard it. Aside from such an economic system (for which I make no claims of automatically perfect functioning), I see no chance of the continued existence of man as he is envisaged in the religious and philosophical traditions of the West. For this reason, I would stand for a free economic order even if it implied material sacrifice and if socialism gave the certain prospect of material increase. It is our undeserved luck that the exact opposite is true.

There is a deep moral reason for the fact that an economy of free enterprise brings about social health and a plenitude of goods, while a socialist economy ends in social disorder and poverty. The "liberal" economic system delivers to useful ends the extraordinary force inherent in individual self-assertion, whereas the socialist economy suppresses this force and wears itself out in the struggle against it. Is the system unethical that permits the individual to strive to advance himself and his neighbor through his own productive achievement? Is the ethical system the one that is organized to suppress this striving? I have very little patience with the moralizing of intellectuals who preach the virtues of the second system, inspired by their ambition to hold commanding places in the vast supervisory machinery such a system entails but too uncritical of themselves to suspect their own *libido dominandi*.[4] It makes virtue appear irrational and places an extravagant demand upon human nature when men in serving virtue in a collectivist economy must act against their own proper interests in ways that, as even the simplest of them can see, do nothing to increase the total wealth. The collectivist state that, in peacetime, supports itself with the patent dishonesties of foreign-exchange control, price ceilings, and confiscatory taxes acts with greater immorality than the individual who violates these regulations to preserve the fruits of his own labor. I cannot believe that it is moral and will make for a better world to muzzle the ox that treadeth out the corn.

The great error of socialism is its steadfast denial that man's desire to advance himself and his family, and to earn and retain

---

[4] Ed. note: "desire to dominate," or "will to power."

what will provide his family's well-being far beyond the span of his own life, is as much in the natural order as the desire to be identified with the community and serve its further ends. They are both in the natural order, both are intrinsic to humanity, and balanced against each other they prevent the excesses that destroy a fit human existence. To deny the elementary force of self-interest in society is an unrealism that eventually leads to a kind of brutal internal *Realpolitik*.[5] The eccentric morality that confuses the eternal teachings of Christianity with the communism of early Christians expecting the imminent end of all things, and calls private property unchristian and immoral, ends by approving a society in which highly immoral means—lying, propaganda, economic coercion, and naked force—are necessities. An economic order which has to rely on propaganda in the press, in moral tracts, and over the radio and on decorations and threats to make people work and save, and which cannot rely on them to see, as peasants do, the self-evident need for work and saving, is basically unsound and contrary to the natural order. An economic system that presupposes saints and heroes cannot endure. As Gustav Thibon says: "Every social system that makes it necessary for the majority of men, in the ordinary conduct of their lives, to display aristocratic virtues reveals itself to be unhealthy." The welfare state, in its rage for egalitarianism, gives its citizens the status and opportunities of slaves, but calls on them to act like heroes.

In speaking of a balance between the elementary drive of self-interest and the urge of the communal sense, I am of course admitting that the former needs taming and channeling. At the very outset, self-interest becomes family interest, and the "civilizing" restraints this sets upon it are too obvious to need mention. Beyond this, a free market operating within a framework of firm legislation seems about as much as is required in the way of economic organization to confine the acquisitive instinct

---

[5] Ed. note: An understanding based primarily on current circumstances rather than moral commitments.

to socially tolerable forms. But this in itself is not enough. The defender of a "liberal" economy must make plain that the realm of economy in which self-interest develops, constrained by legislation and competition, is not set against but enclosed within the realm in which is developed man's capacity for devotion, his ability to serve ends that do not look to his own immediate betterment. Society as a whole cannot be based on the law of supply and demand, and it is a good conservative conviction that the state is more than a joint-stock company. Men who measure their strengths in the competition of the open market have to be united by a common ethic; otherwise competition degenerates into an internecine struggle. Market economy is not in itself a sufficient basis of society. It must, instead, be lodged in an over-all order that not only allows, and is in some measure determined by, supply and demand, free markets, and competition, but that also allows the imperfections and hardships of economic freedom to be corrected and helps man to attain an existence in which he is more than the mere economic animal. For such an existence, man must voluntarily accept the community's prior rights as against certain short-term satisfactions of his own, and he must feel that in serving the community he ennobles his own life with the *philia* by which, according to Aristotle, men are united in political societies. Without this, he leads a miserable existence, and he knows it.

The economist, too, has his occupational disease: restricted vision. I speak from experience when I say that it is not easy for him to look beyond his field and modestly admit that the market is not the whole of the world but only a segment of it, important enough, to be sure, but still merely a part of the larger order for which the theologian and the philosopher, not the economist as such, are competent. Here one could quote a variation on the words of Georg Christoph Lichtenberg, the eighteenth-century physicist: "Whoever understands economics only, understands not even them." My own effort has always been to look beyond the fence enclosing the narrow field of my science, for I have learned that it is not to be worked fruitfully without allowing for the highly complex world in which even the simplest economic law must, in the end, operate. In my own passion for synthesis, I do not think I have forgotten that these laws must be allowed to function according to their own nature; but the more I have inquired into their logic and the effects of ignoring it, the more I have seen that their operating toward humanly good ends presupposes an equivalent function of human goodness. Economic laws will not work to our benefit unless they work within a society that admits of the human virtues which issue in true service (not just "service to the customer"), devotion, charity, hospitality, and in the sacrifices which genuine communities demand.

Two things are absolutely fatal for such a society: mass and centralization. Community, fraternity, charity—they are all possible only in the small, easily comprehended circles that are the original patterns of human society, the village community, the community of small and medium-sized towns, etc. These small circles of human warmth and mutual responsibility increasingly give way to mass and centralization, the amorphous agglutination of the big cities and industrial centers with their deracination, mass organization, and anonymous bureaucracy that end in the monster state by which, with the help of police and tax officials, our crumbling society is now actually held together. This society, paradoxically fragmented and amorphous, at the same time crowned with a vast monolithic superstructure whose irrational weight continues the pulverization that must in time bring the whole thing to collapse, I have tried to describe in *The Social Crisis of Our Time*, in *Civitas Humana*, and in *Beyond Supply and Demand*.

The measures needed to avert this collapse immediately suggest themselves—we must decentralize, put down roots again, extract men out of the mass and allow them to live in forms of life and work appropriate to men. To some this seems a romantic and unworldly program, but I know of no alternative to it that does not threaten to aggravate fatally the disease. Because a suggested treatment is distasteful to the very lethargy induced by the illness it is intended to cure, it does not mean it is impractical. In the gravity of our present situation, there are no easy measures that are going to save man, no gently homeopathic doses that will enable him to shake off his symptoms without effort. If man is to be restored to the possibility of simple, natural happiness, it can only be done by putting him once more in a humanly tolerable existence, where, placed in the true community that begins with the family and living in harmony with nature, he can support himself with labor made purposeful by the institution of private property. The almost desperate character of this effort does not testify against its necessity if we wish to save our civilization. In measure as we see how slight are its chances of acceptance and how serious the present situation is, we can see how badly it is needed.

Here, too, lies one of the basic reasons for the crisis of modern democracy, which has gradually degenerated into a centralized mass democracy of Jacobin complexion and stands more urgently in need of those counterweights of which I spoke in my book *Civitas Humana*. Thus we are led to a political view whose conservative ingredients are plainly recognizable in our predilection for natural law, tradition, *Corps intermediaires*, federalism and other defenses against the flood of modern mass democracy. We should harbor no illusions about the fateful road which leads from the Jacobinism of the French Revolution to modern totalitarianism.

If I find some tendencies of liberal thinking compatible with this conservatism, I think I do so in a manner learned from Lord Acton and Jacob Burckhardt, and without being deceived that certain individual and hard-to-define currents of thought which are commonly thrown together under the heading of "liberalism" are not free of elements of moral and spiritual disintegration. They are the currents of modern "progressivism," the type of rationalism and intellectualism that I have identified with "sinistrismo."

I cannot here draw the portrait of the progress-minded modern who, in my reckoning, accounts for so much that is wrong in our world, but I can list a few of the things that attend him: the dissecting intellect, lacking wisdom and even common sense; the radicalism going in short relays from humanitarianism to bestiality; the nihilism of intellectuals who have lost hold of ultimate convictions and values and ceased to be true *clercs*; the relativism tolerating everything, including the most brutal intolerance; the egalitarianism that, presupposing an omnipotent state machinery, leads to extreme inequality in the most important respect, the distribution of power, and unleashes the soul-corroding forces of envy and jealousy; the grimace of an art called modern whose one achievement is to mirror our society's inner disintegration. Who has seen these things needs no extraordinary illumination to know toward what they tend, for the past twenty years have given us enough examples of its ruin and misery; and no one, seeing all that has been the work of men and not of blind forces, can come to any other conclusion than that men must take council with themselves and set their faces toward another way.

Here my thought comes to its deepest layer, resting on the point from which, in the logical order, all men's thinking must proceed, though in actual life they may be years gaining it. The point is one of religious conviction; I will say it in all candor: the nidus of the malady from which our civilization suffers lies in the individual soul and is only to be overcome within the individual soul. For more than a century, we have made the hopeless effort, more and more baldly proclaimed, to get along without God and vaingloriously to put man, his science, his art, his political contrivances, in God's place. I am convinced that the insane futility of this effort, now evident only to a few, will one day break on most men like a tidal wave, and that they will see that self-idolatry has created a situation in which a moral and spiritual creature cannot exist, a situation in which, despite television, pleasure cruises, and air-conditioned modern architecture, man cannot exist at all. It is as though we had wanted to add to the already existing proofs of God's existence, a new and finally convincing one: the universal destruction that follows on assuming God's non-existence.

For the Catholic, secured in his faith, this poses enviably few personal problems. It is a very different matter for those Protestants who consider the Reformation, or, if you wish, the situation it created, one of the greatest calamities in history, but one that, neither in whole nor in part, can be undone. Such a Protestant has difficulties in finding his religious home either in contemporary Protestantism, which in its disruption and lack of orientation is worse than ever before, or in contemporary, post-Reformation Catholicism. For his own part, he can only try, with whatever grace is allowed him, to re-assemble in himself the essential elements of pre-Reformation, undivided Christianity, and in this I think I am one of a company of men whose good will at least is beyond dispute. But it is a most difficult course and so far a lonely one, since there seems little present hope of establishing thus a religious community that goes much beyond a mutual respect for outward forms. If we have to content ourselves with this for the time being, it is more than ever our duty to work untiringly for our own recollection and to stir others from their indifference.

2

THE PROBLEM*

Grasp the exhaustless life that all men live!
Each shares therein, though few may comprehend:
Where'er you touch, there's interest without end.

— Goethe (*Faust*, Prelude on the Stage)

ORDERED ANARCHY

On the threshold of every scientific speculation about the universe (as the Greek philosophers taught us long ago) is inscribed the word "wonder." Before explaining anything, we must first feel that it needs explanation; before answering questions, we must first learn how to ask them. Science cannot progress where men take the world, their own existence, for granted. If our knowledge of these phenomena is to increase, we must see them naively, with the eyes of children. Unfortunately, if understandably, the more the familiar and commonplace is a given fact, the less does it excite the sensation of "wonder." Is there anything, for instance, more familiar or more humdrum than economic life? What is so usual, even banal, as the

---
*Chapter 1 of Wilhelm Röpke, *Economics of the Free Society*, trans. Patrick M. Boarman (Chicago: Regnery, 1963).

housewife's daily marketing, the farmer's sale of a calf, the workingman's weekly pay check, the sale of a share on the stock exchange? Still, it needs but a moment's reflection to discover behind these banal occurrences something unexplained, even mysterious. Once we have made this discovery, we have already taken the first steps onto the terrain of economics.

Despite the power of the human imagination, it can only feebly picture the economic life of our age in all its variety and complexity. If only we might at this moment have the gift of omnipresence, what an unimaginable number of activities, mutually interacting with and determining each other, we would behold. We would see millions of factories in which thousands of different products are being manufactured; people sowing somewhere, somewhere reaping; a thousand boats and trains hauling to the four corners of the earth cargoes of fantastic variety; shepherds tending flocks in Australia and New Zealand; miners digging copper ore in the Congo or in the American far West and starting it on its way throughout the whole world; the Japanese spinning silk, the Javanese gathering tea—all swelling an unbroken stream of goods flooding across the land into warehouses and factories and from thence into millions of shops. We would see a still finer network of little streams going from the shops into countless households, rivulets of food and clothing and all the other things required by an army of billions: laborers, office workers, clerks, businessmen, farmers—the very ones whose work has created the mighty river of goods. Simultaneously, we would see another current of goods (machines, tools, cement, and similar products not intended for direct consumption) supplying the factories in city and country—the auxiliary goods needed to keep the first stream of consumption goods flowing. And still the panorama would not be complete, for in every direction we would see a host of services being performed: a surgeon beginning an operation, a lawyer making a plea, an economist endeavoring to explain the economic system to a circle of unknown readers. And more than this: we would behold the bewildering moment-to-moment fluctuations of the money market and the securities market—phenomena which we sense are contributing in a mysterious fashion to the movement and progress of our economic system. Finally, our attention would be drawn to small and large ducts labeled "taxes" and "exercises" debouching at all stages of the economic process and serving to divert part of the flow of goods to the state for the maintenance of the army, the administrative agencies of the government, the schools and the courts.

Today, we are witnessing a rapid decline in the number of individuals who satisfy their wants independently of the outside world. The modern farmer manages to retain in a greater degree than any other class the independence of the self-sufficient man, although even he satisfies a growing share of his needs by selling his surplus produce in exchange for the things he does not raise. The rest of mankind, however, is almost completely dependent upon this indirect method of want-satisfaction. Indirect production, in turn, is based upon the principle, familiar to everyone, of the *division of labor*, but it presupposes, nonetheless, a harmonious coordination of the divided elements of the economic process.[1] Who in the countries of the free world is charged with this coordination? What would happen if no one were in charge?

Consider, for a moment, the problem of the daily provisioning of a great city. Its millions of inhabitants must be provided with the basic necessities, to say nothing of the "luxuries" which cheer and brighten existence: so many tons of flour, butter, meat, so many miles of cloth, so many millions of cigars and cigarettes, so many reams of paper, so many books, cups, plates, nails, and a thousand other things must be daily produced in such wise that a surplus or deficiency of any particular good is avoided. The goods must be available hourly, monthly, or annually (according to the kind of good in question) in exactly the quantities and qualities demanded by a population of

---

[1] Ed. note: For the author's original footnote, see Appendix 1: A Glance at Economic History.

several millions. But the people's demand for goods is necessarily dependent upon their purchasing power (money). The existence of purchasing power presupposes, in turn, that the millions who appear in the market as consumers have previously as "producers" (whether employees or independent proprietors) so adjusted their output, both in quantity and quality, to the general demand for goods that they were able to dispose of their stock without loss. Now the highly differentiated modern economic system encompasses not alone a single city, however great, not alone a country however vast, but, in a way to which we shall give our particular attention later, the whole terrestial globe. The craftsman in an optical instrument factory makes lenses for export to the most distant countries, which in turn supply him with cocoa, coffee, tobacco and wool. While he is polishing lenses he is also producing, indirectly, all these things more abundantly and more cheaply than if he produced them directly. This immensely extended and intricate mechanism can function only if all its parts are in such constant and perfect synchronization that noticeable disorder is avoided. Were this not the case, the provisioning of millions would be immediately imperiled.

Who is charged with seeing to it that the economic gears of society mesh properly? Nobody. No dictator rules the economy, deciding who shall perform the needed work and prescribing what goods and how much of each shall be produced and brought to market. Admittedly, people today must perforce accept a great deal more dictation from authorities of all kinds than a few decades ago. Yet by and large the world outside of the Communist bloc—the "capitalist" world, to use a popular if vague expression—still adheres to the principle that decisions about production, consumption, saving, buying and selling are best left to the people themselves. *Thus, the modern economic system, an extraordinarily complex mechanism, functions without conscious central control by any agency whatever.* It is a mechanism which owes its continued functioning really to a kind of anarchy. And yet capitalism's severest critics must admit that all of its parts synchronize with amazing precision. Political anarchy leads invariably to chaos. But anarchy in economics, strangely, produces an opposite result: an orderly cosmos. Our economic system may be anarchic, but it is not chaotic. He who does not find this a wondrous phenomenon and thereby deserving of the most patient study cannot be expected to take much of an interest in economics.

The order which is immanent in our economic system compels recognition even by those who are far from finding it perfect. Indeed, even those who radically disapprove of this kind and degree of order and who wish to replace it with a system of conscious and centralized control (socialism) cannot deny that it exists. Order there is in our economic system; we have a centuries-long proof of it; it is a fact which is beyond debate but which is at the same time compatible with every political faith. Honesty compels the admission that the existence of ordered anarchy is cause for astonishment, that it is something which urgently requires explanation. Further reflection, moreover, must occasion serious doubt as to whether an enormously complicated and differentiated process such as is represented in the economic systems of the advanced industrial nations could be "commanded" in all its details from on high, after the fashion of an army or a factory, without the direst consequences. The existence of order in spite of anarchy—"spontaneous order" if we wish—is not alone an astounding phenomenon in itself. The processes peculiar to economic life in a free society make evident the fundamental superiority of the *spontaneous order* over the *commanded order*. Spontaneous order is not just another variety of order, albeit one with the surprising ability to function, if need be, even without command from on high. For if the organization of the economic system of a free society can be shown to differ fundamentally from the organization of an army, there is reason for believing that a spontaneous economic order is the only possible one. Notwithstanding, our enthusiasm for spontaneous order will be tempered by the realization that as measured against any given ideal, it may leave much to be desired.

OTHER ENIGMAS OF ECONOMICS

Once we have become aware of the element of the mysterious and the problematical in the economic process in which we ourselves are engaged, we are alerted as well to the enigmatic aspects of all the individual parts of the process. Once we have begun to ask questions and have sloughed off the naive unconcern of the unphilosophical man who regards all these things as "given," our intellectual curiosity pushes us ever deeper into the thickets of economics. What about "interest," for example? Here is one of the biggest conundrums of economics and one which will no doubt appear as disconcerting at first sight to the modern tenderfoot as it did to the writer in his own youth. Or again: how many are there who regard money as something self-evident, something on which it is unnecessary to waste much discussion? They know what money is in its concrete form of coin and bank note and that one must have it to survive, but that is the end of the matter for them. It requires a serious monetary disturbance, such as the inflationary crises which developed in some countries after both World Wars, to bring home to people what irreplaceable services are rendered by a healthy monetary system, what fecund and also destructive forces lie hidden in those pieces of paper and those small discs of metal which are passed so nonchalantly from hand to hand. Then, even the uninitiate can see some point in reflecting on the meaning of money. And when once this act of reflection has commenced, how quickly comes insight into and appreciation of the mysteries and the problems which lie hidden here. It is then that the realization comes that money is not something natural and self-evident, but a human invention, and as such an historical phenomenon which acquires significance only at a certain stage of economic development, namely, that of an advanced society founded on the market and the division of labor.

Let us take a step further, leaving aside for the moment the broader interrelationships of economic life (whose problematical aspects are really not so difficult to discern) and confine our attention to a single banal fact, selected at random. Assume that we have a pencil costing $.05 and a watch costing $50. Whence comes this difference in price? There are three possible explanations. *First*: the two prices are simply the result of chance. Chance, clearly, plays a role in the formation of prices as anyone will attest who has ever attended an auction or paid some exorbitant price in an Eastern bazaar. And there is little doubt but that on most of our imperfectly organized markets the formation of prices takes place within a more or less wide range of indeterminacy. Yet no one would seriously maintain that price formation is governed only by the capricious play of chance. It would, at any rate, be difficult to make such an assertion about the pencil and the watch. There is too great a difference between the two prices and too little likelihood of supposing an inversion of the prices. Experience proves that, in reality, prices of all commodities are coordinated in a single system in which each individual price tends to remain stable for a considerable period of time, varying only within relatively narrow limits; a marked change will occur only for good and sufficient reasons.

A *second* explanation is that prices are arbitrarily set by the public authorities. It will be at once evident that this explanation does not apply in our case nor to our experiences, though we are all familiar with a few instances in which the authorities have fixed prices. In wartime, of course, the exception becomes the rule and an elaborate apparatus of price control is set up by the government to prevent a rise in the prices of vitally needed commodities (ceiling price policy). Even in normal times, there are many prices which are fixed (institutional prices). Examples are theatre tickets, taxi fares, etc. But it is precisely our wartime experiences with price control which have made at least one thing clear: a government which fixes prices too far below the level they would have reached in the absence of the official regulations will encounter increasing resistance, ending in complete defiance. It is well to remember that even in these instances of compulsory price fixing, the fixing is linked to factors which have nothing to do with compulsion or chance. It is these factors which provide the *last* and most satisfactory explanation: prices are formed in accordance with inherent social necessities. The elucidation of such price formation is one of the chief tasks of economics.

MARGINAL UTILITY

The preceding examples, which were intended to give us some idea of the tasks of economics, have turned our attention from the narrow confines of our personal experiences to a consideration of the larger fabric of society with which they are mysteriously interwoven. It is as if, all this time, we had been unconcernedly and thoughtlessly drawing water from a brook for our own private needs when, of a sudden, we look up and perceive that our brook is, in reality, a broad and majestic river stretching away upstream into illimitable distances. A recognition of the existence of the great social problems is a long step forward on the road to an understanding of economics.

But we would be traveling, ultimately, in a wrong direction were we not to consider another circumstance which leads us back to ourselves and to our own individual experiences. For it is imperative that we keep clearly in mind that the economic system is not an objective mechanical thing which functions whether we will or no, but a process to which we all contribute in the totality of our reflections and our decisions. At bottom, it is the millions upon millions of subjective events taking place in the mind of each individual which form the substrata of economic phenomena. It is the feelings, judgments, hopes and fears of men which are manifested objectively in such things as prices, money, interest, prosperity and depression. But around what axis do these movements of the human psyche revolve? An answer to this question will provide us with the key to an understanding of all the objective events of economic life—to an understanding, in brief, of the "phenomena of the market."

The meaning of all economic decisions and actions can be summed up in the word *economize*. When we have only a limited quantity of an important or useful commodity, we invariably tend to husband the inadequate supply. When we cannot have as much as we would like of a thing, there must be a certain order in our use of it if "waste" is to be avoided—if we wish, that is, to forestall our acting in an uneconomic manner. Unhappily, we do not live in Cockaigne;[2] there are only a few goods of which there is an inexhaustible supply (free goods). Under normal circumstances, the air of our atmosphere is a free good, though it is at the same time the most essential commodity we know. A calisthenics addict may fill his lungs to bursting with air and no one will label him a glutton. But if he continues his exercise too long, a glance at the gymnasium clock and his own increasing fatigue will soon alert him to the fact that at least two things do not exist in unlimited quantities: time and physical strength. These things must be husbanded. However important and useful breathing exercises are, they cannot be kept up indefinitely without neglecting even more important things. Because time and physical strength are limited in quantity, they are not free goods, but *economic goods*. We are forced to economize them no matter how little importance we attach to life's other activities.

Economic goods and not free goods determine our behavior. Our whole life is made up of decisions which seek to establish a satisfactory balance between our unlimited wants and the limited means at hand to satisfy them. To say that economic goods are limited in quantity is simply to say that the existing stocks of such goods are unable to satisfy the total subjective demand for them. It is important to note that this is not the same thing as objective scarcity. Rotten eggs are, happily, scarce,

---

[2] Ed. note: Cockaigne or Cockayne is an imaginary medieval utopia that does not experience scarcity and, as a result, is a land of unending luxury and idleness. It is described in the poem *The Land of Cokaygne*, one of the Kildare poems from the mid-fourteenth century.

but even so, there are too many of them, economically speaking (Robbins).[3] Not only do we not want them, but energetic efforts are made to see that as few as possible come into existence. They have no value for us, indeed, they are an inconvenience, which is to say that they have a negative value. On the other hand, an economic good which is not objectively scarce can increase infinitely in value, if life itself depends upon its possession. So the sorely-beset hero of Shakespeare's *Richard III* feels compelled to offer his kingdom for a horse. The scale of values of things encompasses, then, all values from minus (negative value) through zero (free goods), through a range of finite values (economic goods) to infinite values (meta-economic goods). The place of any good in this scale of values is determined ultimately by the strength of the subjective demand for it.

Air and water are ordinarily ranked very low on our scale of values, though they are essential to life. On the other hand, a diamond is valued very highly, though it is not in the least an object of vital importance. This circumstance leads us to a further important concept which is indispensable for an understanding of the subjective foundations of economic life. Our preceding discussion has made tacit use of this concept; it behooves us now to give it the most careful scrutiny.

When it comes to assigning a good its place on the scale of values, the determining factor is utility—not a general utility based on the degree of the good's vital importance, but the specific, concrete utility of a definite quantity of the good. The larger the supply of a good at our disposal, the smaller is the amount of satisfaction procured by its individual units, and hence the lower is such a good ranked on our scale of values. The reason for this is that with increasing satisfaction of a want, the utility (satisfaction or enjoyment) furnished by

---

[3] Ed. note: This illustration is originally found in Lionel Robbins, *An Essay on the Nature and Significance of Economic Science* (London: MacMillan, 1932), 45.

each successive dose diminishes. Moreover, take away any one of a number of identical units, and the loss of utility or satisfaction will be the same as if any other had been taken away. It follows that the minimum utility of the last dose or increment determines the utility of every other unit of the supply and therefore the utility of the whole supply. The value we attach to water is not determined by the infinite utility of the single glass of water needed to save us from perishing of thirst; it is determined by the utility of the last dose used to bathe ourselves or to sprinkle the flowers. We call the utility of this last dose *final* or *marginal utility*.

We may now affirm the following theses: (1) marginal utility diminishes with increasing supply, that is, with the increasing possibility of satisfying a want; (2) marginal utility determines the utility of all other units of the supply; (3) as the quantity of a good is increased, there is a corresponding fall in its place on our scale of values, providing our taste (scale of preferences) has not changed in the meantime; (4) the utility of the whole supply (total utility) increases as quantity increases, but at a decreasing rate due to the absolute decline of marginal utility. In fact, if marginal utility diminishes faster than quantity increases, total utility may decline absolutely.

Now it is readily apparent that marginal utility will fall at a different rate for different commodities. Oddly enough, the rate of fall is greater the more vital the commodity. Let us reconsider the example of water. Each of us can remember a long walk on a hot summer's day when we had only one thought in mind: water. We at last reach a spring and, consumed by thirst, fling ourselves down to drink. The first mouthful of water is swallowed greedily, but with the second there is an abrupt lessening of satisfaction. Finally, we bathe our faces, we refill our canteens, and then forget both thirst and water to stretch out on the grass in leisurely contemplation of the countryside of which "we can't get enough." We will observe that as the result of the extremely rapid fall in the marginal utility of water, its total utility can easily become negative. Those unfortunates who, during the Middle Ages, were tortured by forceful infusions of water, could have furnished convincing proof on this point. Or consider the proverbial discontent of the farmer with the weather. He complains as often that it rains too much as that it rains too little—a further proof that water is characterized as much by the urgent need we have for it, as by the extremely rapid fall in its marginal utility.

From the concept of diminishing marginal utility may be deduced still another: *elasticity of demand*. In general, the elasticity of demand for a good varies inversely with the urgency (intensity) of the demand for it. Later, we shall see how this principle underlies important phenomena of the price structure, especially on the markets for agricultural goods.[4] With low elasticity of demand (rapid rate of fall in marginal utility), the total utility of a supply may decrease absolutely, as illustrated in the well-known fact that the income derived from grain production in a given year may be smaller for an abundant harvest than for a lean one.

The meaning of "rapidity of fall in marginal utility" and of "elasticity of demand" will become clearer if we apply these concepts to certain considerations of a practical nature.

Remembering that elasticity of demand varies for different commodities, it is obvious that individuals will tend to consume more nearly the same amounts of a given commodity the less elastic is the demand for it—and this despite differences in income. And inelasticity of demand, we will recall, is the greater, the more essential to life is the commodity in question. Another outcome of these relationships is this: the smaller is one's income, the larger is the share of it which is expended on foodstuffs. This fact was first demonstrated by the Prussian statistician Engel in 1857 (Engel's law). Somewhat later, another statistician, Schwabe, arrived at identical conclusions for housing expenditures (Schwabe's law). We may conclude,

---

[4] Ed. note: See Röpke, *Economics of the Free Society*, 146–50.

therefore, that taxes on basic consumption goods hit the poor more severely than the rich.

A closer scrutiny of the expenditures of the rich will show that the notion of the rich gluttonously stuffing themselves is inexact, the stomach capacity of most individuals being approximately the same. Of course, the larger is a man's income, the greater will be his consumption of luxury goods, such goods having a high elasticity of demand (slow fall in marginal utility). But even such luxury wants are not sufficiently elastic to absorb the whole of a very large income. The result is that the unspent portion of the very large income is saved. This gives us an inkling as to how important is the function of the rich in the formation of capital. It follows that very little can be expected from a redistribution of the large incomes among the poorer classes. For if the rich spend for their vital needs but little more than the poor, the poor will hardly be benefited by such redistribution. Moreover, the amount of money which the rich spend on luxuries is relatively insignificant, in spite of what the lay mind imagines. The rich are so few in number that the amount they expend on luxuries is trifling in comparison with the total expenditures of the rest of the citizens. (For example, of the 58,701,000 individual income tax returns filed in 1958 in the United States, only 236 showed incomes of $1,000,000 or more; only 115,000 income units earned $50,000 or more *[Statistical Abstract of the United States for 1961]*). As for that part of the large income which is saved, it cannot figure in any scheme for the redistribution of the wealth since the cessation of saving will invite general economic decline. It should be remembered that the wealth of a Henry Ford consisted not of money but of factories which were built with his savings, factories which even a Communist state would have built had it the necessary means. Looked at in this light, people like Henry Ford are really public servants who administer our productive resources after the manner of trustees and who, if their trusteeship is bad, undergo the immediate and heavy punishment of financial loss. The problem, then, is not whether the fate of the poor will be appreciably better in a society where there are no rich. The problem is, rather, whether it is preferable to put state functionaries in the place of private entrepreneurs and to convert private enterprises into state enterprises; and further, whether the economic, social, and political power wielded by the rich is such as to result in economic evil or social injustice.

Let us clarify this point by still another illustration. Let us suppose that a poor street cleaner wins first prize in a lottery. How will he dispose of his sudden wealth? We see at once that it is the elasticity of his wants which will play the decisive role. Obviously, he will first satisfy his pressing needs for food, clothing, and shelter. But it is soon apparent that for these inelastic needs the point of satiety is quickly reached. The larger the winnings from the lottery and the richer the individual before his winnings, the smaller will be the percentage of his total income expended on inelastic or vital needs. However, while it is certain that all men will spend a part of their incomes for the basic subsistence goods, we cannot predict how they will distribute the remainder of their incomes among other wants. People will consume more nearly the same amounts of a given commodity the more inelastic is the demand for it. The more elastic is the demand for a commodity, the more probably will its consumption vary with the fluctuations of individual taste. It has been shown, for instance, that during the years 1926–27 the percentage of national income spent for food in Canada, Switzerland, and England was, surprisingly, the same (30–31 percent), while expenditures on other items varied considerably among the three countries.

If it is now the whole population instead of the street cleaner which is enriched, the same sequence of cause and effect will be operative. The percentage of income expended on food (inelastic demand) diminishes, while other needs assume increasing importance. This means that the relative importance of agriculture will ultimately diminish, and that within the agricultural domain itself grain production will become relatively less important than the production of more highly valued foods (milk products, meat, eggs, fowl, vegetables and fruit). Similarly, non-agricultural branches of production satisfying "luxury" wants of a still higher type ("tertiary production") will increase in importance as the general standard of living rises. Trade, transportation, tourism, motion pictures, radio, television, the legitimate theatre, books, art works, concerts, etc. absorb an ever-larger share of the national income as the standard of living rises. Otherwise expressed, rises in living standards go hand in hand with increased production, in the agricultural domain, of butter, meat, fruit, etc. As incomes rise still further, the ultimate stages in the developmental process—urbanization and industrialization—are attained. Our own age clearly reflects this evolution.

Thus far we have sketched the broad outlines of the principle of marginal utility, a clear apprehension of which will show it to be almost a commonplace. But as the above examples indicate, it is a commonplace which is indispensable to an understanding of economics. Indeed, it is upon this principle that the whole edifice of modern economic theory has been built. It is to a group of economists who initiated their researches within the last fifty years that we must assign the credit for this accomplishment.[5]

CHOICE AND LIMITATION:
THE ESSENCE OF ECONOMICS

We have now reached a point in our inquiry where we can begin to grasp the fundamental nature of economics. On every hand we are hemmed in by scarcity: by scarcity of goods, scarcity of time, scarcity of physical strength. We cannot fill one hole without opening another somewhere else. In this world of scarcity we are faced with a twofold task. In the first place, we must choose from among our several wants those which are in most

---

[5] Ed. note: For the author's original footnote, see Appendix 2: Marginal Utility: Foundation of Modern Economic Theory.

urgent need of satisfaction. In the second place, since marginal utility decreases with the increasing satisfaction of a want, we are compelled to interrupt this satisfaction sooner or later. We are under the continual necessity of achieving some kind of balance between our unlimited wants and our limited means. This we do by making a *choice* from among our wants and by *limiting* the extent to which any one of these wants is satisfied.

On what basis shall we make these decisions? It is certain that we shall arrange our purchases in such fashion that the satisfaction procured by the last increment of one commodity will be approximately equal to that afforded by the last increment of any other commodity. This is the abstract explanation of what is, in reality, a very simple process, something we do at every hour of the day without waiting on the proper formula. A very clear illustration of what is involved here is to be found in the otherwise trivial act of packing one's bag for a journey. Since we cannot take all of our possessions with us, we first decide upon the things which we most urgently require (choice). At the same time, we proceed to balance a plus in shirts by a minus in shoes, a plus in books by a minus in suits, in such a way as to arrive at a reasonable proportion among the several items (limitation). Silly as it may sound, it is really true that the traveling bag is ideally packed when the marginal utilities of suits, shirts, socks, handkerchiefs, shoes and books are at the same level and higher than the utilities of the things left behind.

Our example may be objected to on the grounds that it omits the possibility of taking along more and bigger bags. This complicates our problem somewhat, but changes nothing with respect to the principle involved. For how would the size and number of bags be decided on unless by all sorts of utility comparisons between more and bigger bags? Those to whom such an objection occurs have only to consider the plight of the soldier in the field who is restricted to one haversack and consequently must take very seriously indeed the operations of "choosing" and "limiting." Who would have thought that the whole of economic activity is only an endless series of very complicated variations on the simple and fundamental theme of packing a bag? Our whole life is made up of an immense number of similar decisions serving to balance continuously means with wants. Choice, limitation, equalization of marginal utilities—these are the concepts to which we must repeatedly return. They determine how we use our incomes, how we direct our businesses, how we organize production, how we divide up our time between work and leisure, and even between sleep and wakefulness. The utility we renounce constitutes the "costs" of the utility we realize in our private economy as well as in the national economy. *To economize is simply to be constantly making a choice from among different possibilities. Economics is at bottom nothing other than the science of alternatives.* Choosing and limiting are the eternal functions of every human economy, whatever its organization, be it the isolated economy without exchange or our highly developed market economy founded on the division of labor and the circulation of money.

3

THE BASIC DATA OF ECONOMICS*

Je ne connais que trois manières d'exister dans la société: il faut être mendiant, voleur ou salarié.

— Mirabeau[1]

THE MORAL FOUNDATION (THE BUSINESS PRINCIPLE)

The struggle against scarcity (deficiency of means) is the eternal basis of every human economy. It charqacterizes all ages, all climates, all social systems. The forms which this struggle assumes, however, show the greatest diversity. We may divide them into two principal groups: the individual forms and the social forms. The *individual form* of this struggle is exemplified in the isolated, exchangeless economy of a Robinson

---

*Chapter 2 of Wilhelm Röpke, *Economics of the Free Society*, trans. Patrick M. Boarman (Chicago: Regnery, 1963).

[1] Ed. note: The quotation, "I only know three ways of living in society; you have to be a beggar, a thief, or an employee," is attributed to the French statesman Honoré Gabriel Riqueti Mirabeau in Henri Baudillart, "Un Jurisconsule économiste—Charles Renouard," *Revue des Deux Mondes*, 3e période, vol. 40 (1880): 819.

Crusoe with which we are here not concerned. We shall give our attention, therefore, only to the *social form* of the struggle against scarcity.

The *social form of the struggle* is manifested in the different methods men use to obtain those things which nature has not freely supplied. There are, in principle, three such methods, as a result of which we see three kinds of struggle. There is, first, the *ethically negative method* of using violence and/or fraud to procure for ourselves, at others' expense, the means of overcoming scarcity. The second method is the *ethically positive* one of altruism, thanks to which goods and services are supplied to us without our being required to give anything in return. The third method does not lend itself easily to such brief description. It is not founded on egoism, if this implies that individual well-being is achieved at others' expense. Neither is it founded on a selfless altruism, if this implies that individual well-being is neglected in order that others may benefit. It is, rather, an *ethically neutral* method by which, in virtue of a contractual reciprocity between the parties to an exchange, an increase of one's own well-being is achieved by means of an increase in the well-being of others. This method, which may be termed "solidarity," means that an increase in my well-being is achieved in a way which not only does not deprive others of well-being but which yields them, as a by-product of my gain, an increase in their own well-being.

In concrete terms, I may obtain the wherewithal to live either: by selling adulterated butter (first method); or I can be the object (or subject) of a gift of butter (second method); or, by following the axiom "honesty is the best policy," I can acquire a fortune by attracting more and more customers with butter of irreproachable quality, kind and courteous service, finding out where I can buy butter cheapest, keeping a neat and attractive shop, etc. (third method). Whereas people are "handled" in a public facility such as the post office, in our shop they are "served." In this last case I obtain the means which allow me to satisfy my needs neither by violence, exploitation, fraud, nor illicit profit, nor by accepting alms or gifts, but through the supplying of an equivalent service or good (performance principle). It is this method, based on the principle of reciprocity, of value given for value received, which is commonly referred to as "business." It is the business method which characterizes that form of the struggle against scarcity which is based on exchange and the division of labor. Regarding the economic system in this way, however, raises several important questions, and it is upon these that we must focus our attention.

In the first place, the three methods are by no means rigorously separated, but, on the contrary, overlap to a degree. Plainly, there is an essential distinction between defrauding your neighbor in the struggle for survival and accepting a charitable gift from him for the same end: the first and second methods are incompatible and cannot be employed simultaneously. But it is possible to combine the first method (fraud and/or violence) with the third (business), and also the second method (altruism) with the third. "War, trade, and piracy—an inseparable trinity," declares Goethe's Mephistopheles (*Faust*, II, 5), and, in truth, the history of the trading and colonizing nations is a history of invasions, piracies, and oppressive exploitation. It offers us a depressing demonstration of the truth that when left to our own devices, we tend to choose the first method and return nothing in exchange for a service received. Only the powerful influences of religion, morality, and law appear able to induce us to adhere scrupulously to the third method.

There are a variety of procedures for avoiding the rendering of a service equal to one received. Leveling a revolver at someone is one of the quickest but also one of the riskiest ways of getting something for nothing. Much safer and more efficient are the devices of special privilege and monopoly for they can be tricked out in ideological trappings which may make them seem not only innocuous but even beneficial to the general interest. The modern problem of monopoly can ultimately be defined in no other way than as a distortion of the principle of equivalence or reciprocity in exchange effected by means of the method of exploitation. Solving the monopoly problem, therefore, means nothing other than finding a way to eliminate this distortion.

If, as unfortunately happens, the method of "pure business" is often combined with fraud and exploitation, it is just as frequently commingled with elements of altruism. Indeed, business in the real world is not as ethically neutral as we at first supposed. There are businesses which embrace more or less an element of self-sacrifice (and, therefore, of uncompensated "giving") and of genuine service. The medical profession is one example. Then, too, we expect of the scholar and of the artist that they put devotion to their vocations before mere gain, and that in practicing their profession they be not motivated by the principles of the delicatessen-owner. In these cases, the pure business principle is subordinated to a certain moral standard which we may call professional ethics. Members of such professions frequently have or are expected to have a strong service instinct. Expressions such as "trade" or "business," applied to the professions of medicine or law, are felt to be out of place and demeaning. But even the pure businessman who adheres unbendingly to the principle of exact reciprocity in exchange does not, by so doing, remain completely neutral in an ethical sense. His unbending conduct, and the conduct of those with whom he does business, is at bottom conditioned by the acceptance of certain ultimate principles, for the lack of which the business society itself will in the long run founder. It is, therefore, of great importance not to forget the moral reserves which nourish the prosaic and in itself ethically neutral world of pure business, and with which it stands or falls.[2]

The proportions in which the three methods are found and in which they are combined determine in the final analysis what we call the *economic spirit* of an age. The evolution of our own times can be better understood in the light of the dou-

---

[2] Ed. note: For the author's original footnote, see Appendix 3: Economics and Ethics.

ble moral standard which has for so long prevailed: a sterner code is applied within the narrow circle of our own family and friends (internal morality) and a laxer one is employed in our dealings with strangers (external morality). For a soldier to steal from his bunk-mates is regarded as a low form of treachery, while to practice the same theft upon the occupants of a neighboring barrack passes for a feat of cunning. And let the same soldier return laden with loot taken from the citizens of a conquered country and his mates will give him a hero's welcome. The evolution of the last few centuries can then be regarded as a process in which *the domain of internal morality has been continuously enlarged while its content has been simultaneously diluted.* In the Middle Ages, trade among the small group of provincial guilds was rigidly circumscribed while a large place was reserved to charity—a natural outgrowth of the deeply religious spirit of that time. But beyond these confines there was much unscrupulous and unrestrained exploitation. In the course of the development which saw the rebirth of ancient morality (humanism) and the secularization of the substance of Christian morality, the principle of sacrifice lost much of its force, even among members of the same family. In its stead appeared a new principle, and one which served at the same time to reduce the practice of violence and exploitation to negligible proportions, viz., the selfsame business principle we have been discussing.[3]

---

[3] *Capitalism and the Economic Spirit:* The question of the origin of the modern economic spirit (spirit of capitalism) is one that has long interested students of economic history. Investigation has shown that the causes are many and complex and that they cannot be reduced to simple formulations, such as those advanced by Sombart, for example. The question can be studied only in connection with the intellectual history of Europe, in particular, the great movements of the Renaissance, of Humanism, of the Reformation, of nationalism, and of the Age of Enlightenment. Max Weber has drawn attention to the especial influence of Calvinism on the growth of the business spirit in his celebrated and still much discussed work, *The Protestant Ethic and*

Not all of the consequences of this development were happy ones. "Business" has occasionally lain its cold and impersonal hand on the family, requiring children to pay their parents for room and board; and science, art, even religion itself, have become commercialized to a lamentable extent. On the other hand, the general use of the business method has had the effect of narrowly circumscribing the area in which violence and exploitation can be profitably employed and of enlarging the sphere of activities yielding equal benefits to the participants.

A proper appreciation of the differences among the three methods aforementioned will prove helpful in dispelling a double confusion met with today at almost every turn. On the one hand, there is the common mistake of attributing to the third method (business) acts which properly should be put to the account of the first (fraud, exploitation, etc.). Some of us still cling tenaciously to the belief that business is nothing else than a shameless picking of other people's pockets, especially so when it is a question of as abstract and mysterious a business as the modern stock exchange. Just as deeply ingrained is the habit of describing business operations in terms suited only to acts of the first category. People speak of the "conquest" of markets and of the "imperialist exploitation" of foreign countries without realizing that they are confounding two entirely distinct categories of acts.[4] The myth that the employer always

---

the Spirit of Capitalism (New York, 1930). See also R. H. Tawney, *Religion and the Rise of Capitalism* (London, 1926); A. Rüstow, "Die Konfession in der Wirtschaftsgeschichte," *Revue de la Faculté des Sciences Economiques de l'Université d'Istanbul* (1942, nos. 3,4); for more comprehensive discussion of this theme, see Rüstow's major opus, *Ortsbestimmung der Gegenwart* (Vol. III, Zurich, 1957).

[4] *Capitalism and Imperialism:* What has been described in the text as the fusion of the method of exploitation with the method of business is a standard fixture of Marxist theory. Marxists argue that an economic system reposing on the business principle (capitalism) necessarily impels the capitalist countries to expand their political power for purposes of economic exploitation. The truth is that political expansion-

necessarily exploits his employees is another of the same series of errors.

On the other hand, the second and third methods (altruism and business) are also frequently confused. It is a confusion deliberately encouraged by a certain breed of businessman who desires to have people see in him the devotee of self-sacrifice and disinterested service, though in reality he is motivated solely by business considerations. He speaks of "serving the customers," he puts himself "at their disposal," he bids us "be at home," as if, like St. Francis of Assisi, he had nothing in his heart but the disinterested love of his fellow man. Each shop, each factory, becomes a kind of "studio" where work, relieved of its grosser motivations, is carried on on a higher and nobler plane. Cloaking ordinary business operations with such pious phraseology serves not only as effective advertisement, but is in the vanguard of the democratic instincts of our time. There is still, perhaps, unconscious resentment of the old contempt attaching to "people in trade," and it is comforting if the illusion can be created that one is not simply working out his life

---

ism undertaken for the purpose of economic exploitation (economic imperialism) is a phenomenon as old as history itself. Moreover, it is precisely such exploitation to which *our* economic system is opposed. Economic imperialism exists today as at every other period in history and as under every other economic system. Nothing would be more false than to regard it as a necessary element of *our* economic system. The causes of imperialism have their locus in quite another world than that of business. Moreover, the theory which seeks to prove that "capitalism" cannot exist without the incessant conquest of overseas markets will be found upon close examination to be untenable. See J. Schumpeter, *Social Classes and Imperialism: Two Essays* (New York, 1955); S. Rubinstein, *Herrschaft und Wirtschaft* (Munich, 1930); R. Behrendt, "Wirtschaft und Politik im Kapitalismus," *Schmollers Jahrbuch* (Vol. 57, 1933); W. Sulzbach, *National Consciousness* (Washington, D.C., 1943); W. Sulzbach, *Capitalistic Warmongers, A Modern Superstition* (Public Policy Pamphlet No. 35, University of Chicago Press, 1942); L. Robbins, *The Economic Causes of War* (London, 1939); W. Röpke, *International Order and Economic Integration* (Dordrecht, Holland, 1959).

43

within the drab business framework but that he is a dedicated being, a member even of a superior class. The "canonization" of business, if we may use the term, is particularly noticeable in the United States (witness the emergence of the peculiarly American doctrine of the "social responsibility" of business). It is accompanied by a tendency to relegate to a lower class all the professions which do not originate in business (scholars, civil servants, artists, career military officers). It is a process which has been made easier by the commercialization of these professions and the consequent perversion of the true hierarchies of rank and value—a grave American malady and one of which Europe, too, is beginning to exhibit the symptoms.

This complex of problems is one which properly should be of the greatest concern to economists. Indeed, before we pursue our inquiry any farther, it is necessary to stress the artificiality and extreme fragility of the pure reciprocity principle (business principle). "Business" is a product of civilization, and it cannot exist for long in the absence of a specific constellation of conditions, chiefly moral, which support our civilization. The economic ingredient in the constellation is, as we shall see, free competition. But free competition cannot function unless there is general acceptance of such norms of conduct as willingness to abide by the rules of the game and to respect the rights of others, to maintain professional integrity and professional pride, and to avoid deceit, corruption, and the manipulation of the power of the state for personal and selfish ends. The big question of our time is whether we have been so heedless and unsparing in the use of our moral reserves that it is no longer possible to renew these vital props of our economic system and whether it is yet possible to discover new sources of moral strength.

What Are Costs?

The perpetual tension between means and wants (scarcity) at once explains the meaning and fixes the goal of our economic system founded on exchange and the division of labor (business principle). Since we possess only limited means of satisfying our unlimited desires, we are compelled, as we have seen, to make a rigorous selection from among many competing wants and to limit the satisfaction of any one such want in order to make the best use of the means at hand (economic principle). Some will say that this view of economic behavior is quite appropriate to the conduct of the housewife who must hold her expenditures within the limits of a fixed sum of money (use of income, *economics of consumption*), but that it does not apply either to individual economy insofar as it is *economy of acquisition* (procuring of income), nor to the *national economy* since, in these two cases, the means are not fixed but may be increased by production.

Further reflection shows, however, that production changes nothing with respect to the need for practicing economy in the use of means, but that it simply results in the transfer of the problem to a higher level (or levels). Why, for instance, do we not produce as much chocolate or paper as we can consume? Why is production stopped at a certain point—which in our business economy is determined by profitability—when there is still a large and unsatisfied need of paper and chocolate? Is this the result of a stupid organization of our economic system from which socialism will deliver us? Such questions do not merit serious reply, for it is clear that production is tied to "costs." But "costs of production" mean simply that while the quantity of a given consumption good may be increased by production, we encounter a scarcity of certain ultimate factors of production whose quantity cannot be so increased. Ultimately, we are compelled to acknowledge the harsh facts that our capacity for work and our time are strictly limited; that the location and the fertility of the soil are immutable data of Nature; and that even tools and machinery cannot be increased in quantity according to our good pleasure. In using these ultimate factors of production for the production of one good, we thereby renounce the use of the same factors for the production of another good. When we draw a coverlet by one end, the other end does not become longer. We have, then, no other alternative but by means of choice and limitation to allocate the factors of production to the producing of the kinds and quantities of goods which will procure the maximum advantage from the available means.

It follows that the need to make the most economical use of a given supply of means is not the less urgent simply because we can increase this supply by production. The process of equating means and wants takes place in this case merely on a higher level. It is distinguished from the simple process of determining what use is to be made of a given supply of means in the same manner as the traveler's estimation of the relative utilities of taking more and bigger bags on a journey is distinguished from the case of the soldier who must pack his sack with foreknowledge of exactly what articles he must get into it. In the case of the traveler, more trunks and suitcases are taken along only "at the cost" of other pleasures of the trip. Just so, the costs of production are nothing more, in the final analysis, than a faithful reflection of the utility that the factors of production would have furnished had they been otherwise employed—a utility which we renounce in favor of the one we have chosen. *The costs of production, in sum, owe their existence and their amount to the competition of alternative uses for the factors of production.*[5] They stand for utilities which escape us at some other point in the national economy.

This is a principle of such overriding importance that it is worth dwelling on it in some detail. Suppose, for example, that it is planned to build a bridge. What are the problems

---

[5] Ed. note: For the author's original footnote, see Appendix 4: Costs as a Renunciation of Alternative Utilities.

that must be faced here? The first order of business is, generally, for technicians and engineers to calculate the costs of building a bridge of a given type and quality. These costs are subsequently compared with the traffic needs of the projected bridge site on the one hand, and on the other, with the possibility of financing the bridge out of the public purse. That is to say, we take into account the urgency of *other* public needs as this urgency is reflected in the possibility or impossibility of diverting a part of current tax revenue to the construction of the bridge or of increasing taxes in general. Taxes, on their side, represent the personal utility which the taxpayers must renounce in transferring a part of their purchasing power to the state. Thus we see that the "costs" of building a bridge are simply an indication that for the land which must be preempted, for the workmen who must be hired, and for the steel which must be used (including all the resources required in the making of the steel), there are still other uses. And it is the intensity of the competition among these alternative uses which determines the costs, greater or less, of the aforementioned factors of production. The process of production then, analyzed to its foundations, clearly shows the alternative nature of costs. In fine, the construction of the bridge will be justified from an economic point of view if it can be shown that it will result in the best possible use being made of the given means with relation to the national economy.

Our example—the building of a bridge—makes clear the important difference between the economic and the technical (or engineering) point of view. The job of the economist is to decide, first, whether the bridge should be built at all; secondly, whether it should be built on one site rather than another. For the economist the total quantity of means is fixed; his task is to discover the best use that can be made of them. The job of the engineer, on the other hand, is to achieve a given end—in our example, the construction of a bridge of a given quality in a given location—with the least means (technical principle). Here, differently than in economics, the end is given, while the means must be found. The successful solution of the technical problems involved in building a bridge does not in the least imply that its construction is justified economically. Economic justification follows only after costs have been entered on the ledger; only, that is, after the proposed use of means is compared with alternative possible uses and a satisfactory balance established among them. For all of this, confusion of technical with economic problems remains a tenacious undergrowth in the economic thought of our time. Fallacies stemming from it are particularly rife in the field of foreign trade (which is a fertile breeding ground for error in any case).

It is almost an *idée fixe*[6] of contemporary economic policy to see economic advantage for the nation in the exploitation of technical discoveries and inventions and to support the production of synthetic foods or raw materials, even though the synthetic product costs more than the imported natural product and requires special measures to make it "competitive." Apparently, only a minority comprehends that the same reasoning which is used to defend the production of synthetics can be used to justify cotton growing in the Arctic Circle so long as the engineers can supply the necessary greenhouses and artificial heat. Although the manufacture of synthetic materials has registered some notable successes and shows promise, in some cases, of even greater success in the future, the role of costs in this field cannot be ignored. Every so often, the complaint is heard that the limitations set on production by costs are the result of our stupid "capitalist" system, a ball and chain which we ought to shake off once for all and thereby win both riches and freedom. Such naive assumptions would quickly wither, were it more energetically made known that *the problem of costs is nothing other than the problem of deciding whether the productive forces of a country will be better employed in one direction than in another.* Here, certainly, is the most elementary problem confronting any economy, whatever be its organization.

---

[6] Ed. note: "fixed idea," theme, or obsession.

Economic Equilibrium: The Possible Systems

We have now, perhaps, established the truth that in every economic system man is bound by the necessities of choice and limitation. Every economic system consequently must have available to it a device for balancing means with ends. We already have gained some idea of the equilibrium mechanism which is peculiar to our economic system. But for a still clearer apprehension of how this mechanism functions, we must examine briefly the several possible systems of equilibrium.

System of the Queue

System of the queue could as well be called the system of elbowing one's way through the crowd, or the system of first come, first served. It is the simplest and most brutal form of equating supply with demand. It consists in offering the available supply to the public gratis, and it invariably results in a more or less violent use of fist and elbow. This system is so unsatisfactory and so little able to guarantee that the most urgent needs of the community will be met that recourse to it is had only in exceptional cases. We are reminded, perhaps, of those occasions on which the beer runs out at "free beer" parties, or of neighborhood get-togethers at which the refreshments set out are quickly devoured by the first wave of guests to the dismay of those who come after. The experiment undertaken by the Soviet dictatorship in its early years is very instructive in this connection. The streetcars and other means of transport were placed at the disposal of the public free of charge. The result, as was to be expected, was such a crush of passengers that the government was soon compelled to return to the "capitalist" equilibrium mechanism (price system). Anyone who has ever tried to watch a parade through the head of the man in front of him knows that the best viewing spots must be preempted well ahead of time. Indeed, when the crowd is very large—as, for example, at the coronation or the funeral of a monarch—it is common practice to resort to the price system for the disposal of the better places. It is to be noted that the system of the queue is the more undesirable the greater the elasticity of demand for a good or service.[7] Hence, it will prove easier to put the water of the public fountains at the free disposal of the citizens than to allow them, as in the Russian case, to use the streetcars without paying. The proposal to have free medical services supplied by nationalized doctors should be examined in the same light. The experiences of the British with their National Health Service provide a costly lesson of what may be expected from such an arrangement.

A Rationing System

A rationing system shows a certain advance over the system of the queue. Here, too, goods are supplied gratis, but equilibrium is obtained by a systematic distribution of the available goods (rationing). It is such a mechanism which would operate in a pure Communist economy. Even in our economic system, however, it is occasionally necessary to have recourse to this method. Every soldier will recall that in the field not only was food rationed, but also cigars, cigarettes and pipe tobacco. The distribution of food did not involve any great difficulties since individual wants were fairly uniform. But the distribution of tobacco, cigarettes, etc., given the pronounced differences in individual preferences, was regularly followed by a lively private exchange where, under a primitive form, the price system again prevailed. This example shows that under a system of rationing (as well as under the queue system), the difficulties increase with the increase in the elasticity of demand for the rationed product.[8]

---

[7] Ed. note: See p. 32 above.

[8] *The Pure Rationing System*: The interesting lessons of a pure system of rationing operating under conditions of war, and the economic implications thereof, are presented in detail in R. A. Radford, "The Economic Organization of a P.O.W. Camp," *Economica* (November, 1948).

The Mixed System

Where prices are introduced, as in a mixed system, the disadvantages of queueing and rationing are somewhat mitigated. Generally, in such cases, the prices are fixed at levels insufficient to balance supply and demand. Nevertheless, the very existence of these prices tends to bring about a certain limitation of demand. What results, therefore, is a mixture of the price system with one or the other of the systems already described. During both World Wars the mixed system, under the names of "ceiling prices" or "price control," was regularly imposed by the belligerent governments on their respective economies. Experience with this system, however, soon compelled abandonment of the queue-price system in favor of a rationing-price system. For it had become apparent that once the maximum prices were established, the equilibrium mechanism of the price system refused to work. When prices were prevented from rising to the point where supply and demand exactly balanced, a part of demand necessarily remained unsatisfied. The people who were ready to pay the maximum price queued up before the shops, but invariably those at the end of the line went away empty-handed. So intolerable did this situation become that recourse was finally had to a system of ration tickets for a list of selected goods.

Ultimately, of course, the disturbances which price controls provoked on the supply side required government intervention in production itself. Indeed, during World War II, such intervention was universally practiced. The result was that each day that went by saw a further disappearance of the regulating principles of our economic system, ending in a veritable economic muddle. Following World War I, most countries hastened to put an end to the confusion by reestablishing a free economy, i.e., the unhindered price system. And in the post–World War II era, all advanced countries have sought, and rightfully so, to dismantle the system of wartime controls.

Rent controls, the most durable of the wartime price-ceilings, offer a good example of the evolution we have described, beginning with the queue-plus-price system and ending with the rationing-plus-price system. Our experiences with rent control have shown how intolerable in the long run is the situation created by the mixed system. Even in its less noxious form of prices combined with rationing, the marked inferiority of the mixed system vis-à-vis the price system is obvious. This has been publicly acknowledged even in the Soviet Union where the ending of rationing on certain classes of goods was celebrated as an example of progress on the road leading to a more normal situation.

The thoroughly abnormal circumstances of the Great Depression and later of World War II pushed many countries to new experiments with the mixed system. Thus, exchange control is in reality only a variant of the rationing-plus-price system, as is also the control and distribution by government of imported raw materials. The system of ceiling prices was also revived in the foodstuffs markets both under the form of the queue-plus-price system and the rationing-plus-price system. And here again the consensus was that the mixed system is at best only a temporary expedient. The continued repression of a natural force builds up explosive pressures with the result that the price system in one form or another inevitably breaks through the unnatural tensions and rigidities of the mixed system. The greater the amount of unsatisfied demand, the more numerous will be the subterfuges used to circumvent the maximum prices and the bolder will become the disregard for the law. Black markets, under-the-counter deals, illegal currency transactions—a thousand years' experience has shown that these things accompany price control as shadows do the light. Such activities, customarily denounced as "fraud," "smuggling," etc., appear from the objective standpoint of economics merely as corrections of the mixed system by the price system. From the standpoint of ethics these "corrections" are less than edifying and are certainly not the work of the better members of society. Economically speaking, however, they are not always and necessarily harmful. The United States' experience with Prohibition in the prewar era and in the postwar period the collapse of the command economy in Germany, Austria, and France prove that the maintenance of economic regulations to which the bulk of the population is opposed in conscience ends by exercising a strong demoralizing influence. A sort of respectability is attached to breaking the law. An economic system which continues to function thanks only to bootleggers, black marketeers, and smugglers becomes a focus of corruption which, little by little, poisons all the arteries of society. Here is a bitter lesson for those who continually petition for state control of economic life out of their moral indignation at the workings of the free economy.

All too often we hear a system of rationing being justified on the grounds that the goods in question are in "short supply" and that their distribution ought not to be left to the working of the price system. The reader is already aware that this point of view rests on a fundamental misconception. All goods which are not "free goods" are "scarce goods," meaning that not everyone can get as much of them as he would like. To say that a "scarce good" is one for which the demand exceeds the supply can have meaning only in relation to a specific price, namely the price which is held by the public authorities below the so-called equilibrium price at which supply and demand are in equality and whose function it is to bring about this equality. Hence, demand can really exceed supply only in those extraordinary situations in which the shortage of essential commodities is so acute that it is considered advisable to ration the available goods equally among the citizens rather than to permit distribution to take place on the basis of the unequally distributed dollars.

Consider, in this connection, the extreme scarcities which prevailed in practically all types of goods during World War II. The plight of the economy is then comparable to that of a besieged fortress whose commander is compelled to ration bread and water with the utmost severity. In such case, everyone will approve the rationing of the vital commodities. But it is extremely doubtful whether this notion of the "besieged fortress" can be validly applied to the economy in peacetime. We should not forget that what we are concerned with in peacetime is not only fair distribution, but an increase in production itself. The *dilemma* inherent in any system of rationing thus becomes clear: in seeking to distribute the available supply as fairly as possible, we run the risk of causing a constant diminishment of the amount available for distribution until, in the end, we get a system of rationed poverty, or "poorhouse socialism." The more we depart from the situation of the "besieged fortress," the more necessary it is to recommence production and the more self-defeating, therefore, does a policy of rationing with price control become. Keeping the prices of commodities as low as possible for reasons of social justice discourages their production precisely in the degree to which the price-controlled goods are essential. Such a policy ends by requiring the scarcest goods to be sold at the lowest prices. If the policy is not applied uniformly to *all* goods and services, it amounts to the conferring of a premium for nonproduction of the very goods most needed. The result is that in countries where such a policy is pursued, the stores are filled with the most nonessential and useless goods, the prices of which, precisely on this account, the authorities have left uncontrolled.

From the above it might be assumed that a discussion of the mixed system should be reserved for a chapter on economic pathology. But this assumption would be incorrect. For although it is true that this system, when extensively applied, is dangerous and sometimes fatal, in small doses it is relatively harmless. We find it operative in an astonishingly large number of normal economic processes where it appears inopportune, for one reason or another, to use the price system in its pure form. Railroad, bus, and taxi fares, the prices of theatre and movie tickets, as well as many other prices, are ordinarily rigidly fixed, in spite of daily fluctuations in demand (institutional prices). The consequence is that these prices under certain circumstances fulfill only imperfectly their equilibrium function; such prices, for all practical purposes, become maximum prices, proof of which is seen in the block-long queues in front of movie houses and theatres where a hit show is playing, in the throngs that pack trains and busses, in the desperate mien of some *paterfamilias* as, homeward bound from vacation with his numerous offspring and equally numerous valises, he stands before the railroad station waving frantically (and vainly) at passing taxis. Even in these cases, there is a tendency for the price system to reassert itself. So we have the perennial ticket scalper, reserved seats on trains and ... tips. If even these devices fail to correct the disequilibrium in demand, the institutional prices themselves will be changed in the end.

The Price System

The systems analyzed so far show so plainly the nature of the price system that a long explanation seems unnecessary. Its principal characteristic is that equilibrium (choice and limitation) is attained by leaving prices free to adapt themselves to the market situation, so that there is neither an excess of unsatisfied demand nor an excess of unabsorbed supply (equilibrium price). In the systems previously described, the question of who will bear the costs is distinct from the question of whose needs will be satisfied. In the price system, these elements are fused. The cost of satisfying a given want is imposed on the demanding individual in the price itself. But, as we have already seen, the existence of costs shows that the factors of production which are used for one purpose might have been used with equal advantage for some other purpose. Thus, the price system allocates the factors of production in a way which allows us to perceive, in broad outline, the process by which general economic equilibrium is attained.

Since, in a free price system, costs are necessarily borne by consumers, it is the consumers who decide what and how much shall be produced. Hence, it is the consumers who decide how the factors of production themselves are to be used. This mechanism functions ideally when not an iota of productive resources is employed in a way which yields less utility than if it were used in some other way. The tying of prices to costs, which many regard as one of the stupid quirks of "capitalism," thus assumes a function which is central to any economic system, whatever its organization: the function, namely, of effecting the best possible allocation of the nation's productive resources. This does not in the least imply that our economic system, founded for the most part on the price system, is perfect. For in the price system, only those individual demands count which are backed up by the requisite purchasing power. Even if the price system functioned ideally, the factors of production would be employed in the "best possible" manner only in relation to the existing (and unequal) distribution of income. No one will seriously pretend that our present distribution of income is the best possible. As the result of such unequal distribution a rich cat fancier, to take one example, can buy milk to feed her animals while milk is denied to the mother of a family of poor children because she cannot pay for it. We should not make the mistake of equating the explanation of the price system with a glorification of it, for this would be to fall into the error of the classical school which derived from such explanation premature conclusions with respect to economic policy (laissez-faire liberalism).

When we consider economic history, on the other hand, and in particular the recent history of the Soviet Union, we must conclude that the price system, in spite of all its imperfections and in spite of the situations in which it is inapplicable, remains the most natural method of solving the problem of economic equilibrium. Indeed, its essential irrepressibility is shown in the spectacular failure of the efforts to displace it and to frustrate it. An extremely differentiated society such as our own, resting on an intensive division of labor, is inconceivable outside the framework of the price system. Indeed, if the Communist economic experiment, and the National Socialist economic experiment which so closely resembled it, have proven one thing, it is that the most resolute will to impose collectivism is forced, in the end, to capitulate to the elemental equilibrium forces of the price system.

The System of Collective Economy

To understand this last of the possible equilibrium systems, we must take account of a group of special needs to which none of the systems of which we have spoken thus far can be applied. Up to now, we have tacitly supposed that we were concerned only with the needs of individuals which are satisfied by an act of individual consumption (individual demand). But there are still other wants which are experienced by the members of society collectively (collective demand), without it being possible to distinguish the specific utility accruing to individuals from the satisfaction thereof. Some familiar examples are the collectively felt wants for armed forces, for a police force, for protection against epidemics, for street lights. The street light is an indivisible good which cannot be distributed individually to those who declare themselves ready to pay their "share" of the cost. Neither can we deny street lights to the general public because some people, such as lovers or burglars, are annoyed by them. It is the business of the state to satisfy these collective demands. It is the state which assumes the task of choosing and of limiting; it must procure the means of meeting costs in a manner which, contrary to the price system, is completely divorced from benefits accruing to individuals as such. The equity of the procedure resides rather in basing the collection of funds for the given collective demand on the ability of individuals to pay (taxation). All the questions which arise with respect to this collective method of achieving equilibrium belong to the sphere of public finance which is consequently properly studied as part of general economics.[9]

The system of collective economy frequently finds application in cases where collective needs do not actually exist. Although in these cases the other equilibrium mechanisms could be employed, it is regarded as desirable on various grounds to treat the want in question as a collective want. Bridges and

---

[9] *Collective Economy—The Basis of Public Finance.* The essential difference between the price system and the system of collective economy consists in this: in the price system, the equilibration of supply and demand occurs automatically in the market; in the collective economy, it is established as the result of conscious political decision. In the price system, individual preferences are directly manifested; their manifestation in the system of collective economy involves long and complicated detours. The fact that some private persons furnish their homes with Oriental rugs must as a general rule be regarded simply as an expression of their individual preferences. It is something to which no one can take exception, at least within the context of the existing distribution of wealth and income. But where the floors of public buildings are covered with Oriental rugs, we immediately begin to wonder whether waste or graft is being practiced by our public officials. We will have in this case grounds (generally good ones) for suspecting that a collective need is being satisfied at the expense of some more important need of individuals, i.e., of taxpayers. It is obvious that tendencies towards waste are inherent in a system of collective economy, particularly where, as in our age of swollen government budgets, the public sector has been continuously expanded. It is in any case difficult to conceive of any alternative method which would enable governments at all times harmoniously to coordinate the satisfaction of collective wants with the satisfaction of individual wants. Further examination of these problems would carry us deep into the intricacies of public finance. See H. Dalton, *Principles of Public Finance* (London, 1923); W. Röpke, *Finanzwissenschaft* (1929); K. Wicksell, *Finanztheoretische Untersuchungen* (1896); M. Cassel, *Die Gemeinwirtschaft* (1925); W. Gerloff and F. Neumark, *Handbuch der Finanzwissenschaft* (2nd ed., Vol I, 1951); O. Pfleiderer, *Die Staatswirtschaft und das Sozialprodukt* (1930); Ursula K. Hicks, *Public Finance* (London, 1947); R. A. Musgrave, *The Theory of Public Finance—A Study in Public Economy* (New York, 1959).

roads, for example, are, as a general rule, paid for on a collective basis out of taxes, although there is no reason why the price system would not work equally well in such cases. For proof, we need only recall the practice, common enough in former times and now revived in some countries, of charging tolls for the use of highways and bridges. It is our modern concern for social justice that has resulted in the placing of many hitherto individual needs in the category of collective needs. Primary education, for example, is today almost universally supplied on a collective basis. Other wants have become partly collective, such as secondary and university education, the cost of which is met for the greater part by the state.

The case of secondary and university education is particularly instructive. For in the degree in which the state assumes the costs, there arises a danger of oversupplying candidates for the professions, unless a method of limiting the admission of students is developed to replace the older ability-to-pay criterion (for example, *numerus clausus*,[10] or better, a rigorous examination of students' intellectual aptitudes). Hence, the cheaper higher education becomes, the more necessary it will be to increase the difficulty of examinations.

It should be noted, finally, that a system of complete "Communism" is reached when all needs are treated as collective needs and hence are satisfied in accordance with the system of collective economy ("from everyone according to his capacity, to everyone according to his needs").[11] The continued enlargement of the collective sector of the national economy, which is characteristic of the economic evolution of the last one hundred years, must therefore be considered as an enlargement of the "Communist" element in our economic system. The

---

[10] Ed. note: "closed number," i.e., the method of setting a limit on the number of students that may be admitted to an institution.

[11] Ed. note: See Karl Marx, "Critique of the Gotha Programme," in *Karl Marx and Frederick Engels: Selected Works in Two Volumes* (Moscow: Foreign Languages Publishing House, 1958), 2:24.

continued growth of the public sector (system of collective economy) at the cost of the private sector (price system) must, by the same token, be taken as an indication that an increasing number of economic processes are taking place in accordance with laws radically different from those which regulate the market economy.

4

THE CONDITIONS AND LIMITS OF THE MARKET*

The questionable things of this world come to grief on their nature, the good ones on their own excesses. Conservative respect for the past and its preservation are indispensable conditions of a sound society, but to cling exclusively to tradition, history, and established customs is an exaggeration leading to intolerable rigidity. The liberal predilection for movement and progress is an equally indispensable counterweight, but if it sets no limits and recognizes nothing as lasting and worth preserving, it ends in disintegration and destruction. The rights of the community are no less imperative than those of the individual, but exaggeration of the rights of the community in the form of collectivism is just as dangerous as exaggerated individualism and its extreme form, anarchism. Ownership ends up in plutocracy, authority in bondage and despotism, democracy in arbitrariness and demagogy. Whatever political tendencies or currents we choose as examples, it will be found that they always sow the seed of their own destruction when they lose their sense of proportion and overstep their limits. In this field, suicide is the normal cause of death.

---

*Chapter 3 of Wilhelm Röpke, *A Humane Economy: The Social Framework of the Free Market*, trans. Elizabeth Henderson (Chicago: Regnery, 1960).

The market economy is no exception to the rule. Indeed, its advocates, in so far as they are at all intellectually fastidious, have always recognized that the sphere of the market, of competition, of the system where supply and demand move prices and thereby govern production, may be regarded and defended only as part of a wider general order encompassing ethics, law, the natural conditions of life and happiness, the state, politics, and power. Society as a whole cannot be ruled by the laws of supply and demand, and the state is more than a sort of business company, as has been the conviction of the best conservative opinion since the time of Burke. Individuals who compete on the market and there pursue their own advantage stand all the more in need of the social and moral bonds of community, without which competition degenerates most grievously. As we have said before, the market economy is not everything. It must find its place in a higher order of things which is not ruled by supply and demand, free prices, and competition. It must be firmly contained within an all-embracing order of society in which the imperfections and harshness of economic freedom are corrected by law and in which man is not denied conditions of life appropriate to his nature. Man can wholly fulfill his nature only by freely becoming part of a community and having a sense of solidarity with it. Otherwise he leads a miserable existence and he knows it.

Social Rationalism

The truth is that a society may have a market economy and, at one and the same time, perilously unsound foundations and conditions, for which the market economy is not responsible but which its advocates have every reason to improve or wish to see improved so that the market economy will remain politically and socially feasible in the long run. There is no other way of fulfilling our wish to possess both a market economy and a sound society and a nation where people are, for the most part, happy.

Economists have their typical *déformation professionelle*, their own occupational disease of the mind. Each of us speaks from personal experience when he admits that he does not find it easy to look beyond the circumscribed field of his own discipline and to acknowledge humbly that the sphere of the market, which it is his profession to explore, neither exhausts nor determines society as a whole. The market is only one section of society. It is a very important section, it is true, but still one whose existence is justifiable and possible only because it is part of a larger whole which concerns not economics but philosophy, history, and theology. We may be forgiven for misquoting Lichtenberg and saying: To know economics only is to know not even that.[1] Man, in the words of the Gospel, does not live by bread alone. Let us beware of that caricature of an economist who, watching people cheerfully disporting themselves in their suburban allotments, thinks he has said everything there is to say when he observes that this is not a rational way of producing vegetables—forgetting that it may be an eminently rational way of producing happiness, which alone matters in the last resort. Adam Smith, whose fame rests not only on his *Wealth of Nations* but also on his *Theory of Moral Sentiments*, would have known better.

All of this has always been clear to us, and this is why we have never felt quite comfortable in the company of "liberals," even when styled "neo-liberals." But for everything there is season. We have been through years of untold misery and disorders which so many Western countries, including, in particular, Germany, brought upon themselves by their disregard of the most elementary principles of economic order. During

---

[1] Ed. note: Georg Christoph Lichtenberg (1742–1799) was a German physicist and satirist well known for his aphorisms. He was preoccupied with philosophical problems that would affect the proper method and validity of the natural sciences. See J. P. Stern, *Lichtenberg: A Doctrine of Scattered Occasions Reconstructed from His Aphorisms and Reflections* (Bloomington: Indiana University Press, 1959), 75–126.

these years there was a compelling need to put the accent on the "bread" of which the Gospel speaks and on the re-establishment of an economic order based on the market economy. To do this was imperative. Today, when the market economy has been revived up to a point and when even its partial re-establishment more than fulfills our expectations, it is equally imperative to think of the other and higher things here under discussion. That the hour is ripe for this is appreciated by all who are wise enough to sense the danger of stopping short at "bread." It is a sign of the times that those who experience and voice these misgivings have become surprisingly numerous everywhere. They include a growing number of economists in several countries who, independently of each other, are stepping out of the ivory tower of their science to explore the open country "beyond supply and demand."[2] As far as this author is concerned, he is doing no more than returning to scientific work of a kind which he has considered paramount ever since he wrote his book on *The Social Crisis of Our Time*.[3]

---

[2] Among contemporary economists who have turned their attention to the ethical framework of the economy, we may mention J. M. Clark, *The Ethical Basis of Economic Freedom* (The Kazanjian Foundation Lectures, 1955) and David McCord Wright, *Democracy and Progress* (New York, 1948). It is also pertinent to recall the following passages from J. C. L. Simonde de Sismondi's *Nouveaux principes d'économie politique* (2nd ed., Paris, 1827): "The mass of the people, and the philosophers, too, seem to forget that the increase of wealth is not the purpose of political economy but the means at its disposal for insuring the happiness of all." (p. iv) "When England forgets people for thinking of things, is she not sacrificing the aim to the means?" (p. ix) "A nation where no one suffers want, but where no one has enough leisure or enough wellbeing to give full scope to his feelings and thought, is only half civilized, even if its lower classes have a fair chance of happiness." (p. 2) Indeed, the entire first chapter of this book is well worth rereading.

[3] Ed. note: Wilhelm Röpke, *The Social Crisis of Our Time*, trans. Annette Schiffer Jacobsohn and Peter Schiffer Jacobsohn (Chicago: University of Chicago Press, 1950).

To the economist, the market economy, as seen from the restricting viewpoint of his own discipline, appears to be no more than one particular type of economic order, a kind of "economic technique" opposed to the socialist one. It is significant of this approach that the very name of the structural principle of this economic order has been borrowed from the language of technology: we speak of the "price mechanism." We move in a world of prices, markets, competition, wage rates, rates of interest, exchange rates, and other economic magnitudes. All of this is perfectly legitimate and fruitful as long as we keep in mind that we have narrowed our angle of vision and do not forget that the market economy is the economic order proper to a definite social structure and to a definite spiritual and moral setting. If we were to neglect the market economy's characteristic of being merely a part of a spiritual and social total order, we would become guilty of an aberration which may be described as social rationalism.

Social rationalism misleads us into imagining that the market economy is no more than an "economic technique" that is applicable in any kind of society and in any kind of spiritual and social climate. Thus the undeniable success of the revival of the market economy in many countries gave quite a few socialists the idea that the price mechanism was a device which an otherwise socialist economy could well use to its own benefit. In this concept of a "socialist market economy," which Tito seems to want to translate into practice,[4] the market economy is thought of as part of a social system that is best described as an enormous apparatus of administration. In this sense, even

---

[4] Ed. note: Josip Broz Tito was a Yugoslav communist revolutionary and statesman who served as president of Yugoslavia from 1953 to 1980. Beginning in 1950, and with Tito's support, Yugoslavia began a series of economic reforms called "workers' self-management" (*radničko samoupravljanje*) including elements of profit sharing and workplace democracy absent in other centrally planned and managed communist states. See David Prychitko, *Marxism and Workers' Self-Management: The Essential Tension* (New York: Greenwood, 1991).

the Communist economic system of Soviet Russia has always had a "market sector," although it is undoubtedly no more than a technical device and contrivance and not a living organism. How could a genuine market, an area of freedom, spontaneity, and unregimented order, thrive in a social system which is the exact opposite in all respects?

The same social rationalism is evident in the attitude of certain contemporary economists who, while not open partisans of socialism and sometimes speaking in the name of the market economy, work out the most elaborate projects for regulating the movements of the circular flow of the economy. They seem to be prepared to transform the economy into an enormous pumping engine with all sorts of ducts and valves and thermostats, and they not only seem confident that it will function according to the instructions for use, but they also seem to be unaware of the question of whether such a machine is compatible with the atmosphere of the market, to which freedom is essential.

All of these protagonists of social rationalism—socialists and circular-flow technicians alike—have a common tendency to become so bemused by aggregate money and income flows that they overlook the fundamental significance of ownership. The market economy rests not on one pillar but on two. It presupposes not only the principle of free prices and competition but also the institution of private ownership, in the true sense of legally safeguarded freedom to dispose of one's own property, including freedom of testation.

To grasp the full significance of ownership to a free society, we must understand that ownership has a dual function. Ownership means, as in civil law, the delimitation of the individual sphere of decision and responsibility against that of other individuals. But ownership also means protection of the individual sphere from political power. It traces limits on the horizontal plane, and also vertically, and only this dual function can fully explain the significance of ownership as an indispensable condition of liberty. All earlier generations of social philosophers agreed on this point.

But ownership is not only a condition of the market economy, it is of the essence. This becomes evident from the following considerations. We start out from competition. We all realize its central importance for a free economy, but the concept is obscured by a confusing ambiguity. Communist governments, too, claim that they are using competition extensively and successfully. We have no reason to doubt that in the factories of Soviet Russia, the managers, and even the workers and employees, have ample opportunity for competitive performance. And in Yugoslavia, Tito made a whole system of the "decentralization" of public enterprises whereby the latter were divided up into independent and mutually competing units; he seems to regard this system, with some pride, as a sort of "socialist market economy." There can be no doubt that such an introduction of competition into a collectivist economic system may raise productivity. Is this not the same virtue which we have in mind when we ascribe the rapid recovery of the German economy chiefly to the re-establishment of competition?

There is obviously some confusion here, which calls for clarification. The confusion is due to neglect of the dual nature of competition and to the lumping together of things which should be kept strictly separate. Competition may have two meanings: it may be an institution for stimulating effort, or it may be a device for regulating and ordering the economic process. In the market economy, competition is both, and it constitutes, therefore, an unrivaled solution of the two cardinal problems of any economic system: the problem of continual inducement to maximum performance and the problem of a continual harmonious ordering and guidance of the economic process. The role of competition in the market economy is to be mainspring and regulator at one and the same time, and it is this dual function which is the secret of the competitive market economy and its inimitable performance.

If we now return to the question of whether a collectivist economic order can take advantage of competition and thus appropriate the secret of the market economy's success without impairing the collectivist nature of the economic order, we know that the answer depends upon which aspect of competition is meant. Competition as a stimulant is simply a psychological technique that is as applicable in a collectivist economy as in a market economy or, indeed, in any group, be it a school or a regiment or any other. We may even note that as far as the effects of competition on human destinies are concerned, it may, in collectivist systems, be hardened in a way that is unknown and impossible in the market economy. But the other function of competition, which is at least equally important for its economic effectiveness, the function of selection in the area of material means of production, meets with the greatest obstacles in collectivist systems. In relation to people, the carrot and the stick are ruthlessly applied, but it is quite another question whether in collectivist systems competition can accomplish so uncompromising, undeviating, and continual a selection of products and firms as takes place in the market economy.

Even on the unwarrantedly charitable assumption that collectivist public authorities resist the temptation to hush up investment errors and have the honest intention to carry out such a continual selection in accordance with the dictates of competition, they would lack the indispensable criterion. This brings us to the other function of competition: to serve as an instrument of the economic order as a whole and as a regulator of the economic process. Unlike the market economy, the collectivist economy is necessarily debarred from such use of competition because no collectivist system can create the necessary precondition without losing its own identity. This precondition is genuine economic independence of firms. Only on this condition is the formation of genuine scarcity prices for capital and consumer goods conceivable, but there can be no independence of firms without private ownership and related freedom of action.

Thus everything is interlocked: competition as a regulator of the economy presupposes free market prices; free market prices are impossible without genuine independence of economic units, and their independence stands and falls by private ownership and freedom of decision, unimpaired and undisturbed by government planning. No collectivist economy can possibly satisfy the last of these conditions without ceasing to be collectivist, and therefore it cannot enjoy the advantages of the regulatory and guiding functions of competition. To try to arrange such competition artificially would be as absurd for a collectivist system as it would be for me to want to play bridge with myself. It follows that "socialist competition" can, at best, stimulate (economically not necessarily rational) performance but cannot rule and guide the economic process. It is only half of what competition is in the market economy, and we may well ask whether this bisection does not reduce the effectiveness of even that half of competition which alone is accessible to collectivism, namely, the stimulating effect. Be that as it may, it remains a serious weakness in any collectivist economy that competition can, at best, fulfill only one of its functions, and even that less than optimally. And it is the incomparable strength of the market economy that it alone can take advantage of the dual nature of competition, which is genuine and fully effective only when it is whole. Just as unavoidable limitation to one aspect of competition gravely handicaps collectivism, so does the combination of both aspects of competition give the market economy a start which cannot be overtaken. This is the prerogative of the market economy, but this prerogative stands and falls by private ownership of the means of production.

The economic function of private ownership tends to be obstinately underestimated, and even more so is its moral and sociological significance for a free society. The reason is, no doubt, that the ethical universe in which ownership has its place is hard for social rationalism even to understand, let alone to find congenial. And since social rationalism is in ascendancy everywhere, it is not surprising that the institution of ownership has been badly shaken. Even discussions on questions concerning the management of firms are often conducted in terms which suggest that the owner has followed the consumer and the taxpayer into the limbo of "forgotten men."[5] The true role of ownership can be appreciated only if we look upon it as representative of something far beyond what is visible and measurable. Ownership illustrates the fact that the market economy is a form of economic order belonging to a particular philosophy of life and to a particular social and moral universe. This we now have to define, and in so doing the word "bourgeois"[6] imposes itself, however much mass public opinion (especially of the intellectual masses) may, after a century of deformation by Marxist propaganda, dislike this designation or find it ridiculous.

In all honesty, we have to admit that the market economy has a bourgeois foundation. This needs to be stressed all the more because the romantic and socialist reaction against everything bourgeois has, for generations past, been astonishingly successful in turning this concept into a parody of itself from

---

[5] Ed. note: The concept of the "forgotten man" comes from an essay of the same name by American social scientist William Graham Sumner (1840–1910): "As soon as A observes something which seems to him to be wrong, from which X is suffering, A talks it over with B, and A and B then propose to get a law passed to remedy the evil and help X. Their law always proposes to determine what C shall do for X or, in the better case, what A, B and C shall do for X. As for A and B, who get a law to make themselves do for X what they are willing to do for him, we have nothing to say except that they might better have done it without any law, but what I want to do is to look up C. I want to show you what manner of man he is. I call him the Forgotten Man." William Graham Sumner, *The Forgotten Man and Other Essays*, ed. Albert Galloway Keller (New Haven: Yale University Press, 1918), 466.

[6] The word "bourgeois" is here used to correspond to the German word *bürgerlich*, in a completely non-pejorative and non-political sense. As will be seen from the context, the word is used to designate a particular way of life and set of values.

which it is very difficult to get away. The market economy, and with it social and political freedom, can thrive only as a part and under the protection of a bourgeois system. This implies the existence of a society in which certain fundamentals are respected and color the whole network of social relationships: individual effort and responsibility, absolute norms and values, independence based on ownership, prudence and daring, calculating and saving, responsibility for planning one's own life, proper coherence with the community, family feeling, a sense of tradition and the succession of generations combined with an open-minded view of the present and the future, proper tension between individual and community, firm moral discipline, respect for the value of money, the courage to grapple on one's own with life and its uncertainties, a sense of the natural order of things, and a firm scale of values. Whoever turns up his nose at these things or suspects them of being "reactionary" may in all seriousness be asked what scale of values and what ideals he intends to defend against Communism without having to borrow from it.

To say that the market economy belongs to a basically bourgeois total order implies that it presupposes a society which is the opposite of proletarianized society, in the wide and pregnant sense which it is my continual endeavor to explain, and also the opposite of mass society as discussed in the preceding chapter. Independence, ownership, individual reserves, saving, the sense of responsibility, rational planning of one's own life—all that is alien, if not repulsive, to proletarianized mass society. Yet precisely that is the condition of a society which cherishes its liberty. We have arrived at a point where we are simply forced to recognize that here is the true watershed between social philosophies and that every one of us must choose for himself, knowing that the choice is between irreconcilable alternatives and that the destiny of our society is at stake.

Once we have recognized this necessity of a fundamental choice, we must apply it in practice and draw the conclusions in all fields. It may come as a shock to many of us to realize how much we have already submitted to the habits of thought of an essentially unbourgeois world. This is true, not least, of economists, who like to think in terms of money flows and income flows and who are so fascinated by the mathematical elegance of fashionable macroeconomic models, by the problems of moving aggregates, by the seductions of grandiose projects for balanced growth, by the dynamizing effects of advertising or consumer credit, by the merits of "functional" public finance, or by the glamor of progress surrounding giant concerns—who are so fascinated by all this, I repeat that they forget to consider the implications for the values and institutions of the bourgeois world, for or against which we have to decide. It is no accident that Keynes—and nobody is more responsible for this tendency among economists than he—has reaped fame and admiration for his equally banal and cynical observation that "in the long run, we are all dead."[7] And yet it should have been obvious that this remark is of the same decidedly unbourgeois spirit as the motto of the *ancien régime*: *Après nous le déluge*.[8] It reveals an utterly unbourgeois unconcern for the future, which has become the mark of a certain style of modern economic policy and inveigles us into regarding it as a virtue to contract debts and as foolishness to save.

A most instructive example is the modern attitude toward an institution whose extraordinary development has caused it to become a much-discussed problem. I have in mind installment buying, or consumer credit. In its present form as a mass habit and in its extreme extent, it is certainly a conspicuous expression of an "unbourgeois" way of life. It is significant, however, that this view and the misgivings deriving from it are hardly listened to nowadays, let alone accepted. It is not, as we are often told, mere "bourgeois" prejudice but the lesson of millennial experience and consonant with man's nature and dignity and

---

[7] Ed. note: John Maynard Keynes, *A Tract on Monetary Reform* (London: MacMillan, 1923), 80.

[8] Ed. note: "after us the deluge."

with the conditions of a sound society to regard it as an essential part of a reasonable and responsible way of life not to live from hand to mouth, to restrain impatience, self-indulgence, and improvidence alike, to think of the morrow, not to live beyond one's means, to provide for the vicissitudes of life, to try to balance income and expenditure, and to live one's life as a consistent and coherent whole extending beyond death to one's descendants rather than as a series of brief moments of enjoyment followed by the headaches of the morning after. To depart conspicuously from these precepts has always and everywhere been censured by sound societies as shiftless, spendthrift, and disreputable and has carried the odium of living as a parasite, of being incompetent and irresponsible. Even so happy-go-lucky a man as Horace was of one mind on this subject with Dickens' Mr. Micawber: "Annual income twenty pounds, annual expenditure nineteen nineteen and six, result happiness. Annual income twenty pounds, annual expenditure twenty pounds ought and six, result misery."[9]

Installment buying as a mass habit practiced with increasing carelessness is contrary to the standards of the bourgeois world in which the market economy must be rooted, and jeopardizes it. It is, at the same time, an indicator of how much of the humus of the bourgeois existence and way of life has already been washed away by social erosion, as well as an infallible measure of proletarianization, not in the sense of the material standard of living but of a style of life and moral attitude. The representatives of this style of life and moral attitude have lost their roots and steadfastness; they no longer rest secure within themselves; they have, as it were, been removed from the social fabric of family and the succession of generations. They suffer, unconsciously, from inner non-fulfillment, their life as a whole is stunted, they lack the genuine and essentially non-material conditions of simple human happiness. Their existence is empty,

---

[9] Ed. note: Charles Dickens, *The Personal History of David Copperfield*, ed. Edward Chauncey Baldwin (Chicago: Scott, Foresman, 1919), 218.

and they try to fill this emptiness somehow. One way to escape this tantalizing emptiness is, as we have seen, intoxication with political and social ideologies, passions, and myths, and this is where Communism still finds its greatest opportunity. Another way is to chase after material gratifications, and the place of ideologies is then taken by motor scooters, by television sets, by quickly acquired but unpaid-for dresses—in other words, by the flight into unabashed, immediate, and unrestrained enjoyment. To the extent that such enjoyment is balanced not only by corresponding work but also by a reasonable plan of life, saving and provision for the future, and by the non-material values of habits and attitudes transcending the moment's enjoyment, to that extent the emptiness, and with it the "unbourgeois" distress, is, in fact, overcome. But unless this is the case, enjoyment remains a deceptive method of filling the void and is no cure.[10]

The incomprehension, and even hostility, with which such reflections are usually met nowadays is one more proof of the predominance of social rationalism, with all its variants and offshoots, and of the implied threat to the foundations of the market economy. One of these offshoots is the ideal of earning a maximum amount of money in a minimum of working time and then finding an outlet in maximum consumption, facilitated by installment buying, of the standardized merchandise of modern mass production. *Homo sapiens consumens* loses sight of everything that goes to make up human happiness apart from money income and its transformation into goods. Two of the important factors that count in this context are how people work and how they spend their life outside work. Do people regard the whole of the working part of their life as a liability, or can they extract some satisfaction from it? And how do they live outside work, what do they do, what do they think, what part have they in natural, human existence? It is a false anthropol-

---

[10] Cf. my two treatises, *Borgkauf im Lichte sozialethischer Kritik* (Köln and Berlin, 1954) and *Vorgegessen Brot* (Köln and Berlin, 1955).

ogy, one that lacks wisdom, misunderstands man, and distorts the concept of man, if it blinds us to the danger that material prosperity may cause the level of simple happiness not to rise but to fall because the two above-mentioned vital factors are in an unsatisfactory condition. Such anthropology also prevents us from recognizing the true nature of proletarianism and the true task of social policy.

It is, for instance, a superficial and purely materialist view of proletarianism to believe complacently that in the industrialized countries of the West the proletarians are becoming extinct like the dodo simply because of a shorter working week and higher wages, wider consumption, more effective legal protection of labor and more generous social services, and because of other achievements of current social policy. It is true that the proletariat, as understood by this kind of social rationalism, is receding. But there remains the question of whether, concurrently with this satisfactory development and perhaps because of it, ever wider classes are not engulfed in proletarianism as understood in a much more subtle sense, in the sense, that is, of a social humanism using other criteria which are really decisive for the happiness of man and the health of society. The criteria I have in mind are those which we know well already, the criteria beyond the market, beyond money incomes and their consumption. Only in the light of those criteria can we assess the tasks of genuine social policy, which I advocated fifteen years ago in my book on *The Social Crisis of Our Time* and for which Alexander Rüstow has recently coined the felicitous term of "vital policy."[11]

The circle of our argument closes. It is, again, private ownership which principally distinguishes a non-proletarian form of life from a proletarian one. Once this is recognized, the social rationalism of our time has really been left behind. We

---

[11] Ed. note: Alexander Rüstow, "Sozialpolitik oder Vitalpolitik?" *Mitteilungen der Industrie- und Handelskammer zu Dortmund*, November 15, 1951, 453–59.

shall see in a later chapter how direct and short a road leads from here to the great problem of our era's constant inflationary pressure, which has developed into a danger to the market economy plain for all to see.[12]

THE SPIRITUAL AND MORAL SETTING

One of the oversimplifications by which social rationalism distorts the truth is that Communism is a weed particular to the marshes of poverty and capable of being eradicated by an improvement in the standard of living. This is a fatal misconception. Surely everyone must realize by now that the world war against Communism cannot be won with radio sets, refrigerators, and widescreen films. It is not a contest for a better supply of goods—unfortunately for the free world, whose record in this field cannot be beaten. The truth is that it is a profound, all-encompassing conflict of two ethical systems in the widest sense, a struggle for the very conditions of man's spiritual and moral existence. Not for one moment may the free world waver in its conviction that the real danger of Communism, more terrible than the hydrogen bomb, is its threat to wipe these conditions from the face of the earth. Anyone who rejects this ultimate, apocalyptic perspective must be very careful, lest, sooner or later, and perhaps for no worse reason than weakness or ignorance, he betray the greatest and highest values which mankind has ever had to defend. In comparison with this, everything else counts as nothing.

---

[12] Another apposite example of the progressive decline of the significance of ownership and related norms and institutions is the deteriorating morale of debtors at the expense of creditors. This development can be observed in many countries. The courts are lenient in cases of default and bankruptcy, and the result is that the creditor is often deprived of his rights and property in the name of mistaken "social justice." It should hardly be necessary to point to the expropriation of landlords because of rent control in many countries or to the effects of progressive personal taxes.

If we want to be steadfast in this struggle, it is high time to bethink ourselves of the ethical foundations of our own economic system. To this end, we need a combination of supreme moral sensitivity and economic knowledge. Economically ignorant moralism is as objectionable as morally callous economism. Ethics and economics are two equally difficult subjects, and while the former needs discerning and expert reason, the latter cannot do without humane values.[13]

Let us begin with a few questions which we, as economists, may well put to ourselves. Are we always certain of our calling? Are we never beset by the sneaking doubt that although the sphere of human thought and action with which we deal is one of primary necessity, it may, for that very reason, be of a somewhat inferior nature? *Primum vivere, deinde philosophari*[14]—certainly. But does this dictum not reflect an order of precedence? And when the Gospel says that man does not live by bread alone, does this not imply an admonition that once his prayer for his daily bread is fulfilled, man should direct his thoughts to higher things? Should we be free of such scruples and doubts—and this is not a matter for pride—others will assuredly bring them to our attention.

I myself had a characteristic experience in this respect. Some years before his death, I had the privilege of a discussion with Benedetto Croce, one of the greatest minds of our age.[15] I had

---

[13] From the characteristically plentiful recent literature, we may mention, apart from the works cited in Note 2 above: F. H. Knight, *The Ethics of Competition* (London, 1935); K. E. Boulding, *The Organizational Revolution* (New York, 1953); Daniel Villey, "The Market Economy and Roman Catholic Thought," *International Economic Papers* (No. 9, 1959); G. Del Vecchio, *Diritto ed Economia* (2nd ed., Rome, 1954); W. Weddigen, *Wirtschaftsethik* (Berlin-Munich, 1951); A. Dudley Ward (ed.), *The Goals of Economic Life* (New York, 1953); and D. L. Munby, *Christianity and Economic Problems* (London, 1956).

[14] Ed. note: "Live first, then philosophize."

[15] Ed. note: Benedetto Croce (1866–1952) was an Italian philosopher, historian, and statesman. An idiosyncratic political liberal, he

put forward the proposition that any society, in all its aspects, is always a unit in which the separate parts are interdependent and make up a whole which cannot be put together by arbitrary choice. I had maintained that this proposition, which is now widely known and hardly challenged, applied also to the economic order, which must be understood as part of the total order of society and must correspond to the political and spiritual order. We are not free, I argued, to combine just any kind of economic order, say, a collectivist one, with any kind of political and spiritual order, in this case the liberal. Since liberty was indivisible, we could not have political and spiritual liberty without also choosing liberty in the economic field and rejecting the necessarily unfree collectivist economic order; conversely, we had to be clear in our minds that a collectivist economic order meant the destruction of political and spiritual liberty. Therefore, the economy was the front line of the defense of liberty and of all its consequences for the moral and humane pattern of our civilization. My conclusion was that to economists, above all, fell the task, both arduous and honorable, of fighting for freedom, personality, the rule of law, and the ethics of liberty at the most vulnerable part of the front. Economists, I said, had to direct their best efforts to the thorny problem of how, in the aggravating circumstances of modern industrial society, an essentially free economic order can nevertheless survive and how it can constantly be protected against the incursions or infiltrations of collectivism.

 This was my part of the argument on that occasion, during the last war. Croce's astonishing reply was that there was no necessary connection between political and spiritual freedom on the one hand and economic freedom on the other. Only the first mattered; economic freedom belonged to a lower and independent sphere where we could decide at will. In the economic sphere, the only question was one of expediency in the

---

was skeptical of liberal economic policy including free trade. He was nominated for the Nobel Prize in Literature sixteen times.

manner of organizing our economic life, and this question was not to be related with the decisive and incomparably higher question of political and spiritual freedom. The economic question was of no concern to the philosopher, who could be liberal in the spiritual and political field and yet collectivist in the economic. The important movement for the defense of spiritual and political freedom was *liberalismo*, as Croce called it, to distinguish it from *liberismo*, by which slightening term he designated the defense of economic freedom.[16]

Croce's view hardly needs to be refuted today, and even his followers will not be inclined to defend it. But Croce's error has had a fatal influence on the development of Italian intellectuals and has smoothed the way to Communism for many of them. The mere fact that so eminent a thinker could be so utterly wrong about the place of economic matters in society proves how necessary it is to thresh this question out over and over again.

Naturally nobody would dream of denying that the aspect of society with which the economist deals belongs to the world of means, as opposed to ends, and that its motives and purposes therefore belong to a level which is bound to be low, if only because it is basic and at the foundation of the whole structure. This much we must grant a man like Croce. To take a drastic example, what interests economics is not the noble beauty of a medieval cathedral and the religious idea it embodies, but the worldly and matter-of-fact question of what place these monuments of religion and beauty occupied in the overall economy of their age. It is the complex of questions which, for instance, Pierre du Colombier has discussed in his charming book *Les chantiers des cathédrales*.[17] We are fully aware that what concerns us as economists is, as it were, the prosaic and bare

---

[16] The relevant discussion has been fully reported by Carlo Antoni in A. Hunold (ed.), *Die freie Welt im kalten Krieg* (Erlenbach-Zürich, 1955).

[17] Ed. note: Pierre du Colombier, *Les chantiers des cathedrals* (Paris: Picard, 1953).

reverse side of the *décor*. When the materialistic interpretation of history regards the spiritual and political life of nations as a mere ideological superstructure on the material conditions of production, we are, as economists, very sensitive to the damning revelations of a philosophy of history that reduces higher to lower—a feeling which proves our unerring sense of the genuine scale of values.

All of this is so obvious that we need not waste another word on it. But equally obvious is the argument with which we must safeguard a proper place in the spiritual and moral world for the economy, which is our sphere of knowledge. What overweening arrogance there is in the disparagement of things economic, what ignorant neglect of the sum of work, sacrifice, devotion, pioneering spirit, common decency, and conscientiousness upon which depends the bare life of the world's enormous and ever growing population! The sum of all these humble things supports the whole edifice of our civilization, and without them there could be neither freedom nor justice, the masses would not have a life fit for human beings, and no helping hand would be extended to anyone. We are tempted to say what Hans Sachs angrily calls out to Walter von Stolzing in the last act of *Die Meistersinger*: "Do not despise the masters!"[18]

We are all the more entitled to do so if, steering the proper middle course, we guard against exaggeration in the opposite direction. Romanticizing and moralistic contempt of the economy, including contempt of the impulses which move the market economy and the institutions which support it, must be as far from our minds as economism, materialism, and utilitarianism.

When we say *economism*, we mean one of the forms of social rationalism, which we have already met. We mean the incorrigible mania of making the means the end, of thinking only of bread and never of those other things of which the Gospel

---

[18] Ed. note: "Verachtet mir die Meister nicht" from *Die Meistersinger von Nürnberg*.

speaks. It is economism to succumb to those aberrations of social rationalism of which we have spoken and to all the implied distortions of perspective. It is economism to dismiss, as Schumpeter does, the problem of giant industrial concerns and monopoly with the highly questionable argument that mass production, the promotion of research, and the investment of monopoly profits raise the supply of goods, and to neglect to include in the calculation of these potential gains in the supply of material goods the possible losses of a non-material kind, in the form of impairment of the higher purposes of life and society.[19] It is economism to allow material gain to obscure the danger that we may forfeit liberty, variety, and justice and that the concentration of power may grow, and it is also economism to forget that people do not live by cheaper vacuum cleaners alone but by other and higher things which may wither in the shadow of giant industries and monopolies. To take one example among many, nowhere are the economies of scale larger than in the newspaper industry, and if only a few press lords survive, they can certainly sell a maximum of printed paper at a minimum of pennies or cents; but surely the question arises of what there is to read in these papers and what such an accumulation of power signifies for freedom and culture. It is economism, we continue, to oppose local government, federalism, or decentralization of broadcasting with the argument that concentration is cheaper. It is economism, again, to measure the peasant's life exclusively by his money income without asking what else determines his existence beyond supply and demand, beyond the prices of hogs and the length of his working day; and the worst economism is the peasant's own. It is, finally, that selfsame economism which misleads us into regarding the problem of economic stability merely as one of full employment, to be safeguarded by credit and fiscal policy, forgetting that besides equilibrium of national aggregates, equal

---

[19] Ed. note: See Joseph A. Schumpeter, *Capitalism, Socialism and Democracy*, 3rd ed. (New York: Harper, 2008), 87–106.

importance should be attached to the greatest possible stability of the individual's existence—just as the springs of a car are as important for smooth driving as the condition of the road.[20]

When we say *materialism,* we mean an attitude which misleads us into directing the full weight of our thought, endeavor, and action towards the satisfaction of sensual wants. Almost indissolubly linked therewith is *utilitarianism,* which, ever since the heyday of that philosophy, has been vitiating our standards in a fatal manner and still regrettably distorts the true scale of values. One of the more likable of the high priests of that cult, Macaulay, wrote in his famous essay on Francis Bacon, the ancestor of utilitarianism and pragmatism, that the production of shoes was more useful than a philosophical treatise by Seneca;[21] but once more we must ask the familiar question of whether shoes—not to mention the latest products of progress—are likely to be of much help to a man who, in the midst of a world devoted to that cult, has lost the moral bearings of his existence and who therefore, though he may not know why, is unhappy and frustrated. It is indeed our misfortune that mankind has, but for a small remnant, dissipated and scattered the combined spiritual patrimony of Christendom and antiquity, to which Seneca contributed a more than negligible portion. This is what our reaction should be today to a

---

[20] The idea here expressed is treated more fully in my book *The Social Crisis of Our Time,* 225–27.

[21] Ed. note: Lord Thomas Babington Macaulay (1800–1859) was a British Historian and Whig politician. The passage referenced is: "For our own part, if we are forced to make our choice between the first shoemaker, and the author of the three books On Anger, we pronounce for the shoemaker. It may be worse to be angry than to be wet. But shoes have kept millions from being wet; and we doubt whether Seneca ever kept any body from being angry." Thomas Babington, Lord Macaulay, "LORD BACON. (July, 1837.)," in *Critical and Historical Essays Contributed to the Edinburgh Review,* 5th ed., 3 vols. (London: Longman, Brown, Green, and Longmans, 1848), 2:375–76.

passage in another and no less famous of Macaulay's essays,[22] bursting with derision and indignation about Southey, who, at the dawn of British industry, had had the temerity to say that a cottage with rosebushes beside the door was more beautiful than the bleak workers' houses which were sprouting all over the place—"naked, and in a row."[23]

Economism, materialism, and utilitarianism have in our time merged into a cult of productivity, material expansion, and the standard of living. This cult proves once again the evil nature of the absolute, the unlimited, and the excessive. Not too long ago, André Siegfried[24] recalled Pascal's dictum that

---

[22] Ed. note: The passage referenced is: "Here is wisdom. Here are the principles on which nations are to be governed. Rose-bushes and poorrates, rather than steam-engines and independence. Mortality and cottages with weather-stains, rather than health and long life with edifices which time cannot mellow. We are told, that our age has invented atrocities beyond the imagination of our fathers; that society has been brought into a state, compared with which extermination would be a blessing; and all because the dwellings of cotton-spinners are naked and rectangular." Thomas Babington, Lord Macaulay, "SOUTHEY'S COLLOQUIES. (Jan. 1830.)," in *Critical and Historical Essays Contributed to the Edinburgh Review*, 1:233.

[23] The economist who rejects utilitarianism finds himself in the distinguished company of J. M. Keynes, who has this to say about the Benthamite tradition: "But I do now regard that as the worm which has been gnawing at the insides of modem evolution and is responsible for its present moral decay." (J. M. Keynes, *Two Memoirs* [London, 1949], 96) In connection with the passage from Macaulay's *Essays* mentioned in the text, we recall Bentham's remark: "While Xenophon was writing his history and Euclid teaching geometry, Socrates and Plato were talking nonsense under pretence of talking wisdom and morality." (Quoted from *Time and Tide* [May 19, 1956]) There is a clearly visible road from this kind of Philistine utilitarianism to positivism and the philosophy of logical analysis.

[24] Ed. note: André Siegfried (1875–1959) was a French academic, geographer, and political writer who was elected to the *Académie française* in 1944.

man's dignity resided in thought, and Siegfried added that although this had been true for three thousand years and was still valid for a small European elite, the real opinion of our age was quite different. It is that man's dignity resides in the standard of living. No astute observer can fail to note that this opinion has developed into a cult, though not many people would, perhaps, now speak as frankly as C. W. Eliot, for many years President of Harvard University, who, in a commemoration address in 1909, enounced the astonishing sentence: "The Religion of the Future should concern itself with the needs of the present, with public baths, play grounds, wider and cleaner streets and better dwellings."[25]

This cult of the standard of living scarcely needs further definition after what we have already said. It is a disorder of spiritual perception of almost pathological nature, a misjudgment of the true scale of vital values, a degradation of man not tolerable for long. It is, at the same time, very dangerous. It will, eventually, increase rather than diminish what Freud calls the discontents of civilization.[26] The devotee of this cult is forced into a physically and psychologically ruinous and unending race with the other fellow's standard of life—keeping up with the Joneses, as they say in America—and with the income necessary for this purpose. If we stake everything on this one card and forget what really matters, freedom above all, we sacrifice more to the idol than is right, so that, if once the material standard of living should recede by an inch or fail to rise at the rate the cult demands, we remain politically and morally disarmed and baffled. We are deprived of firmness, resistance, and valor in today's world struggle, where more than the standard of life (though it, too) is at stake; we become hesitant and cowardly, until it may be too late to realize that exclusive concentration

---

[25] Ed. note: See Charles W. Eliot, "The Religion of the Future," in *The Durable Satisfactions of Life* (New York: Crowell, 1910), 179.

[26] Ed. note: See Sigmund Freud, *Civilization and Its Discontents* (New York: Norton, 2010).

on the standard of living can lose us both that standard and freedom as well. This road to happiness is bound to lead to a dead end sooner or later. As we approach the limits of reasonable consumption, the cult of the standard of life must end up in disillusionment and eventual repugnance. Even now we are told by Riesman[27] and other American sociologists that the mass of consumers is becoming so blasé that the most spectacular advertising effort can hardly break through. Color television, the second car in the family, the television screen in the private swimming pool—all right, but what then? Fortunately, the moment seems near when people begin to rediscover the charms of books and music, of gardening and the upbringing of their children.

One thing that makes the standard-of-life cult so dangerous is that it obscures the issue in the struggle between the free world and Communism. Again and again experience has shown how grave an error it is to believe that the counterforce to Communism which must form the moral core of the defense behind the West's military and political battle lines resides in faith in the power of the standard of living. It would be foolish, of course, to belittle or deny the importance of the standard of living in this contest. But one has not understood much about the phenomenon of modern totalitarianism if one still regards as an evil fruit of poverty this infernal mixture of unbridled power and deception of the masses—with spells concocted by morally unsettled and mentally confused intellectuals.

No, the source of the poison of Communist totalitarianism is our era's social crisis as a whole, which has now spread also to the colored peoples; it is the disintegration of the social structure and its spiritual and moral foundations. Communism thrives wherever the humus of a well-founded social order and true community has been removed by proletarianization, social erosion, and the disappearance of the bourgeois and peasant

---

[27] Ed. note: See David Riesman, *The Lonely Crowd: A Study of Changing American Character*, rev. ed. (New Haven: Yale University Press, 2001).

classes; it thrives where men, and intellectuals above all, have lost their roots and solidity and have been pried loose from the social fabric of the family, the succession of generations, neighborliness, and other true communities. Communism finds the most fertile soil of all wherever these processes of social disintegration are associated with religious decline, as first in China and now in the Moslem world and in Japan.

Totalitarianism gains ground exactly to the extent that the human victims of this process of disintegration suffer from frustration and non-fulfillment of their life as a whole because they have lost the true, pre-eminently non-material conditions of human happiness. For this reason it is certain that the decisive battle between Communism and the free world will have to be fought, not so much on the field of material living conditions, where the victory of the West would be beyond doubt, but on the field of spiritual and moral values. Communism prospers more on empty souls than on empty stomachs. The free world will prevail only if it succeeds in filling the emptiness of the soul in its own manner and with its own values, but not with electric razors. What the free world has to set against Communism is not the cult of the standard of living and productivity or some contrary hysteria, ideology, or myth. This would merely be borrowing Communism's own weapons. What we need is to bethink ourselves quietly and soberly of truth, freedom, justice, human dignity, and respect of human life and the ultimate values. For these we must set our course unerringly; we must cherish and strengthen the spiritual and moral foundations of these values and vital goods and try to create and preserve for mankind such forms of life as are appropriate to human nature and support and protect its conditions.[28]

The material prosperity of the masses is not an absolute standard, and a warning against regarding it as the West's principal weapon in the cold war is nowhere more justified than in the

---

[28] For more detail, see my essay "Gegenhaltung und Gegengesinnung der freien Welt," in *Die freie Welt im kalten Krieg*, 183–211.

underdeveloped countries. For one thing, their case makes it particularly clear that the belief that people can be preserved from Communism by higher standards of living is dangerously superficial because it grossly exaggerates a factor which in itself is not unimportant and because it forgets the decisive spiritual and moral problems. In the underdeveloped countries, another factor assumes importance. The road to higher living standards is sought in industrialization, urbanization, and general emulation of the advanced Western nations' society and civilization; but, even more than in the Western world, this usually leads at once to a revolutionary upheaval in all the traditional forms of life and thought. What happens then is ominously manifest, for instance, in Japan, where the dissolution of the old forms, powerfully promoted after the last war by an obtuse victor, has prepared the ground for the Communist seed in a manner which poverty and material destruction could never have achieved. For the same reason, it is regrettable that India seems to follow Nehru's materialist socialism rather than Gandhi's humane wisdom. Finally, as regards the present advance of Communism in the Arab countries, it is unfortunately clear that it owes much less to the poverty of the masses than to the incompetence of the ruling classes, hysterical hatred of the West, and to immature intellectuals bewildered by the decline of Islam.[29]

So there is a grave danger that in the especially vulnerable field of underdeveloped countries the free world may lose, by proletarianization, urbanization, intellectualization, disintegration of family and religion, and disruption of the ancient forms of life, everything it may hope to wring from Communism by modernization, mechanization, and industrialization. There is a possibility that the non-material consequences of "economic

---

[29] For an exposition of the overall problem, see my study "Unentwickelte Länder," *ORDO, Jahrbuch für die Ordnung von Wirtschaft und Gesellschaft* (1953), 63–113. For the topical case of the Arab world, see Walter L. LaQueur, *Communism and Nationalism in the Middle East* (London, 1957).

development" may cause more losses than its material consequences cause gains, and this possibility is enhanced by the West's arrogant tendency to underestimate these nations' loyalty to their traditions. Thus we play into the hands of Communism the trump card of unnecessarily hurt national, religious, and cultural susceptibilities that are already exacerbated by a pathological feeling of inferiority vis-à-vis the Western countries. What we should do instead is to use the entirely admirable loyalty of a people to its own traditions as a bulwark against Communism; we should encourage and respect this loyalty and set its forces of preservation against the dissolving and eroding effects of material Westernization.[30]

Let us return to our main theme. Whatever may be the proper place of the economy in the universal order, what is the ethical place of the specific economic order proper to the free world? This economic order is the market economy, and it is with its relationships that economics as a science is largely concerned. What, then, are the ethical foundations of the market economy?

"Supply and demand," "profit," "competition," "interest," "free play of forces," or whatever other words we may choose to characterize the free economic system prevailing, even if in

---

[30] Apart from LaQueur's book, see also Emil Brunner, "Japan heute," *Schweizer Monatshefte* (March, 1955); Ramswarup, *Gandhism and Communism* (New Delhi, 1955), in which we find this statement: "Our intellectualized leftist conscience sees nothing but illiteracy, inadequacy, misery and frustration around and hopes to remove these by the blueprints of 5-year plans. Gandhiji, on the other hand, brought a message of hope and suggested ways of improvement, not by destroying existing patterns but by bearing with them, by improving them." (p. 11); Harry D. Gideonse, "Colonial Experience and the Social Context of Economic Development Programs," in R. A. Solo (ed.), *Economics and the Public Interest* (New Brunswick, 1955); F. S. C. Northrop, *The Taming of Nations* (New York, 1952); Eugene Staley, *The Future of Underdeveloped Countries* (New York, 1954); M. R. Masani, "The Communist Party in India," *Pacific Affairs* (March, 1951).

imperfect form, outside the Communist world—do they not, to say the least, belong to an ethically questionable or even reprehensible sphere? Or to put it more bluntly, are we not living in an economic world or, as R. H. Tawney says, in an "acquisitive society"[31] which unleashes naked greed, fosters Machiavellian business methods and, indeed, allows them to become the rule, drowns all higher motives in the "icy water of egotistical calculation" (to borrow from the *Communist Manifesto*),[32] and lets people gain the world but lose their souls? Is there any more certain way of desiccating the soul of man than the habit of constantly thinking about money and what it can buy? Is there a more potent poison than our economic system's all-pervasive commercialism? Or can we still subscribe to that astonishing eighteenth-century optimism which made Samuel Johnson say: "There are few ways in which man can be more innocently employed than in getting money"?[33]

Economists and businessmen who have a distaste for such questions or who would, at any rate, prefer to hand them over, with a touch of irony, to theologians and philosophers are ill advised. We cannot take these questions too seriously, nor must we close our eyes to the fact that it is not necessarily the most stupid or the worst who are driven into the camp of collectivist radicalism for lack of a satisfactory answer to these questions. Among these men are many who have a right to call themselves convinced Christians.

There is another and no less important reason why we should examine the ethical content of everyday economic life. This reason is that the question concerns us most intimately because it reaches down to the levels from which our roots draw their

---

[31] Ed. note: See R. H. Tawney, *The Acquisitive Society* (London: Bell, 1952).

[32] Ed. note: Karl Marx and Friedrick Engels, *Manifesto of the Communist Party*, trans. Samuel Moore (Chicago: Kerr, 1906), 16.

[33] Ed. note: James Boswell, *The Life of Samuel Johnson, L.L.D.*, ed. William Wallace (Edinburgh: Nimmo, Hay, and Mitchell, 1890), 240.

life-giving sap. *Navigare necesse est, vivere non est necesse,*[34] says an inscription on an old sailor's house in Bremen; we may generalize this into saying: Life is not worth living if we exercise our profession only for the sake of material success and do not find in our calling an inner necessity and a meaning which transcends the mere earning of money, a meaning which gives our life dignity and strength. Whatever we do and whatever our work, we must know what place we occupy in the great edifice of society and what meaning our activity has beyond the immediate purpose of promoting material existence. We must answer to ourselves for the social functions for which society rewards us with our income. It is a petty and miserable existence that does not know this, that regards the hours devoted to work as a mere means of earning money, as a liability to be balanced only by the satisfactions which the money counterpart of work procures.[35]

This feeling for the meaning and dignity of one's profession and for the place of work in society, whatever work it be, is today lost to a shockingly large number of people. To revive this feeling is one of the most pressing tasks of our times, but it is a task whose solution requires an apt combination of economic analysis and philosophical subtlety. This is, perhaps, truer of commerce than of other callings because the merchant's functions are more difficult to place in society than others. An activity which, at first sight, seems to consist of an endless series of purchases and sales does not display its social significance and professional dignity as readily as do the peasant's or the sailor's pursuits. The merchant himself is not easily aware

---

[34] Ed. note: "To sail is necessary; to live is not."

[35] Admirably apposite is Theodor Mommsen's summing up of the staleness of ancient Rome, which formed the background for a personage like Catiline: "When a man no longer enjoys his work but works merely in order to procure himself enjoyments as quickly as possible, then it is only an accident if he does not become a criminal." (Quoted from Otto Seel, *Cicero* [Stuttgart, 1953], 66.)

of them, nor are others, who all too often treat him as a mere parasite of society, an ultimately redundant intermediary whose "trading margins" are resented as an irksome levy and whom one would like to eliminate wherever possible. How infinitely more difficult must it be, then, to explain to a layman the functions of stock-exchange speculation and to defeat the almost ineradicable prejudices which fasten onto this favorite subject for anti-capitalist critics?

This is the place, too, to note that the hard-boiled business world, which ignores such questions or leaves them, with contempt, to the "unbusinesslike" intellectuals, and these same intellectuals' distrust of the business world match and mutually exacerbate each other. If the business world loses its contact with culture and the intellectuals resentfully keep their distance from economic matters, then the two spheres become irretrievably alienated from each other. We can observe this in America in the anti-intellectualism of wide circles of businessmen and the anti-capitalism of equally wide circles of intellectuals. It is true that intellectuals have infinitely less social prestige in America than in Europe and that they are much less integrated in the network of society and occupy a much more peripheral place than their brothers in Europe. They retaliate for this seating plan at the nation's table with their anti-capitalism, and the businessmen and entrepreneurs repay the intellectuals' hostility by despising them as "eggheads."

In so dynamic a competitive economy, the American intellectuals have to admit that the gulf between education and wealth, which is derided in Europe in the person of the *nouveau riche*, is the rule rather than the exception, as it should be; on the other hand, American businessmen easily fall into the habit of treating the intellectual as a pompous and would-be-clever know-all who lacks both common sense and a sound scale of values. Since in both cases the caricature is often not very far from the truth, the result is a vicious circle of mutually intensifying resentment which threatens to end up in catastrophe. One has to break out of this vicious circle by making the world of the mind as respectable to the business world as, conversely, the business world to the world of the mind.

Naturally, there is no question of taking sides with American intellectuals when they rebel against a predominantly commercial society with which they have little in common. But it must be conceded that it will not be easy to hold down this rebellion as long as the tension between business and culture is not considerably diminished. This tension is particularly obvious in the United States and in all the overseas territories of European expansion. It would be unfair to expect the diminution to come from only one side, and the task would become harder if we were simply to blame the American anti-capitalist intellectuals and not try also to understand their point of view. The chain reaction between the business world's distrust of intellectuals and the intellectuals' retaliating resentment should be broken by both sides: the intellectuals should abandon untenable ideologies and theories, and the "capitalists" should adopt a philosophy which, while rendering unto the market the things that belong to the market, also renders unto the spirit what belongs to it. Both movements together should merge into a new humanism in which the market and the spirit are reconciled in common service to the highest values. It need hardly be mentioned that we Europeans have no reason to strike any holier-than-thou attitudes about these problems. If things are, on the whole, still a little better in Europe, this is due to no merit of ours but to an historical heritage which beneficially slows down a development we share with "Europe overseas."[36]

---

[36] Wilhelm Röpke, "A European Looks at American Intellectuals," *The National Review* (November 10, 1956). The literature on this important subject reflects the facts, for it is divided into the two extremes of anti-capitalist intellectuals on the one hand and anti-intellectual capitalists on the other. This means that the problem as such is lost to view. This weakness is also apparent in F. A. Hayek (ed.), *Capitalism and the Historians* (Chicago, 1954), however valuable this book is in other respects as a corrective of our ideas about economic history. Cf. my

What, then, is our answer to the great question we asked at the beginning? At what ethical level, in general, must we situate the economic life of a society which puts its trust in the market economy?

It is rather like the ethical level of average man, of whom Pascal says: "L'homme n'est ni ange ni bête, et le malheur veut que qui veut faire l'ange fait la bête."[37] To put it briefly, we move on an intermediate plane. It is not the summit of heroes and saints, of simon-pure altruism, selfless dedication, and contemplative calm, but neither is it the lowlands of open or concealed struggle in which force and cunning determine the victor and the vanquished.

The language of our science constantly borrows from these two contiguous spheres to describe modern economic processes, and it is characteristic of our uncertainty that we usually reach either too high or too low. When we speak of "service" to the consumer, we obviously have in mind not St. Elizabeth but the assistant who wipes the windshield of our car at the filling station, and the "conquest" of a market brings to mind the traveling salesman, tempting prospectuses, and rattling cranes rather than thundering tanks or booming naval guns.[38] It is true that in our middle plateau of everyday economic life there is, fortunately, as much room for elevations into the higher sphere of true devotion as there is for depressions of violence and fraud; nevertheless, it will generally be granted that the

---

review ("Der 'Kapitalismus' und die Wirtschaftshistoriker") in *Neue Zürcher Zeitung*, No. 614 (March 16, 1954).

[37] Ed. note: "Man is neither angel nor brute, and the unfortunate thing is that he who would act the angel acts the brute." Blaise Pascal, *Pensées*, in *Pensées and The Provincial Letters*, trans. W. F. Trotter (New York: Modern Library, 1941), 118.

[38] On the ethical "middle level" of the market economy, see M. Pantaleoni, *Du caractère logique des differences d'opinions qui séparent les économistes* (Geneva, 1897); Wilhelm Röpke, *Die Lehre von der Wirtschaft* (8th ed., Erlenbach-Zürich, 1958), 41–46; and *idem, Internationale Ordnung-heute*, 116–35.

world in which we do business, bargain, calculate, speculate, compare bids, and explore markets ethically corresponds by and large to that middle level at which the whole of everyday life goes on. Reliance on one's own efforts, initiative under the impulse of the profit motive, the best possible satisfaction of consumer demand in order to avoid losses, safeguarding one's own interests in constant balance with the interests of others, collaboration in the guise of rivalry, solidarity, constant assessment of the weight of one's own performance on the incorruptible scales of the market, constant struggle to improve one's own real performance in order to win the prize of a better position in society—these and many other formulations are used to characterize the ethical climate of our economic world. They are imperfect, groping, and provisional, perhaps also euphemistic, but they do express what needs to be said at this point in our reflections.

This ethical climate, we must add at once, is lukewarm, without passions, without enthusiasm, but also, in the language of one of Heine's poems, without "prodigious sins" and without "crimes of blood";[39] it is a climate which, while not particularly nourishing for the soul, at least does not necessarily poison it. On the other hand, it is a favorable climate for a certain atmosphere of minimal consideration and for the elementary justice of a certain correspondence of give and take and most favorable, whatever one may say, for the development of productive energy. That this energy is applied not to the construction of pyramids and sumptuous palaces but to the continual improvement of the well-being of the masses and that this happens because of the effect of all-powerful forces proper to the structure and ethical character of our free economic order is perhaps the greatest of the assets in its overall balance sheet.

This view of the ethical climate of the market has distinguished ancestors. In 1748, Montesquieu wrote in his book

---

[39] Ed. note: Heinrich Heine, "Anno 1829," in *Heine's Poems*, ed. Carl Edgar Eggert (Boston: Ginn, 1906), 115–16.

L'Esprit des Lois of the spirit of our market economy (which he calls *esprit de commerce*): "It creates in man a certain sense of justice, as opposed, on the one hand, to sheer robbery, but on the other also to those moral virtues which cause us not always to defend our advantage to the last and to subordinate our interest to those of others" (Book XX, Chapter 2). We may add that our era's market-economy society may claim to be less subject to compulsion and power than any other society in history, though it is perhaps for that very reason all the more prone to deception as a means of persuasion. We shall have more to say about this later.

The poem by Heine to which we alluded is "Anno 1829," and the lines we referred to are these:

> Prodigious sins I'd rather see
> And crimes of blood, enormous, grand,
> Than virtue, self-content and fat,
> Morality with cash in hand.

Who does not know such moments of despair in the face of Philistine self-satisfaction and ungenerousness? But this should not cause us to forget the real issue here, namely, the eternal romantic's contempt of the economy, a contempt shared often enough by reactionaries and revolutionaries, as well as by aloof aesthetes. Nevertheless, there remains the question of whether we really prefer to do away with "virtue" and go hungry, to give up "morality" and go bankrupt.

As a matter of fact, a certain opprobrium was attached for many centuries to that middle level of ethics which is proper to any essentially free economy. It is the merit of eighteenth-century social and moral philosophy, which is the source of our own discipline of political economy, to have liberated the crafts and commercial activities—the banausic (the Greek βάναυσος means "the man at the stove") as they were contemptuously called in the slave economy of Athens—from the stigma of the feudal era and to have obtained for them the ethical position to which they are entitled and which we now take for granted.

It was a "bourgeois" philosophy in the true sense of the word, and one might also legitimately call it "liberal." It taught us that there is nothing shameful in the self-reliance and self-assertion of the individual taking care of himself and his family, and it led us to assign their due place to the corresponding virtues of diligence, alertness, thrift, sense of duty, reliability, punctuality, and reasonableness. We have learned to regard the individual, with his family, relying on his own efforts and making his own way, as a source of vital impulses, as a life-giving creative force without which our modern world and our whole civilization are unthinkable.

In order to appreciate just how important this "bourgeois" spirit is for our world, let us consider the difficulty of implanting modern economic forms in the underdeveloped countries, which often lack the spiritual and moral conditions here under discussion. We in the West take them for granted and are therefore hardly aware of them, but the spokesmen of the underdeveloped countries frequently see only the outward economic success of Western nations and not the spiritual and moral foundations upon which it rests. A sort of human humus must be there, or at least be expected to form, if Western industry is to be successfully transplanted. Its ultimate conditions remain accuracy, reliability, a sense of time and duty, application, and that general sense of good workmanship which is obviously at home in only a few countries. With some slight exaggeration, one might put it this way: modern economic activity can thrive only where whoever says "tomorrow" means tomorrow and not some undefined time in the future.[40]

In the Western world, "interested" activity has, without doubt, a positive value as the mainspring of society, civilization, and culture. Some may still protest in the name of Christian teaching, but in so doing, they merely reveal that they have, for their part, not yet overcome the eschatological communism of the

---

[40] Cf. my essay "Unentwickelte Länder," *ORDO, Jahrbuch für die Ordnung von Wirtschaft und Gesellschaft* (1953).

Acts of the Apostles.[41] After all, "the doctrine of self-reliance and self-denial, which is the foundation of political economy, was written as legibly in the New Testament as in the *Wealth of Nations*," and Lord Acton, the distinguished English historian to whom we owe this bold statement, rightly adds that this was not realized until our age.[42] The history of literature is very revealing: for Molière, the bourgeois was still a comic figure, and when for once Shakespeare introduces a merchant as such, it is Shylock. It is a long way to Goethe's *Wilhelm Meister*, where we move in the bourgeois trading world and where even double-entry bookkeeping is transfigured by philosophy and poetry.

To make this even clearer, let us turn the tables and see what happens when we give free rein to those who condemn the market, competition, profit, and self-interest in the name of a "higher" morality and who deplore the absence of the odor of

---

[41] How Christianity overcame this phase in the course of its development as a dogma and a church and how it came once more to acknowledge the cultural value of "loving oneself" is very evident from Augustine's example. Cf. Hans von Soden, *Urchristentum und Geschichte* (Tübingen, 1951), 56–89.

[42] Lord Acton, *The History of Freedom and Other Essays* (London, 1907), 28. Lord Acton was a Catholic and might well have invoked St. Thomas Aquinas: "Ordinatius res humanæ tractantur, si singulis immineat propria cura alicuius rei procurandæ; esset autem evolutio, si quilibet indistincte quælibet procuraret." ["Human affairs are conducted in more orderly fashion if each man is charged with taking care of some particular thing himself, whereas there would be confusion if everyone had to look after any one thing indeterminately."—Ed.] (*Summa Theologiae*, II, II, 66, 2. Quoted from Joseph Höffner, "Die Funktionen des Privateigentums in der freien Welt," in E. von Beckerath, F. W. Meyer, and A. Müller-Armack (eds.), *Wirtschaftsfragen der freien Welt* [Erhard-Festschrift, Frankfurt a. M., 1957], 122.)

We might also recall the Pilgrim Fathers, the first English colonizers of New England, who, devout Calvinists as they were, thought they could set up a purely communist system of agriculture; but a few years later, they were forced by the catastrophic decline in yields to change over to a market system and private ownership.

sanctity in individual self-assertion. They clearly do violence to one side of human nature, a side which is essential to life and which balances the other, nobler side of selfless dedication. This kind of moralism asks too much of ordinary people and expects them constantly to deny their own interests. The first result is that the powerful motive forces of self-interest are lost to society. Secondly, the purposes of this "higher" economic morality can be made to prevail only by doing something eminently immoral, namely, by compelling people—by force or cunning and deception—to act against their own nature. In all countries in which a collectivist system has been set up, in the name of many high-sounding purposes and not least of an allegedly "higher" morality, police and penalties enforce compliance with economic commands, or else people are kept in a state of permanent intoxication by emotional ideologies and rousing propaganda—as far and as long as it may be possible.

This, as we all know, regularly happens whenever the market is replaced by a collectivist economy. The market economy has the ability to use the motive power of individual self-interest for turning the turbines of production; but if the collectivist economy is to function, it needs heroes or saints, and since there are none, it leads straight to the police state. Any attempt to base an economic order on a morality considerably higher than the common man's must end up in compulsion and the organized intoxication of the masses through propaganda. To cite Pascal again, "… et qui veut faire l'ange fait la bête."[43] This is one of the principal reasons for the fact, with which we are already familiar, that a free state and society presuppose a free economy. Collectivist economy, on the other hand, leads to impoverishment and tyranny, and this consequence is obviously the very opposite of "moral." Nothing could more strikingly demonstrate the positive value of self-interested action than that its denial destroys civilization and enslaves men. In "capitalism" we have a freedom of moral choice, and no one is

---

[43] Ed. note: "He who would act the angel acts the brute." See 93n37.

forced to be a scoundrel. But this is precisely what we are forced to be in a collectivist social and economic system. It is tragically paradoxical that this should be so, but it is, because the satanic rationale of the system presses us into the service of the state machine and forces us to act against our consciences.

However, to reduce the motives of economic action solely to the desire to obtain material advantage and avoid material loss would result in too dark a picture of the ethical basis of our free economic system. The ordinary man is not such a *homo œconomicus*, just as he is neither hero nor saint. The motives which drive people toward economic success are as varied as the human soul itself. Profit and power do move people, but so do the satisfactions of professional accomplishment, the wish for recognition, the urge to improve one's performance, the dream of excavating Troy (as in the famous example of Schliemann)[44], the impulse to help and to give, the passion of the art or book collector, and many other things.[45] But even

---

[44] Ed. note: Heinrich Schliemann (1822–1890) was a German businessman and archeologist. Convinced that the events recounted in Homer's *Iliad* were historical, he began excavating near the modern Turkish city Çanakkale in 1871 discovering many ruins and artifacts from the Bronze Age (3300–1200 BC). Many scholars today agree with Schliemann's judgment at the time that this site is the location of ancient Troy.

[45] The part played by the art collector's passion in the lives of American multimillionaires of the past generation is described in an entertaining biography of the art dealer who supplied them: S. N. Behrman, *Duveen* (London, 1952). Their names are immortalized in the art galleries they created, which include the National Gallery in Washington, the Frick Gallery, and special collections at the Metropolitan Museum in New York. It seems as if this back door to immortality was one of Duveen's most effective selling points.

On the other hand, even supreme intellectual achievements are not always free from the profit motive, as Goethe's example shows. It seems that it was an attractive offer by his publisher, Cotta, which finally led Goethe to complete his *Faust*. Schiller had solicited this offer behind Goethe's back; we have his letter to Cotta of March 24, 1800: "I am

if we discover nothing better than the motive of bare material advantage, we should never forget that the man who decently provides for himself and his family by his own effort and on his own responsibility is doing no small or mean thing. It should be stated emphatically that he is more deserving of respect than those who, in the name of a supposedly higher social morality, would leave such provision to others. This applies also to that further category of people who pride themselves on their generosity at others' expense and shed tears of emotion about themselves when their advocacy of a well-oiled welfare state earns them a place in the hearts of the unsuspecting public—and, at the same time, on some political party's list of candidates.

Anyone who knows anything about economics will realize at once that these considerations suggest a familiar answer to an obvious question. What will happen when these individualist motives induce people to do things which are manifestly harmful to others?

Again we turn to the social philosophy of the eighteenth century and its lessons. An economy resting on division of labor, exchange, and competition is an institution which, in spite of its occasionally highly provocative imperfections, does tend, more than any other economic system, to adjust the activities governed by individual interests to the interests of the whole community. We know the mechanism of this adjustment. The individual is forced by competition to seek his own success in serving the market, that is, the consumer. Obedience to the market ruled by free prices is rewarded by profit, just as dis-

---

afraid Goethe will completely neglect his Faust, into which so much work has already gone, unless some stimulus from outside in the form of an attractive offer stirs him to take up this great work once more and finish it.... However, he expects a large profit, for he knows that this work is awaited with suspense in Germany. I am convinced that you can get him, by means of a brilliant offer, to complete this work in the coming summer." Goethe's prompt reaction can be seen in his letter to Schiller of April 11, 1800. But who would therefore deprecate the profit motive?

obedience is punished by loss and eventual bankruptcy. The profits and losses of economic activity, calculated as precisely and correctly as possible by the methods of business economics, are thus at the same time the indispensable guide to a rational economy as a whole. Collectivist economies, of whatever degree of collectivism, try in vain to replace this guidance by planning.

These simplified formulations are, of course, highly inadequate, although the truth they contain is undeniable. We need not waste many words over this or over the large and perhaps increasing number of cases where even the market and competition fail to discharge the enormous task of adjusting individual economic action to the common interest. It hardly needs to be stressed, either, how difficult it is to keep competition as such free and satisfactory. Any more or less well-informed person knows that these unsolved tasks and difficulties constitute the thorny problems of an active economic and social policy and that they cannot be taken too seriously.

However, this is not the place to discuss them. There is something else, though, which does need stressing in this context. Have we said all there is to say when we have underlined the importance of competition, and of the price mechanism moved by competition, in regulating an economic system whose principle it is to leave individual forces free? Is it enough to appeal to people's "enlightened self-interest" to make them realize that they serve their own best advantage by submitting to the discipline of the market and of competition?

The answer is decidedly in the negative. And at this point we emphatically draw a dividing line between ourselves and the nineteenth-century liberal utilitarianism and immanentism, whose traces are still with us. Indeed, there is a school which we can hardly call by any other name but liberal anarchism, if we reflect that its adherents seem to think that market, competition, and economic rationality provide a sufficient answer to the question of the ethical foundations of our economic system.

What is the truth? The truth is that what we have said about the forces tending to establish a middle level of ethics in our economic system applies only on the tacit assumption of a modicum of primary ethical behavior. We have made it abundantly clear that we will have no truck with a sort of economically ignorant moralism which, like Mephistopheles in reverse, always wills the good and works the bad. But we must add that we equally repudiate morally callous economism, which is insensitive to the conditions and limits that must qualify our trust in the intrinsic morality of the market economy. Once again, we must state that the market economy is not enough.

In other words, economic life naturally does not go on in a moral vacuum. It is constantly in danger of straying from the ethical middle level unless it is buttressed by strong moral supports. These must simply be there and, what is more, must constantly be impregnated against rot. Otherwise our free economic system and, with it, any free state and society must ultimately collapse.

This also applies in the narrower sense of competition alone. Competition is essential in restraining and channeling self-interest, but it must constantly be protected against anything tending to vitiate it, restrict it, and cause its degeneration. This cannot be done unless everybody not only accepts the concept of free and fair competition but in practice lives up to his faith. All individuals and groups, not excluding trade-unions (as must be stressed in view of a widespread social priggishness), who take part in economic life must make a constant moral effort of self-discipline, leaving as little as possible to an otherwise indispensable government-imposed compulsory discipline. It is by no means enough to invoke the laws of the market in appealing to people's enlightened self-interest and their economic reason, for within certain limits, cartels, labor unions, pressure groups, and trade associations serve their members' interests very well indeed when they exercise monopoly power or pressure on the government's economic policy in an attempt to get more than genuine and fair competition would give them. There must be higher ethical values which we can invoke successfully: justice, public spirit, kindness, and good will.[46]

So we see that even the prosaic world of business draws on ethical reserves by which it stands and falls and which are more important than economic laws and principles. Extra-economic, moral, and social integration is always a prerequisite of economic integration, on the national as on the international plane. As regards the latter, it should be especially emphasized that the true and ultimate foundation of international trade, a foundation of which our textbooks have little to say, is that unwritten code of normal ethical behavior which is

---

[46] "The Benthamite delusion that politics and economics could be managed on considerations purely material has exposed us to a desolate individualism in which every man and every class looks upon all other men and classes as dangerous competitors, when in reality no man and no class can continue long in safety and prosperity without the bond of sympathy and the reign of justice." (Russell Kirk, "Social Justice and Mass Culture," *The Review of Politics* [October, 1954], 447) If we want to understand fully this error of liberal immanentism, which we first meet in such disarming purity in Say's youthful work *Olbie*, then in the writings of Bentham and his school, and which had a last bright flicker in Herbert Spencer's work, we must remember that at that time the liberation from really constrictive bonds was an absorbing task, while the moral reserves were still intact enough to be taken for granted. A similar situation existed in Germany after 1945, when it was necessary to give priority to the need of overcoming intolerable poverty by releasing the economic forces weakened by repressed inflation. The one-sidedness of nineteenth-century individualism was paralleled by the equally conspicuous one-sidedness of political individualism, whose fatal ideal of utilitarian democracy can be understood as a reaction to the pluralistic petrification of the *ancien regime*.

The roots of the moral blindness of individualism and utilitarianism naturally reach far back into the eighteenth century, to Helvétius, Holbach, Lamettrie, and D'Alembert, just as its ramifications ultimately reach forward to Marx and Engels.

epitomized in the words *pacta sunt servanda* [agreements must be kept—Ed.].[47]

The market, competition, and the play of supply and demand do not create these ethical reserves; they presuppose them and consume them. These reserves have to come from outside the market, and no textbook on economics can replace them. J. B. Say was mistaken in his youthful work *Olbie ou Essai sur les moyens de réformer les moeurs d'une nation*, a liberal utopian fantasy published in 1800, when he naively proposed to hand the citizens of his paradise "un bon traité d'économie politique" as a "premier livre de morale."[48] That valiant utilitarian Cobden also seems to have thought in all seriousness that free-trade theory was the best way to peace.[49]

Self-discipline, a sense of justice, honesty, fairness, chivalry, moderation, public spirit, respect for human dignity, firm ethical norms—all of these are things which people must possess before they go to market and compete with each other. These are the indispensable supports which preserve both market and competition from degeneration. Family, church, genuine communities, and tradition are their sources. It is also necessary that people should grow up in conditions which favor such moral convictions, conditions of a natural order, condi-

---

[47] Cf. my book *International Economic Disintegration* (3rd ed., London, 1950), 67ff., and my course of lectures on "Economic Order and International Law" at The Hague Academy of International Law (*Recueil des Cours* 1954 [Leiden, 1955]).

[48] Ed. note: "A good deal of political economy" as a "first moral book." Jean-Baptiste Say, *Olbie, ou Essai sur les moyens de réformer les moeurs d'une nation* (Paris: Crapelet, 1799), 25.

[49] Ed. note: "I see in the Free-trade principle that which shall act on the moral world as the principle of gravitation in the universe,—drawing men together, thrusting aside the antagonism of race, and creed, and language, and uniting us in the bonds of eternal peace." Richard Cobden, "Free Trade. VII. Manchester, October 19, 1843," in *Speeches on Questions of Public Policy by Richard Cobden, M.P.*, ed. John Bright and J. E. Thorold Rogers, 2 vols. (London: Unwin, 1908), 1:187.

tions promoting co-operation, respecting tradition, and giving moral support to the individual. Ownership and reserves, and a feeling for both, are essential parts of such an order. We have, a little earlier, characterized such an order as "bourgeois" in the broadest sense, and it is the foundation upon which the ethics of the market economy must rest. It is an order which fosters individual independence and responsibility as much as the public spirit which connects the individual with the community and limits his greed.

The market economy is a constantly renewed texture of more or less short-lived contractual relations. It can, therefore, have no permanence unless the confidence which any contract presupposes rests on a broad and solid ethical base in all market parties. It depends upon a satisfactory average degree of personal integrity and, at the margin, upon a system of law which counteracts the natural tendency to slip back into less-than-average integrity. Within that legal framework, the market's own sanctions undeniably foster the habit of observing certain minimum rules of behavior and thereby also integrity. Whoever always lies and deceives and breaks contracts will sooner or later be taught that honesty is the best policy. For all its resting on utilitarian calculation, this pattern of behavior is valuable and reliable, as we can see in the extreme example of Soviet Russia, which, in its relations with the outside world of the market, has tried systematically and successfully to acquire the reputation for prompt payment while adhering, in other respects, to the ethical code of gangsters. Even if we conscientiously credit the market with certain educational influences, we are, therefore, led back to our main contention that the ultimate moral support of the market economy lies outside the market. Market and competition are far from generating their moral prerequisites autonomously. This is the error of liberal immanentism. These prerequisites must be furnished from outside, and it is, on the contrary, the market and competition which constantly strain them, draw upon them, and consume them.

We would, of course, again err on the side of unrealistic and unhistorical moralism if we were to apply to modern economic behavior moral standards which would have been enough to condemn mankind at any time because men can never live up to them. Such moralism is least tolerable when it self-righteously pretends that the moralist is a better man for the mere reason that his standards are so strict. This should always be remembered whenever the talk turns to the questionable aspects of competition. Ruthless rivalry has never and in no circumstances been banned from human society. The young Torrigiani, spurred by jealousy and professional rivalry, smashed Michelangelo's nasal bone and thereby disfigured him for life; in our days, a leading German trade-union intellectual, no doubt a valiant detractor of the "capitalist jungle," tried to get rid of a rival by means of forged letters—it is always the same thing and always equally unedifying. But we get nowhere by raising our eyebrows because the market economy does not always display the sporting spirit of a tennis tournament; we would do better to reflect that no small advantage of the market economy is that it channels men's natural rivalry into forms which, by and large, are preferable to broken noses and forged letters—and also to mass executions, as in Communist countries.

But we cannot, in good conscience, let the matter rest there. It cannot be denied that the market places the constant competitive struggle for self-assertion and self-advancement in the center of the stage. Nor can it be denied that such all-pervasive competition has a disturbing tendency to lead to consequences to which we cannot remain indifferent, especially from the moral point of view. Those who are in the rough-and-tumble of the competition of modern economic life, with its nerve-racking claims on time, effort, and susceptibility, and who are worn down by this endless struggle are more sensitive than most to the questions raised thereby, and it would be both unjust and uncivil therefore to treat them as monopoly-mongers.

We all acknowledge the validity and justice of such questions when we accept as a model of a higher form of rivalry the way in which certain professions, above all the medical, submit to strict rules of competition to the point of including them among the standards of professional behavior. Unfortunately, this example of the medical profession's deontology cannot be applied to industry and trade. But it shows what a blessing for all it would be if a definite code of competitive behavior, resting on professional standards, binding for all and violable only at the price of outlawry, were to dampen competition everywhere and withdraw it from the laws of "marginal ethics,"[50] without appeal to the state but in full appreciation of the positive potentialities of professional solidarity.

In acknowledging these potentialities, we express the idea that we should aim at compensating the socially disintegrating effects of competition by the integrating forces outside the market and outside competition. There is, however, the danger of abuse. On no account must competition be corrupted by its economically most questionable and morally most reprehensible perversion, namely, monopoly in any shape or form. Monopoly is precisely the worst form of that commercialism which we want to combat by trying to mitigate competition by integrating counterforces.

The truth is that competition, which we need as a regulator in a free economy, comes up on all sides against limits which we would not wish it to transgress. It remains morally and socially dangerous and can be defended only up to a point and with qualifications and modifications of all kinds. A spirit of ever alert and suspicious rivalry, not too particular in the choice of its means, must not be allowed to predominate and to sway society in all its spheres, or it will poison men's souls, destroy civilization, and ultimately disintegrate the economy.

To assert oneself all the time by ubiquitous advertising, day and night, in town and country, on the air and on every free square foot of wall space, in prose and in verse, in word and

---

[50] Cf. Goetz Briefs, "Grenzmoral in der pluralistischen Gesellschaft," in *Wirtschaftsfragen der freien Welt*.

picture, by open assault or by the subtler means of "public relations," until every gesture of courtesy, kindness, and neighborliness is degraded into a move behind which we suspect ulterior motives; to fashion all imaginable relations and performances on the principle of supply and demand and so to commercialize them, not excluding art and science and religion; forever to compare one's own position with that of others; always to tryout something new, to shift from one profession and from one place to the next; to look with constant jealousy and envy upon others—such extreme commercialization, restlessness, and rivalry are an infallible way of destroying the free economy by morally blind exaggeration of its principle. This is bound to end up in an unhealthy state of which the worst must be feared.

The curse of commercialization is that it results in the standards of the market spreading into regions which should remain beyond supply and demand. This vitiates the true purposes, dignity, and savor of life and thereby makes it unbearably ugly, undignified, and dull. We have had occasion earlier to note this. Think of Mother's Day, a day set aside to honor mothers and motherhood; the most tender and sacred human relationship is turned into a means of sales promotion by advertising experts and made to turn the wheels of business. Father's Day soon followed, and if we did not fortunately know better, the latest forms of Christmas might make us suspect that this whip which makes the top of business spin is also a creation of modern advertising techniques. Not long ago it happened that an automobile race, which, to the horror of the spectators, led to a fatal accident, was nevertheless continued because of its commercial and technical purposes, so that even death had to defer to business and technology.

All of this cannot be castigated too severely—with the intention, not of condemning the market economy, but of stressing the need to circumscribe and moderate it and of showing once more its dependence upon moral reserves. This circumscription and moderation can take many forms. One of them is that we do not allow competition to become the dominating principle and that we keep an eye on all the circumstances which tend to mitigate it. Let me illustrate my point. Has any sociologist ever bothered to discover why there is usually fierce rivalry among actors and singers, while circus folk tend to live in an atmosphere of kindly good-fellowship? Would it not be a rewarding task to examine the whole texture of modern society for such differences in competition and their presumable causes?[51]

Nobilitas Naturalis

It cannot be said often enough that in the last resort competition has to be circumscribed and mitigated by moral forces within the market parties. These constitute the true "countervailing power" of which the American economist J. K. Galbraith speaks in his book of the same title, and not the mechanics of organized buying power, to which he mistakenly looks for the containment of competition and its monopolistic perversions. Without a fund of effective convictions regarding the moral limits of competition, the problem cannot find a genuine solution.

In a sound society, leadership, responsibility, and exemplary defense of the society's guiding norms and values must be the exalted duty and unchallengeable right of a minority that forms and is willingly and respectfully recognized as the apex of a social pyramid hierarchically structured by performance. Mass society, such as we have described it earlier, must be counteracted by individual leadership—not on the part of original geniuses or eccentrics or will-o'-the-wisp intellectuals,

---

[51] The problems of competition and the dilemma it so often involves can be studied very well in the example of universities. If one knows the system of those countries where the lecturer draws attendance fees and therefore has a financial interest in the outward success of his lectures, one realizes how poisonous an atmosphere of rivalry can thus be created and how the teacher is tempted to court outward success more than is right and proper. On the other hand, this system provides a good stimulant for weaker characters who are not sufficiently conscious of the obligations of their office.

but, on the contrary, on the part of people with courage to reject eccentric novelty for the sake of the "old truths" which Goethe admonishes us to hold on to and for the sake of historically proved, indestructible, and simple human values. In other words, we need the leadership of genuine *clercs* or of men such as those whom the distinguished psychiatrist Joachim Bodamer[52] recently described as "ascetics of civilization," secularized saints as it were, who in our age occupy a place which must not for long remain vacant at any time and in any society. That is what those have in mind who say that the "revolt of the masses" must be countered by another revolt, the "revolt of the elite."

The conviction is rightly gaining ground that the important thing is that every society should have a small but influential group of leaders who feel themselves to be the whole community's guardians of inviolable norms and values and who strictly live up to this guardianship. What we need is true *nobilitas naturalis*. No era can do without it, least of all ours, when so much is shaking and crumbling away. We need a natural nobility whose authority is, fortunately, readily accepted by all men, an elite deriving its title solely from supreme performance and peerless moral example and invested with the moral dignity of such a life. Only a few from every stratum of society can ascend into this thin layer of natural nobility. The way to it is an exemplary and slowly maturing life of dedicated endeavor on behalf of all, unimpeachable integrity, constant restraint of our common greed, proved soundness of judgment, a spotless private life, indomitable courage in standing up for truth and law, and generally the highest example. This is how the few, carried upward by the trust of the people, gradually attain to a position above the classes, interests, passions, wickedness, and foolishness of men and finally become the nation's conscience. To belong to

---

[52] Ed. note: Joachim Bodamer (1910–1985) was a German neurologist and writer most famous for naming the disorder prosopagnosia, the selective inability to recognize faces.

this group of moral aristocrats should be the highest and most desirable aim, next to which all the other triumphs of life are pale and insipid.

No free society, least of all ours, which threatens to degenerate into mass society, can subsist without such a class of censors. The continued existence of our free world will ultimately depend on whether our age can produce a sufficient number of such aristocrats of public spirit, aristocrats of a kind which was by no means rare in the feudal age. We need businessmen, farmers, and bankers who view the great questions of economic policy unprejudiced by their own immediate and short-run economic interests; trade-union leaders who realize that they share with the president of the national bank the responsibility for the country's currency; journalists who resist the temptation to flatter class tastes or to succumb to political passions and court cheap success and instead guide public opinion with moderation, sound judgment, and a high sense of responsibility. In turn, it will be of crucial importance for the ultimate fate of the market economy whether this aristocracy includes, above all, people who, by position and conviction, have close ties with the market economy and who feel responsible for it in the moral sphere here under discussion.[53]

---

[53] The idea of *nobilitas naturalis* is, of course, so old that it is difficult to trace its spiritual genealogy. It may be worth noting, though, that the idea was quite familiar to a democrat like Thomas Jefferson, who is above any suspicion of reactionary opinions. On October 28, 1813, Jefferson wrote to John Adams, who was a conservative: "I agree with you that there is a natural aristocracy among men. The grounds of this are virtue and talents.... The natural aristocracy I consider as the most precious gift of nature, for the instruction, the trusts and government of society. And indeed it would have been inconsistent in creation to have formed man for the social state, and not to have provided virtue and wisdom enough to manage the concerns of society." (A. Koch and W. Peden, *The Life and Selected Writings of Thomas Jefferson* [Modern Library, New York], 632–33) The application to the particular case of

Evidently, many and sometimes difficult conditions must be fulfilled if such a natural aristocracy is to develop and endure and if it is to discharge its tasks. It must grow and mature, and the slowness of its ripening is matched by the swiftness of its possible destruction. Wealth gained and lost overnight is a stony ground on which it cannot prosper but on which thrive plutocracy and newly rich parvenus—the very opposite of what is desirable. Yet without wealth and its inheritance, whereby a spiritual and moral tradition is handed down together with its material foundation, a natural aristocracy is equally impossible, and it would be shortsighted egalitarian radicalism to overlook this.[54] One generation is often, indeed usually, not sufficient to produce the flower and fruit of aristocratic public spirit and leadership, and this is why the almost confiscatory limitation of the testator's rights, which today is the rule in some major Western countries, is one of the most harmful measures imaginable and contrary to the spirit of sound policy.[55]

But *richesse oblige*.[56] Any privilege, be it a privilege of birth, mind, honor and respect, or of wealth, confers rights only in

---

the market economy can be found in my book *The Social Crisis of Our Time*, 134ff. See also Wright, *Op. cit.*, 25ff.

[54] We again quote an author beyond suspicion: "[The legislator] has not fulfilled his task if, in his desire to insure equal satisfaction of all needs, he renders impossible the full development of outstanding individuals, if he prevents anyone from rising above his fellows, if he cannot produce anyone as an example to the human race, as a leader in discoveries which will benefit all." (Simonde de Sismondi, *Op. cit.*, II, 2) The same idea is forcefully expressed by Alexis de Tocqueville in his *Democracy in America*. See also L. Baudin, "Die Theorie der Eliten," in *Masse und Demokratie*, 39–54.

[55] Ed. note: A testator is a person who has written and executed a last will and testament in effect at the time of his or her death. Testator's rights are the rights of the testator to distribute his or her property according to the terms specified in the last will and testament. Estate taxes preempt and violate testator's rights.

[56] Ed. note: "wealth obliges."

exactly the same measure in which it is accepted as an obligation. It will not do to hide one's talent in the earth; each must remain conscious of the responsibilities which his privileged position entails. If ever the much-abused words "social justice" are appropriate, it is here.

One of the obligations of wealth, which need not be enumerated, is to contribute to the filling of the gaps left by the market because they are in the realm of goods outside the play of supply and demand, but which gaps must not be left for the state to fill if we want to preserve a free society. I have in mind the patronage of art in the widest sense, generous grants for theatre, opera, music, the visual arts, and science—briefly, for everything whose existence and development would be jeopardized if it had to "pay." We would be hard put to name a single supreme work of art in any period of history which did not owe its origin to patronage, and it is even more difficult to think of a theatre, opera house, or orchestra which bowed to the laws of supply and demand without damage to its quality or which, therefore, could have maintained its quality without patronage. The tragedies of Aeschylus, Sophocles, and Euripides are as unthinkable without the public donations of the rich Athenians as are the plays of Shakespeare without his patrons. Conversely, in so far as in our age the laws of supply and demand determine the level of artistic performance—in extreme form, in the film industry—the devastating effects are plain for all to see.

This function is to be fulfilled by the rich in the same spirit in which in the old days the Hanseatic burghers of Bremen used to pay property taxes: in honest self-assessment of one's ability to pay and in voluntary fulfillment of an honorary duty.[57] Here it is appropriate to emphasize that this spirit is smothered by the modern welfare state and its fiscal socialism. It may also be pointed out that the rich cannot exercise their function of patronage of the arts unless they are at home in the realm of

---

[57] H. K. Röthel, *Die Hansestädte* (Munich, 1955), 91.

the spirit and of beauty as much as in the world of business—which brings us back to what we said earlier in this chapter.

The task of leadership falls to the natural aristocracy by virtue of an unwritten but therefore no less valid right which is indistinguishable from duty. Washington's successor, the great American statesman John Adams, had some very pertinent things to say about this. According to him, a member of the "natural aristocracy of virtues and talents"[58] was anyone who disposed not only of his own vote but, at the same time, of the votes of those whose opinions he influenced by his example, acknowledged authority, and persuasion. But since this is unfortunately true not only of the "natural aristocracy of virtues and talents" but of everybody who, by foul means or fair, influences the formation of political opinion, we must add the qualification that the unwritten plural franchise which actually exists in any democracy is the more justified the more we can rely on the existence and effectiveness of a genuine natural aristocracy. The latter therefore appears all the more indispensable.

Finally, we have to speak of science, whose leadership functions and responsibility are obvious. There can be no doubt that here, too, rights and duties are inextricably linked. Here, too, authority—and it is authority of the highest rank—has to be gained and held by achievement and character. But what, precisely, is the deontology of science, especially, in this context, of the social sciences?

Boswell has recorded an apposite remark by Samuel Johnson, that great eighteenth-century Englishman. Certain professions, Johnson said, principally the sailor's and the soldier's, had the dignity of danger. "Mankind reverence those who have got over

---

[58] Ed. note: "Few men will deny that there is a natural aristocracy of virtues and talents in every nation and in every party, in every city and village. Inequalities are a part of the natural history of man." John Adams, "Letters to John Taylor II," in *The Works of John Adams*, ed. Charles Francis Adams, 10 vols. (Boston: Little, Brown, 1856), 6:451–52.

fear, which is so general a weakness."[59] Conversely, the honor of those professions whose dignity is danger cannot be more deeply wounded than by casting doubt on their courage.

The esteem in which science is held certainly does not rest on such a dignity of danger. We do not expect of a Sanskrit scholar the bravery of a soldier or sailor who, professionally, has to face physical danger of losing his life, but we do expect men of science to be courageous and intrepid in another sense, which we recognize when we have grasped that the "dignity of science" is truth. This sounds a little pompous, but it is meant to express something very simple. It does not mean that science is respected because it has to offer "truth" like ripe plums. What we mean is this: just as much as fear, another universal human failing is a tendency to allow the prospect of advantages or the threat of disadvantages to deflect one from the pursuit of the "true" facts and, even more, from the free announcement of facts recognized as "true." The dignity of science is that its genuine apostles constantly have to overcome this human weakness of interested squinting at truth. Only those who fulfill this requirement can partake in the dignity of science. Only they discharge the obligation put upon them by the privilege of being the servants of science, and only they can hope to attain to natural nobility and to render to the community those services which it has a right to expect from them.

Since men of science, too, are generally neither saints nor heroes, it is no doubt hard for them to live up to this standard without faltering and occasional aberrations. It is hardest for those who, unlike the Sanskrit scholar, have chosen a field of knowledge which gives them occasion and indeed obliges them to defend the "dignity of truth" in the rough-and-tumble of interests and passions. Economic policy, of which we are treating here, is such a battlefield, and the scholars involved are the

---

[59] Ed. note: Boswell, *Life of Samuel Johnson*, 369.

jurists and economists.[60] Economists also have this in common with jurists: their scientific authority, whose moral foundation is the "dignity of truth," is appealed to in controversial questions. Such activities by scholars are as old as the history of science and the universities; we have but to remember that in the fourteenth century, Louis of Bavaria called on the famed scholars of the Universities of Bologna and Paris for opinions in his struggle with Pope John XXII.[61] Curiously enough, this is not usually held against jurists, although the delicate nature of such a task is obvious. It always presents the man of science with a question of conscience which he must decide in the light of the "dignity of truth."

The answer should not be in doubt. Such a commission can be accepted—and indeed has point for the questioner—only if it is discharged in such a manner that the scholar's answer does not deviate in the slightest respect from that which he would have pronounced without the commission and without the ensuing advantages (which may include such things as enhanced prestige or public honors). The answer must be strictly in line with his scientific convictions, and if there is the slightest doubt about this, the scholar should withdraw. The economist, in particular, should make it a rule to put his scientific work at the service of any precise commission, originating from the government or from international or non-governmental organizations, only on condition that this work can serve

---

[60] W. H. Hutt, *Economists and the Public* (London, 1936); Wilhelm Röpke, "Der wissenschaftliche Ort der Nationalökonomie," *Studium Generale* (July, 1953).

[61] Ed. note: The Holy Roman Emperor Louis IV (1282–1347) was crowned emperor in 1328 and three months later issued a decree declaring Pope John XXII (1244–1334) deposed on the grounds of heresy. The emperor appealed to the Franciscan scholars William of Ockham and Michael of Cesena who had earlier clashed with Pope John XXII over the doctrine of the Absolute Poverty of Christ, then prominent in the Franciscan Order, which maintained Christ and the apostles had no individual or shared property.

his own convictions also and on the further condition that he may hope thereby to promote a good cause threatened by overwhelming forces. In the absence of these conditions, the economist has every reason to ask himself whether the counsel expected of him in the struggle of economic interests and social passions is not a mortgage on his conscience, considering the social function of his science.

If a task so undertaken also happens to involve some private interests, the economist can congratulate himself. Aims of economic policy which lack such a solid anchor have little prospect of being taken seriously in our world of overwhelming material interests and stormy passions. To take an important example, liberal trade policy would be in a bad way indeed if there did not, fortunately, exist groups which have a material interest in it and thereby form a natural counterweight to the fatal combination of protectionist interests and political passions such as nationalism and socialism. To help such groups may be regarded as a legitimate duty by the economist who weighs the opposing forces against each other.

The economist has all the less right to evade the duty of bringing his authority to bear on the controversies of economic policy since this duty has an important characteristic in common with every genuine duty. This is that it tends to be beset by vexations, and to withstand these vexations requires that same courage which is indispensable for defending the "dignity of truth." By putting his view onto one of the scales, he lessens the relative weight of the other, and the interest and passions involved on the other side will feel provoked. They have a perfect right to resist by trying to prove that the reasons, assumptions, and conclusions of the inconvenient scientific verdict are wrong and that the scientific judgment against them is a misjudgment. The scholar would be foolish if he thought himself in possession of objective truth, and it is no dishonor for him to be disproved. But he has a right to expect that his search for truth, his intellectual integrity, is not suspected. Like the judge, he has an absolute claim, which should be effectively protected, to the assurance that factual criticism of his sentence will not be replaced by an attempt to smear his reputation with accusations of bribery, cowardice, or political prejudice.

Bad experiences of this kind do not seem to have been spared even Adam Smith, the father of economics and contemporary of Samuel Johnson. In a famous passage of his *Wealth of Nations* (Book IV, Chapter 2), he says that anyone who opposes unconquerable private interests or has authority enough to be able to thwart them must expect that "neither the most acknowledged probity, nor the highest rank, nor the greatest public services can protect him from the most infamous abuse and detraction, from personal insults, nor sometimes from real danger."

THE ASYMMETRY OF THE MARKET ECONOMY

The role of natural nobility in general, and of science in particular, is seen with special clarity if we consider a very important circumstance which often does not receive sufficient attention. I have in mind what we might call the asymmetry of the market.

We know well enough that it would be foolish to regard the market, competition, and the play of supply and demand as institutions of which we can always expect the best in all circumstances. Nobody has better reasons to bear this in mind than the friend of the market economy. This general recognition leads us to a more particular one. The market frequently weights the scales in vital questions because it favors activities which are the source of gain and does not give sufficient scope to reasons which oppose these activities and should, in the general interest, have the greatest weight. The market thereby loses its authority in the ultimately most important decisions. It would be shortsighted of us to invoke the market or rely on it in such cases, and it becomes inevitable that we should seek decisions outside the market, beyond supply and demand. It is precisely for this purpose that the weight of authoritative opinions is needed. The highest interests of the community and the indispensable things of life have no exchange value and are neglected if supply and demand are allowed to dominate the field. We shall illustrate this point with a few particularly important examples.

The first example is advertising, a matter which repeatedly demands attention because it separates our era from all earlier ones as little else does, so much so that we might well call our century the age of advertising. A vast industry with enormous turnover figures lives on advertising, and it has generated such a colossus of influence and vested interests that it is hard to raise one's voice against it except in a book, all other instruments of public opinion having moved so close to the colossus that, to say the least, they can no longer be regarded as free agents.

We do not have to be told that advertising fulfills indispensable functions. Far be it from us to inveigh against it.[62] But only the blind could fail to notice that commercialism, that is, the

---

[62] See my *Mass und Mitte*, 200–218. Since that book was published, I have become even more firmly convinced that advertising, in all of its forms and with all of its effects, one of the foremost of which is to encourage the concentration of firms, is one of the most serious problems of our time and should receive the most critical attention of those few who can still afford to speak up without fear of being crushed by the powerful interests dominating this field. However, the interested parties are likely to put up fierce resistance, as we know from experience. To give a sample of it, and at the same time to illustrate the point of view developed in the text, I quote the following sentences from an article against the limitation of outdoor advertising: "With all due respect to the tidiness of our towns and landscapes and to the need of protecting monuments of nature, art, and culture, the aesthete's susceptibilities must today yield to the very concrete claims of life.... Undoubtedly, town and country would be prettier without posters and obviously also without the rush of traffic and all the other well-known inevitable troubles and distinguishing marks of modern business activity. But all of this, whether good or unpleasant, cannot be painted out of modern public and business life by, as it were, faking the picture with the brush of a buildings-preservation policy." (*Niedersächsische Wirtschaft* [July 20, 1954]) It is hardly possible to state more crudely an opinion whose power is, unfortunately, only too easy to imagine.

luxuriance of the market and its principles, causes the beauty of the landscape and the harmony of cities to be sacrificed to advertising. The reason that the danger is so great is that although money can be made from advertising, it cannot be made from resistance to advertising's excesses and perversions. Thousands get hard cash out of advertising, but the unsalable beauty and harmony of a country give to all a sense of well-being which cannot be measured by the market.

Yet the non-marketable value, while incomparably higher than the marketable one, is bound to lose unless we come to its assistance and put on its scale enough moral weight to make up for the deficiency of mercantile weight. The market's asymmetry opens a gap which has to be closed from without, from beyond the market, and it would be sheer suicide on the part of the market economy's friends to leave to others the cheap triumph of this discovery. In one of the loveliest parts of Germany there lives an old man who has dedicated his life to fighting against the excesses of advertising; it is a downright desperate fight against ignorance, greed, and obtuseness, and he carries on this struggle out of love for beauty and harmony and out of devotion. This old man is a living embodiment of our proposition that the market economy is not enough and, at the same time, proof that it needs such wise and public-spirited men as much as competition and the free play of supply and demand.

Another closely related example is installment buying, of which we have already spoken in another context. Again, there is no symmetry in the market economy between the forces favoring this extraordinarily widespread modern form of sales promotion and the forces which impede it. Yet the warmest supporter of installment buying will not deny that it is in danger of excess and degeneration. As in the first case, the asymmetry is due to the fact that the impulses originating in the market work to the benefit of consumer credit because the interests of those who want to sell their wares are joined by the special interests of the finance institutes making money out of installment-plan sales. But no money is to be made by organizing cash purchases because they need no organization. Nevertheless, not to make debts is the sound practice and the one which should primarily be encouraged. So the cause of reasonable conduct, which is threatened from all sides, needs our support and encouragement, and we should do well to reinforce the brakes, which are none too strong. We can count ourselves fortunate that this almost abandoned cause still finds some active supporters in a few economic groups, such as the savings banks and isolated industrial and trading companies, whose own interests seem to lie there. Even so, cash trade will remain in a bad enough way, thanks to the above-mentioned asymmetry of the market.[63]

One last example: the free world's trade with the Communist countries, euphemistically called East-West trade.[64] Here we meet a familiar state of affairs. This trade is highly dangerous and objectionable and is apt to strengthen the power which the free world, if it is not to delude itself, must recognize as its own worst enemy and which, indeed, never misses an opportunity of stating this with brutal frankness or of making it clear by its attitude. But money can be made only by expanding East-West trade, not by restricting it. We have a paradoxical situation: on the one side, Moscow is anxious to make good the deficiencies of the Communist economic system by getting supplies of the most wanted goods from the market economies of the free world while, at the same time, plotting these economies' destruction; on the other side, Moscow has no stauncher allies in these designs than the Western businessmen, precisely the people who represent an economic system that is the diametric opposite of Communism and who would be the first to be eliminated if Communism were to win.

---

[63] See Note 10 above and the works to which it refers.

[64] On East-West trade, see Wilhelm Röpke, "Aussenhandel im Dienst der Politik," *ORDO, Jahrbuch fur die Ordnung von Wirtschaft und Gesellschaft* (1956), 45–65.

The cultural and political ideal for which the West fights and the defense of which is the meaning of its struggle against Communism is the ideal of freedom in the precise sense that politics must not encroach upon the whole of life and society but must leave a large part of them independent. In other words, the West opposes its own pluralistic system to Communism's monolithic one. This is the pride and the strength of the West and one of the essential conditions of the world of freedom in which alone we can breathe. The freedom of society resides in its pluralism and is defined by it; and one of the areas which must remain independent is, of course, the economy. By contrast, it is of the essence of the Communist empire that its economy and also its economic relations, as well as its cultural and all other relations with the Western world, are subordinated to the paramount purposes of politics.

We are faced with a totalitarian world empire which draws all matters, and above all the economy, into politics. It follows that each and every economic transaction with the Communist empire is an act of international politics, for the simple reason that the other party regards it as such. For this reason, any appeal to separate East-West trade discussions from politics reveals either unusual ignorance or an intention to further Communist aims, for it admirably suits Moscow's game to represent the matter as harmless. It is a weakness of the West that the decisively political character of East-West trade is easy to obscure by invoking the principle of pluralistic liberty. For monolithic Communism, trade with the West is primarily a political act: for the pluralistic West, it is primarily an opportunity for business and profit. It is precisely the habit of respecting business interests which leads Western politicians to lend their ears to businessmen who profit from East-West trade and want to transpose into this political mine field the functions of business which are legitimate and proved in our own economic and social order. There are but few who stop to think whether in this case their business interests are not in conflict with overall political interests and with political interests, at that, which are a matter of life and death for all of us and most of all for Western "capitalists."

The fact that the wind of private business interests fills the sails of the Western business world's eagerness to expand East-West trade is no proof that it has political reason on its side—and political reason must, here, have the last word. On the contrary, just because these private interests are strong, any attempts at justifying East-West trade need to be scrutinized with the greatest suspicion. Market and profit are not competent in the decision; the decision lies with higher political interests, and business must submit to them. Businessmen should really regard it as an insult to their intelligence when Moscow tries to catch them with the bait of profit. They should remember Lenin's statement that when it was time to hang the world's capitalists, they would trip over each other in their eagerness to sell the Communists the necessary ropes.[65] Unless they are completely blinded by their short-term interests, Western businessmen should not find it so very difficult to see through Moscow's dishonest game. They should realize that this is another case of asymmetry in the market, one to be stressed especially by the market's friends.

Seeing that we are, here, up against one of the limits of the market economy, it is, perhaps, hardly to be expected that businessmen themselves will exercise self-restraint for the sake of higher political interests, especially since competition works against such self-restraint; but we certainly have a right to expect

---

[65] Ed. note: "They [capitalists] will furnish credits which will serve us for the support of the Communist Party in their countries and, by supplying us materials and technical equipment we lack, will restore our military industry necessary for our future attacks against our suppliers. To put it in other words, they will work on the preparation of their own suicide." Vladimir Lenin as reported by I. U. Annenkov, "Remembrances of Lenin," *Novyi Zhurnal/New Review*, September 1961, 147.

that any restrictions imposed by the government in the exercise of its proper functions will be recognized as necessary, reasonable, and binding. The supporters of the market economy do it the worst service by not observing its limits and conditions, as clear in this case as in the others, and by not drawing the necessary conclusions.

THE POLITICAL FRAMEWORK OF THE MARKET ECONOMY

What happens if governments, in this as in other instances, fail to make independent decisions based on objective assessment of all relevant facts and designed to serve the common interest? What if governments give way to pressures for another decision?

These questions touch upon a very sore spot. It is one to which we cannot pay too much attention in this field beyond supply and demand. To put it briefly, the problem is whether, in a mass democracy, with its many kinds of perversions, it is at all possible for policy to serve the common interest. In effect, policy has to withstand not only the pressure of powerful interest groups but also mass opinions, mass emotions, and mass passions that are guided, inflamed, and exploited by pressure groups, demagogy, and party machines alike. All these influences are more dangerous than ever when the decisions in question, to be reasonable, require unusual factual knowledge and the just assessment of all circumstances and interests involved. This applies above all to the wide field of economic policy.[66]

---

[66] On economic policy in a mass democracy, see Lippmann, *Essays in the Public Philosophy* (Boston, 1955); Felix Somary, *Democracy at Bay: A Diagnosis and a Prognosis* (New York, 1952); Lord Percy of Newcastle, *The Heresy of Democracy* (London, 1954); René Gillouin, *Man's Hangman Is Man* (Mundelein, Illinois, 1957); Kirk, "Social Justice and Mass Culture," *The Review of Politics* (October, 1954); and David McCord Wright, *Democracy and Progress* (New York, 1948). Modern "television democracy" is the nadir of the downward development so far.

Of these influences, we shall first single out interest groups. We shall have to be careful not to throw out the baby with the bath water. Such groups had no place in the original concept of the modern democratic state. The idea was that there was no room for legitimate separate interests beside what was called the common interest. The state was supposed to represent an indivisible common interest through co-operation between the executive, organized in the civil service, and parliamentary parties, which, in their turn, were to be divided by ideas rather than by material interests.[67] It is well known that actual developments were less and less in line with this concept. Governments and political parties everywhere progressively became subject to the influence of groups and associations either pressing their particular claims upon both the legislative body and the administration or at least obstructing what did not suit them. One result is that political parties are swayed more by interests than by ideas; another, that the internal authority of the state and its claim to represent the common interest are impaired.

Thus the monistic state of democratic doctrine has developed into the pluralistic state of democratic practice. Although the written constitution proclaims the theory, it is complemented by the unwritten paraconstitutional influence of particular groups embodied in vast mass organizations and interest groupings, in powerful concerns and cartels, in farmers' unions and labor unions. The Capitol is besieged by pressure groups, lobbyists, and veto groups, to use the American political jargon. The structure of the modern state is the result of this interplay of constitutional institutions and paraconstitutional economic and social power. It is obvious that the discrepancy between democratic idea and constitutional law on the one hand and the hard facts of reality on the other puts a heavy strain on the modern democratic state. The idea itself appears compromised, and any responsible government must examine carefully all the

---

[67] Bertrand de Jouvenel, *Du Pouvoir, histoire naturelle de sa croissance* (Geneva, 1945), 390ff.

possible means of resisting this pluralistic disintegration of the state. This process has accompanied the development of the modern state since its origins; more than a hundred years ago, Benjamin Constant, the great theoretician of constitutional government, warned against its dangers.[68] But it was only in the last quarter of the nineteenth century that it gained conspicuously in extent and pace, and in our day it has reached a degree critical for democracy and for rational economic policy. No legislative act, no import duty, no important administrative measure escapes the attention of the pressure groups and their frequently successful attempts to deflect the government's action to their own advantage.

It would be preaching to the converted to inveigh against the dangers of this development, but a few dispassionate remarks may be all the more useful.

The first circumstance which should give us cause for reflection is that the expression "pluralism," which is here used in a derogatory sense, has a positive meaning in the Anglo-Saxon countries and has been used by ourselves more than once in that meaning. In this positive sense it implies something which is a source of pride and satisfaction: the salutary existence of counterweights to the overweening power of the democratic doctrine's monistic state, the *république une et indivisible*. Has not Montesquieu, too, spoken of the *corps intermédiaires*,[69] whose necessary function it is to loosen the giant unity of the state

---

[68] Benjamin Constant, *Oeuvres politiques* (ed. Louandre, Paris, 1874), 248f.

[69] Ed. note: "The intermediate, subordinate, and dependent powers constitute the nature of monarchical government; I mean of that in which a single person governs by fundamental laws. I said, the intermediate, subordinate, and dependent powers: and indeed, in monarchies, the prince is the source of all power, political and civil. These fundamental laws necessarily suppose the intermediate channels through which the power flows; for, if there be only the momentary and capricious will of a single person to govern the state, nothing can be fixed, and of course there is no fundamental law." Charles Louis de Secondat,

by geographical or professional separatism? Is it not our own conviction that the centralist monistic state is to be rejected? Is it not one of the distinguishing marks of a sound state to allow as much social, political, and intellectual independence as possible and to leave room for local government and autonomy, institutions and corporations, private groups with particular interests and particular rights? Is this not desirable in order to contain the state's own striving for power, especially the democratic state's, which is all the more dangerous for posing as the representative of the "will of the people"? Are we, then, not entangling ourselves in a grave contradiction when we criticize "pluralism"?

The contradiction is resolved if we distinguish two kinds of pluralism, one justified and one unjustified, one sound and one unhealthy.

By sound pluralism we mean the case of particular groups defending themselves and their rights against the power of the state and the claims of other groups represented therein. This is a salutary limitation. A clear case in point is the landlords' effort to prevent themselves, a politically weak minority, from being expropriated by the votes of the politically strong majority of tenants. Unhealthy pluralism, on the other hand, is not defensive but offensive. It does not limit the power of the state but tries to use it for its own purposes and make it subservient to these purposes. The state is opposed only when it crosses the interests of this kind of pluralism, which, for the rest, merely tries to exploit its power.

The immense danger of this unhealthy pluralism is that pressure groups covetously beset the state—the modern suitors of Penelope. The wider the limits of the state's competence and the greater its power, the more interesting it becomes as an object of desire. The fewer the groups sharing the booty, the better it is for the participants in the marauding expedition. The

---

Baron de Montesquieu, "The Spirit of Laws," in *The Complete Works of M. de Montesquieu*, 4 vols. (London: Evans, 1777), 1:19.

ideal of such pluralism would be to maximize the power of the state in the economy and to minimize the number of those competing for the conquest and exploitation of that power. This ideal is achieved in the collectivist state, with the important difference, however, that it is usual in this case for an entirely new power group to triumph, which cheats all others of the booty.

These characteristics of unhealthy (offensive) pluralism explain why, during the last thirty or forty years, it has gained ground in exactly the same measure in which liberal economic policy has been displaced by centralist socialist policies. In the same measure, too, the opposite, defensive and sound pluralism, which we welcome, has lost influence and weight. State power on the one hand and economic and social power on the other have grown continuously and have progressively merged. The counterweights against this accumulation and alliance of power are federalism, local government, family, market economy, ownership, private enterprise, well-earned rights, *corps intermédiaires*—but they have become ever lighter during that period and by virtue of the same development.

If we want to understand fully the nefarious effects of offensive interest groups, we must consider what I have called "pluralism of the second degree" (*The Social Crisis of Our Time*, p. 131). By this I mean that the mass organizations of interested parties dangerously increase the already alarming power of separate interests, to the detriment of the common interest. Moreover, the representation of these interests tends to stray into dubious paths because the officials of these organizations make a living from the representation of interests and therefore have a particular concern to justify their profession as ostentatiously as possible. They therefore not only tend to be more ruthless than those whose interests it is their business to defend, but they are constantly tempted to do so in a manner which demonstrates the useful and indispensable nature of their office as clearly as possible. It is obvious that this professional vested interest of the representatives of particular interests tends to interpret the latter in the light of the former and that the two need not necessarily coincide. There is a refraction of the interests represented as they pass through the prism of the officials' own particular interest.

The matter can be illustrated by an example which is of paramount importance today, namely, trade-unions. The prime interest of trade-union leaders is a continuous rise in money wages because this is a tangible and patent result of their efforts; they generally have only a secondary interest in raising real wages through price reductions or in other purposes which, for the well-being and happiness of workers and employees, may well be more important than wage increases. It is quite possible for price reductions to further the true interests of trade-union members better than wage increases, but from the point of view of the trade-union leaders themselves, price reductions have the disadvantage of obscuring their own merits. We shall see presently that this is undoubtedly one of the chief sources of the permanent inflation which characterizes the Western world today and also the reason why a "labour standard," as Hicks says, has come to replace the old gold standard—though not at all to our benefit.[70]

So much for the power of pressure groups. If we now add the power of mass opinions, mass emotions, and mass passions, the combined effect of these forces and influences on economic policy will hardly seem surprising. A first result is that economic policy will tend to be irrational, that is, determined by what is "politically feasible" rather than by what is economically rational and just. The most spectacular example is that rent control, an irrational, ill-considered, and at the same time unsocial and inequitable intervention if ever there was one, can carry the day against unexceptionable arguments and against the better judgment of honest and intelligent politicians. Rent

---

[70] On pressure groups, see Boulding, *Op. cit.*, and A. Rüstow, *Ortsbestimmung der Gegenwart* (Erlenbach-Zürich, 1957), Vol. III, 171ff. On the "labour standard," see J. R. Hicks, "Economic Foundations of Wage Policy," *Economic Journal* (September, 1955), 391.

control is really nothing but the protection of one privileged special kind of tenants, those with old leases, at the expense of the landlords and later tenants alike. Yet it persists, and the explanation is no doubt that, on the one hand, it does need a little reflection and intelligence to see its full implications and that, on the other hand, politicians are afraid to renounce this object of cheap demagogy.[71]

A second result is that the power of pressure groups and the power of mass opinions, emotions, and passions mutually support each other and that group interests can be furthered by exploiting and mobilizing the ignorance, thoughtlessness, and vague feelings of the masses. This leads to the third result: that economic policy suffers from contradictions and degenerates into a sum of disconnected measures lacking a consistent principle. A telling example of the ensuing makeshift opportunism is that of a French finance minister who recently attacked, not the causes of inflation, but only its statistics, namely, the cost-of-living index, which determines the wage level in France. Where there are no principles or where principles cannot be effectively implemented, economic policy is at the mercy of the day's political whims and so becomes a dangerous source of uncertainty, which merely aggravates nervousness and vacilla-

---

[71] Wilhelm Röpke, *Wohnungszwangswirtschaft—ein europäisches Problem* (Düsseldorf, 1951); M. Friedman and George J. Stigler, "Roofs or Ceilings?" *Popular Essays on Current Problems*, Vol. I, No. 2 (September, 1946); Alfred Amonn, "Normalisierung der Wohnungswirtschaft in grundsätzlicher Sicht," *Schweizer Monatshefte* (June, 1953). A comprehensive postwar exposition of this hair-raising chapter of economic policy has yet to be written. The true state of affairs became clear to me recently when I received a letter from a German socialist politician. He wrote that by now everybody was of one mind about this troublesome matter but that he would be glad to hear from me concerning what one could do about it in practice. I replied that that was not my business but his. I expected of him, I said, that he should openly defend in public the view which he had expressed in his letter to me, and I proposed that as a beginning we publish our correspondence. I received no reply.

tion. All of this together is bound to impart to economic policy one overriding quality: it will follow political expediency, the line of least social resistance, the motto *après nous le deluge*[72] (or, to quote Keynes again: "In the long run, we are all dead.")

This means that contemporary economic policy tends to prefer what Walter Lippmann calls "soft" solutions, solutions which appear cheapest and most convenient at the moment, even if at the expense of the future. One of these is protectionism; to bar inconvenient foreign competition is often the solution which comes to mind first among other reasons because it is, politically, the easiest. A second type of "soft" solution is reliance on the public treasury, powerfully supported by the "fiscalism" of our times. This reliance, incidentally, is, like the demand for protective tariffs and other import restrictions, nourished by the people's obstinate inclination to believe in a sort of "fourth dimension" of economic and social policy and to forget that someone has to foot the bill, in one case the consumer, in the other the taxpayer. The consumer and the taxpayer become the "forgotten men" of our age—together with the saver and the other victims of the erosion of the value of money. The third "soft" solution, as everybody knows, is inflation—and the "softer" for starting more mildly. This is the real key to the Western countries' chronic inflation, which therefore, for reasons still to be discussed, deserves the name of "democratic-social inflation."

This diagnosis must be pronounced with ruthless honesty because recognition of the danger is the first condition of overcoming it and also because this is the best service that can be rendered to a democracy threatened by its own excesses. The danger can be countered only by a long-term and comprehensive program.

A solution must be found to the problem of how the executive can gain in strength and independence so that it can become the safeguard of continuity and common interest without

---

[72] Ed. note: "after us the deluge."

curtailing the essentials of democracy, namely, the dependence of government upon the consent of those governed, which alone makes government legitimate, and without giving rise to bureaucratic arbitrariness and omnipotence. It is urgently necessary to strengthen the feeling for the imponderable nature of community surpassing all separate interests and immediate claims and commanding the individual's loyalty, even unto death; it is equally necessary to strengthen the feeling for the unchallengeable authority and power of government legitimately entrusted with managing the affairs of the community. At the same time, however, people must be liberated from the fear—only too justified in our days—of being at the mercy of a Leviathan. It is an enormously difficult problem. There can be no solution unless the state's overgrown functions are drastically pruned and its economic, financial, and social policies are once more made subject to firm, simple, and universally understood rules inspired by the common interest and by a free economic order, without which there can be no protection against arbitrary power.

The most important aspect is, again, the spiritual and moral one. Individualism and utilitarianism, which give the individual's interests and material profit so damaging a predominance, and legal positivism, which sees no further than the written law, must be counterbalanced by all the imponderables which ultimately are the basis of the nation as a permanent entity and without which disintegration is inevitable: the immutable standards of natural law, continuity, tradition, historical awareness, love of country, all the things which anchor a community in the hearts of men. The younger the state is and the more provisional it appears, the more pressingly must all efforts be directed toward this aim.

To this end, it is invaluable to have independent institutions beyond the arena of conflicts of interests—institutions possessing the authority of guardians of universal and lasting values which cannot be bought. I have in mind the judiciary, the central bank, the churches, universities, and foundations, a few newspapers and periodicals of unimpeachable integrity, an educational system which, by cultivating the universal and the classical, sets up a barrier to the teachings of utilitarianism and the specialization of knowledge, and, finally, that natural nobility of which we have already spoken.

In conclusion, I want to say a little more about the tasks and responsibilities falling to the academic representatives of economics in an age in which the conditions of rational economic policy serving the interests of the community and of a free society are more than ever threatened by the forces of mass democracy. Some people seem to think that the principal function of economics is to prepare the domination of society by "specialists" in economics, statistics, and planning, that is, a situation which I propose to describe as economocracy—a horrible word for a horrible thing. We have already gone quite far along this path, although it is no less dangerous to deliver state and society into the hands of such economists than into the hands of generals.[73]

The true task of economics appears to me to be quite different, especially in a modern mass democracy. Its unglamorous but all the more useful mission is to make the logic of things heard in the midst of the passions and interests of public life,

---

[73] The prototype of the modern economocrat is the eighteenth-century physiocrat. The physiocrats—or *économistes*, led by Quesnay—are clearly the ancestors of all the power-thirsty, cocksure, and arrogant planners and organizers. Walter Bagehot (*Biographical Studies* [London, 1881], 269f.) paints a vivid picture of them. He says that a contemporary of Quesnay's wrote of him that he was convinced that he had reduced economic theory to a mere calculation and to axioms of irrefutable evidence. Tocqueville (*L'ancien régime et la révolution* [1856], Chapter 3) says of the physiocrats: "They not only abhor certain privileges, but all diversity: they would worship equality even if it meant general slavery. Whatever does not fit in with their designs has to be smashed. They have little respect for contracts and none for private rights; or rather, they do not, strictly speaking, admit private rights at all, but only the common benefit."

to bring to light inconvenient facts and relationships, to weigh everything and assign it its due place, to prick bubbles and expose illusions and confusions, and to counter political enthusiasm and its possible aberrations with economic reason and demagogy with truth. Economics should be an anti-ideological, anti-utopian, disillusioning science. It could then render society the invaluable service of lowering the temperature of political passions, counteracting mass myths, and making life difficult for demagogues, financial wizards, and economic magicians. But economics must not itself become the willing servant of passions, of whose stultifying effects Dante says in canto 13 of his *Paradiso*: "E poi l'affetto lo intelletto lega."[74]

The mission of economics is understood even better if we consider a problem which is peculiar to modern democracy and keeps recurring in economic policy. I have in mind the delay between some economic or social claim and its demagogic exploitation, on the one hand, and the moment, on the other, when the price of its fulfillment can no longer be concealed. If the economist repeatedly succeeds in reducing this delay by timely and effective explanation, he renders society a service which cannot be valued too highly, for in economic policy, as elsewhere, Chateaubriand's words are true: "Le crime n'est pas toujours puni dans ce monde; les fautes le sont toujours."[75]

This does not by any means imply that we economists may retire into the ivory tower of scientific neutrality. Least of all can social scientists be spared a decision at the cross-roads of our civilization; we must not only be able to read the signs, but we must know which way to point and lead: the road to free-

---

[74] Ed. note: "One's own opinion binds, confines the mind." Dante Alighieri, "Canto XIII," in *Paradiso*, trans. Allen Mendelbaum (Berkeley: University of California Press, 1982), 116.

[75] Ed. note: "Crime is not always punished in this world; faults always are." François-René de Chateaubriand, *Mémoires d'outre-tombe*, vol. 6 (Paris: Garnier, 1910), 120.

dom, humanity, and unswerving truth or the road to serfdom, violation of human nature, and falsehood. To evade this decision would be just as much *trahison des clercs*[76] as to sacrifice the dignity of our science, which is truth, to the political and social passions of our time.

---

[76] Ed. note: "treason of the intellectuals." See Julien Benda, *The Treason of the Intellectuals (La trahison de clercs)*, trans. Richard Aldington (New York: Morrow, 1928).

5

CENTRISM AND DECENTRISM[*]

THE DIVIDING LINES IN SOCIAL PHILOSOPHY AND ECONOMIC POLICY

I return once more to the subject of inflation, which we have just examined from all sides,[1] in full awareness of its overwhelming importance. I would like to relate an experience I had a few years ago. It so happened that on one and the same day I came across two statements, both of which concerned money but which arrived at such completely divergent and indeed irreconcilable conclusions that they were explicable only as being derived from two opposing social philosophies. One was made by a distinguished American economic expert. The very title of the article which contained it was provoking: "Inflation or Liberty?" It was an early warning of the danger of progressive inflation, the kind of warning which must now be recognized by all as justified. The author came to the conclusion that a nation can preserve its freedom only with the help

---

[*] Chapter 5 of Wilhelm Röpke, *A Humane Economy: The Social Framework of the Free Market*, trans. Elizabeth Henderson (Chicago: Regnery, 1960).

[1] Ed. note: See Röpke, *Humane Economy*, 151–221.

of sound money, but that in a modern mass democracy the monetary system could not remain sound if it was at the mercy of government, parliament, political parties, and powerful pressure groups in the absence of sufficient countervailing forces. The other statement reached me through a German news agency. A university professor of moderate socialist tendencies violently criticized the "fatal deflationary policy" of the German central bank and demanded that "the democratic means of guiding the economy, namely, money and credit, should be placed in the hands of democracy."

It is unlikely that this socialist would repeat today what he then propounded so passionately. The American, on the other hand, would have every reason not simply to warn but to implore. It follows that the socialist was wrong on a matter of economic policy, while the American was right. The inflationary pressure which the latter feared has now become so obvious that even the socialists must subordinate all other considerations to the need for an effective barrier to inflation.

But this is not what interests us in this context. The point I wish to make is the sharp and irreconcilable clash of two opinions on one of the most important questions of the economic and social order. It is difficult to think of a compromise between the two principles here involved. Either it is right and desirable that monetary and credit policy should be operated like a switchboard by a government directly dependent upon a parliamentary majority or, worse still, upon some non-parliamentary group posing as the representative of public opinion. Or, conversely, it is right and desirable to counteract such dependence. Either it is wise to put all the eggs into one basket or it is not. It is perfectly obvious that the German professor's opinion, which rested on a characteristic though, as we know today, unfounded fear of deflationary policies on the part of the central bank, was as firmly grounded on profound social convictions as was the American economist's contrary opinion.

We are in the presence of a case which reveals a fundamental cleavage of thought within social philosophy and economic policy. It teaches us how important it is to mark the dividing lines clearly in the everyday strife and conflicts of political opinion. The better we succeed in doing so, the more we may hope to understand the meaning of political differences and to reduce the conflict to an honest and generally recognized opposition of basic convictions. Not the least of the merits of such an undertaking is that it leads us to examine our own conscience and make our own choice. What are we, really? Liberals? Conservatives? Socialists? And if we are one or the other, why? And whither does it lead us?

Our example suggests that we may begin with a contrast which, while not the most important, is closely connected with other and more profound contrasts. We might say that a man whom we would call an inflationist is here in conflict with another whom we might call a deflationist. There is some justification in putting things in this manner. Each of us obviously tends, by temperament, either to think that inflation is a lesser evil than deflation or vice versa; or, in other words, either to fear deflation more than inflation, or vice versa; or, in yet other words, to be quicker in recognizing the dangers either of inflation or deflation. The reader will, at this stage of the book, not be in the dark about the author's views. I would go so far as to deny the justice of calling anyone a deflationist in the same sense in which his opposite number may be called an inflationist, for the simple reason that, as we know, there exists an asymmetry between inflation and deflation. Inflation is a poison whose initial effects are mostly pleasant and which reveals its destructive powers only later, while deflation is a process of general disadvantage from the outset; for this reason it is possible to want inflation, but deflation can at best be accepted as a possibly lesser evil. Hence we may speak of inflationism as an attitude not only of defending but possibly desiring inflation, and it is, in fact, a powerful and ancient current in economic history. Nothing of the kind can be said of deflationism.

To examine inflationism and deflationism in detail and to analyze their motives is a task which is as rewarding as it has hitherto been neglected. Let us look at some of the most important factors. First of all, inflationism has an exaggerated predilection for continuous growth, for rising figures (including the population figure), for quantitative progress—in short, it has a tendency to make sacrifices to expansion within limits which are too widely drawn. We are again reminded of Faust, in his old age this time: this kind of expansionism wishes, as he did, to "see such a throng" and "furnish soil to many millions." It rejoices in steeply rising curves and is prepared to pay for them by letting the curve of the value of money go down, at least for longer than is safe. Such expansionism implies very many other things, too: if necessary, it is willing to sacrifice the more remote future to the present, whether its adherents say, with the eighteenth century, *après nous le deluge*[2] or, in Keynes's more modern terms, "in the long run we are all dead"; it has no feeling for those invaluable reserves of society which ought not to be used up as fuel to keep the boiler of expansion going, including one of the most precious reserves of all, namely, respect for money and the inviolability of its value; it is against anything bourgeois, against the creditor, against the *rentier*, to whom, like Keynes, it wishes at best a painless death. Expansionism is futuristic, optimistic, and much else besides; the deflationist, or, as we would prefer to say, the anti-inflationist, is the opposite in all respects.

At this point of our argument we are anxious to probe deeper. We want to resolve the contrast between inflationism and anti-inflationism into a wider and more general one so that we may gain a vantage point from which to view the ultimate conflict between two social philosophies and two currents of economic policy. I have in mind the conflict between "left" and "right" in thought, between a tendency towards what I called "progressivism" and discussed in detail in my earlier book *Mass und Mitte* and one towards "conservatism"—although I hardly like

---

[2] Ed. note: "after us the deluge."

to use this expression nowadays because in most countries of the Western world it carries undesirable associations.

In order to make the transition from our example to this more general and important dividing line, we recall once more that our unhappy socialist, expansionist or inflationist as he was, objected to the independence of the central bank and demanded that it be subjected to the will of "democracy." Our American, on the other hand, who was convinced that inflation is a danger which always lurks in the background and now threatens us immediately, felt quite certain that a barrier must be erected against government domination of money. This was precisely the essence of the gold standard; after its demise, the only barrier remaining is the independence of the central bank, and it must be defended all the more obstinately. One of our spokesmen wants to concentrate responsibility for money in the hands of government and to subject it to politics; the other wants a division of power, an articulated system of checks and balances, decentralization, and hence the withdrawal of money from politics.

The first talks of the need to put money, the "democratic means of guiding the economy," into the hands of a government acting at its own discretion and according to a comprehensive plan, so that the government may conduct an economic policy which is called "progressive," guarantee "full employment" and thereby the power of trade-unions, and guide the course of the economy according to the wishes of the "people." In advocating all this, our German professor expresses a certain social philosophy diametrically opposed to that of his American counterpart. In this particular question, as in others, he takes a line common to the Jacobins of the French Revolution and all of their many spiritual heirs. The ideal of democracy is seen, not in a well-articulated state with balanced and therefore mutually limiting powers, but in centralized power of a kind which is unlimited in principle and can in practice be wielded all the more freely as it is supported by the fiction of the sovereign will of the people. This Jacobin excludes or repudiates the idea that, in so far as, like Montesquieu (*Esprit des Lois*, Book XI, Chapter 2), we attach more value to the freedom of the people than to its imaginary "power," democracy can derive nothing but benefit when power, of whatever origin, is split up and its mistakes and abuses thereby limited. A man who looks with suspicion upon a central bank which has not yet become a pliable tool of centralized state power reveals himself as one of those "eternal Jacobins" to whom any manifestation of independence and autonomy is a thorn in the flesh, whether it be the free market, free local government, private schools, independent broadcasting, or even the family itself.[3] Any institutions which still preserve some independence, whether central banks or

---

[3] Here is one of these Jacobin opinions: "We proscribe the regional spirit, whether of the department or the commune; we hold that it is odious and contrary to all principles that some municipalities should be rich and others poor, that some should have vast possessions and others nothing but debts." (*Mémoires de Carnot*, I, 278, quoted from H. Taine, *La révolution*, III, 107) "We want no more local interests, memories, dialects, or patriotism. There must be only one bond among individuals, namely that which ties them to society as a whole. We shall break all the others; we cannot tolerate individual groupings, and we shall do our best to disintegrate the most tenacious of them all, the family." This is how Taine acutely sums up this Jacobin ideology. It is no accident that Carnot is the man who later became the creator of the mass armies based on compulsory military service. Few other institutions are so conducive to centralization and concentration of power; Bertrand de Jouvenel (*Du Pouvoir, histoire naturelle de sa croissance*, 11ff.) says it results in a modern Minotaur. A democracy inspired by the Jacobin myth of the sovereignty of the people rather than by the liberal idea that those governed should control government is bound to develop into a centralist "democratic despotism." There is fairly general agreement on this point today, but a little more alertness is called for to detect the underlying social philosophy in the contemptuous talk of the detractors of federalism, small nations, or small firms. We should look upon this kind of talk, which is now fashionable among so-called progressives, as a half-open door through which we get a glimpse of a house furnished in the Jacobin-Napoleonic style.

pension funds or anything else, are, to repeat the simile, so many *Bastilles* which have to be razed to the ground.

Clearly, we are faced by two types of social thought to which most specific conflicts may be reduced without difficulty. We seem to be standing on a ridge from which we have a wide view into the valleys on both sides. Here is the parting of minds. Some are attracted towards collectivity, the others to the members which compose it. The former look at the structure of society from the top downwards, the latter from the bottom upwards. The first seek security, happiness, and fulfillment in the subordination of the individual and the small group to a deliberately and strictly organized community, which, from this point of view, is all the more attractive the larger it is; the others seek these benefits in the independence and autonomy of the individual and the small group. The difference in social outlook closely resembles another difference between two modes of thought: one which has a strange predilection for everything contrived, man-made, manufactured, organized, and intricately constructed, for the drawing board, blueprint, and ruler; and another which prefers what is natural, organic, time-tested, spontaneous, and self-regulating, and which endures through long eras. Still another difference in outlook is connected with this. On the one side are those who believe that society and economy can be reconstructed from above and without considering the fine web of the past. They believe in radical new beginnings; they are reformers inspired by an optimism that is apparently proof against any failure. On the other side are those who possess a sense of history and are convinced that the social fabric is highly sensitive to any interference. They deeply distrust every kind of optimistic reforming spirit and do not believe in crusades to conquer some new Jerusalem; they hold, with Burke, that the true statesman must combine capacity for reform with the will to prudent preservation.

Before continuing with this attempt to characterize the two types of social thought, we must confess that while we are most anxious to find a name for them, the task is a somewhat embarrassing one. We tried to give a provisional indication with the expressions "progressivism" and "conservatism," but we had to desist at once because the label "conservatism" is too discredited, at any rate on the European continent. Even with all kinds of qualifications, tiresome misunderstandings would still be inevitable. We do not get much further by contrasting "individualism" and "collectivism" because this would imply some sort of exaggeration in both cases. Nor are "liberalism" and "socialism" the right words. They have both become indispensable in the vocabulary of politics, but for this very reason they have become blurred by use and have collected so many shades of meaning and associations that they are useless for our purpose, especially since they signify something different in nearly every country.[4] What we need is a terminology which

---

[4] The term "liberalism" may be interpreted in a number of ways. In Switzerland, for example, political parties call themselves liberal when they are just as much conservative, in the sense in which Jacob Burckhardt and Alexandre Vinet may be called both conservative and liberal. Liberalism is the basic concept of the Swiss state, and anyone who defends it today against collectivist tendencies calls himself a liberal. In Italy, the liberals are, on the one hand, anti-collectivist conservatives and, on the other, anti-clerical progressives who are anxious not to lose their connections with the Left. In Germany, the government's policy is liberal, but its chief exponent is a party which calls itself Christian Democratic, while the "liberals" are in the opposition. Such concepts are comparable to a musical instrument of a certain compass: in the highest and lowest registers it reaches into the range of another instrument, as does the viola into the ranges of the violin and the violoncello, but we still associate with each instrument the idea of a definite range which characterizes its sound. Thus the concept of liberalism has, in Europe, a considerable breadth within which its significance fluctuates. Much the same is true of America, except that the compass there is shifted considerably to the Left. Certain border notes are common to both variants of liberalism, but the average range is so different in America and Europe that the two concepts are almost the opposite of each other. The American associates with liberalism mostly notes which we in Europe would associate with the Social Demo-

is not only new, fresh, and unburdened by associations but which also characterizes at least some essentials of the great contrast. What we have said so far in this chapter suggests the solution of calling the Montagues and Capulets of our play by the names "centrists" and "decentrists."

It should be clear by now that we are in the presence of two contrary principles which determine and mark all aspects of social life—politics, administration, economy, culture, housing, technology, and organization. If we take both concepts in a broad sense and explore their implications to the end, they will be revealed as two principles which express what is perhaps the most general contrast in social philosophy. Whether our ideal is centralization or decentralization, whether we regard as the primary element in society the individual and small groups or the large community, that is, the state, the nation, and the collective units up to the utopian world state—these are the questions which ultimately constitute the watershed between all the currents of thought and points of view which we have so far confronted with each other.[5]

---

cratic register. The New Deal, trade-unionism, planning, centralism, inflationary policies, radical taxation of income and wealth—all that is known as "liberal" in America, though this term certainly covers a lot of things which we in Europe would call by the same name. Confusion is even worse confounded by the fact that the concept is usurped by people and movements that are distinguished from Communists only by pretending that they are not.

[5] No less a man than Proudhon has said the same thing: "Thus the systems of centralization, imperialism, communism, absolutism—all of these words are synonymous—derive from popular ideals. In the social contract, as conceived by Rousseau and the Jacobins, the citizen divests himself of his sovereignty; the town council, the departmental and provincial administrations are absorbed by central authorities and are no more than agencies under the direct control of the ministry.... State power invades every sphere, lays its hands on everything and usurps everything finally, forever: army and navy, administration, jurisdiction, police, education, public building; banks, stock exchanges, credit, insurance, public assistance, saving, charity; forests, canals,

This is where federalism and local government clash with political centralization. It is here that the friends of the peasantry, the crafts, and middle classes, and the small firm and of widely distributed private property and the lovers of nature and of the human scale in all things part company with the advocates of large-scale industry, technical and organizational rationality, huge associations, and giant cities. This is the moat across which the eternal dialogue goes on: on one side are those who think that the economy is best planned by the market, competition, and free prices and who regard the decentralization of economic decisions among millions of separate producers and consumers as the indispensable condition of freedom, justice, and well-being; on the other side are those who prefer planning from above, with the state's compulsory powers. And so it goes on.

The centrist is none other than the social rationalist, whom we met before. Seen from his central point, the individual is small and eventually dwindles to a statistical figure, a building brick, a mathematical magnitude encased in equations, something that can be "refashioned," in short, something that may well be lost sight of. We know with what optimism our social rationalist views the success of his constructions and refashioning. By contrast, the decentrist, who thinks in terms of human beings and also knows and respects history, is skeptical or pessimistic and in any case bases his arguments realistically and unsentimentally upon human nature. The centrist is doctrinaire, the decentrist undoctrinaire and unideological. The latter prefers to hold on to established principles; he is swayed more by a hierarchy of norms and values, by reason and sober reflection, than by passions and feelings; he is firmly rooted in ulti-

---

rivers; religion, finance, customs, trade, agriculture, industry, transport. *And on top of everything heavy taxation, which takes one-fourth of the nation's gross social product.*" (*Du principe fédératif* [Paris, 1863], 69) I have italicized the last sentence in order to direct the reader's attention to Proudhon's perspicacity. It is easy to see why the centrist Marx hated this decentrist from the bottom of his heart.

mate and absolute convictions for which he requires no proof because he would regard it as absurd not to believe in them.

We see also that the centrist is what we have called a moralist, a moralist of the cheap rhetorical kind, who misuses big words, such as freedom, justice, rights of man, or others, to the point of empty phraseology, who poses as a paragon of virtues and stoops to use his moralism as a political weapon and to represent his more reserved adversary as morally inferior. Since, again, he looks at things from on high, well above the reality of individual people, his moralism is of an abstract, intellectual kind. It enables him to feel morally superior to others for the simple reason that he stakes his moral claims so high and makes demands on human nature without considering either the concrete conditions or the possible consequences of the fulfillment of those demands. He does not seem capable of imagining that others may not be lesser men because they make things less easy for themselves and do take account of the complications and difficulties of a practical and concrete code of ethics within which it is not unusual to will the good and work the bad.

The "left" moralist all too often reaches the point where his big words of love and freedom and justice serve as a cover for the exact opposite. The moralist, with his lofty admonitions, becomes an intolerant hater and envier, the theoretical pacifist an imperialist when it comes to the practical test, and the advocate of abstract social justice an ambitious place-hunter. These moralists are a world apart from the decentrists' attitude, of which the hero's father in Adalbert Stifter's *Nachsommer* says that man does not primarily exist for the sake of human society but for his own sake, "and if each one of us exists in the best possible manner for his own sake, he does so for society as well."[6] I used to know an old servant who had discovered this wisdom for herself; she always wondered why so many people

---

[6] Ed. note: Adalbert Stifter (1805–1868) was an Austrian writer, poet, and painter. *Der Nachsommer* (The Indian Summer) is a *Bildungsroman* (coming-of-age story) and a fine example of bourgeois realism.

kept racking their brains about how to do good to others, while, so she thought, it would surely be better if everyone simply and decently did his duty in his own station. The centrist's moral ideal frequently enough amounts to a desire to make the world into a place where, to quote Goethe again, everyone is nursing his neighbor—which presupposes a centralized compulsory organization.

The further we proceed with our analysis of the two modes of thought, the more we are led to assign each attitude to one or the other camp. The contrast between centrism and decentrism is, in fact, unusually comprehensive. In the economic sphere, the contrast is most clearly epitomized by monopoly and competition, and the collectivist economy corresponds to the centrist's ideal, just as the market economy corresponds to the decentrist's. Every economic intervention is a concession to centrism—made lightheartedly and in pursuit of his own ideal by the centrist and unwillingly by the decentrist. The latter demands strict justification for all concessions, and the burden of proof is on their advocates because it is his principle that there is always a presumption in favor of shifting the center of gravity of society and economy downwards, so that every act of centralization and every upward shift of the center of gravity requires convincing proof before the decentrist will condone such deviation from his ideal.

The position of equality and inequality cannot be in doubt. Equality and uniformity obviously belong to centrism; inequality, diversity, multiformity, and social articulation to decentrism. This requires no further explanation, but there is a special problem here upon which we touched earlier,[7] namely, the particular form of "equality of opportunity." This problem reminds us that life is not an equation which is soluble without a remainder; unless we are very careful, decentrism might involve itself in self-annihilating contradictions on this point. The ideal of decentrism, in common accord with one of the unchal-

---

[7] Ed. note: See Röpke, *Humane Economy*, 285–86.

lenged aims of liberalism, certainly demands that individuals should try their strength against each other in free competition, and this implies that they start the race from the same starting line and on the same conditions. Is it, then, to be a continuous race of all for everything? Do we always have to be on the lookout for better opportunities, wherever they may appear? Do we always have to regret the opportunities we missed and always chase after those we think are better? This cannot be the true meaning of the ideal. If it were so, it would obviously be a dangerous ideal and one most uncongenial to the decentrist, and to pursue it would cause general unhappiness. Our star witness, Tocqueville, observed long ago that the Americans, in whose country equality of opportunity always held pride of place, are so dedicated to the restless hunt after better opportunities that they end up as nervous and ever dissatisfied nomads.[8]

---

[8] "In America I saw the freest and most enlightened men placed in the happiest circumstances that the world affords; it seemed to me as if a cloud habitually hung upon their brow, and I thought them serious and almost sad, even in their pleasures.... Their taste for physical gratifications must be regarded as the original source of that secret disquietude which the actions of the Americans betray and of that inconstancy of which they daily afford fresh examples.... If in addition to the taste for physical well-being a social condition be added in which neither laws nor customs retain any person in his place, there is a great additional stimulant to his restlessness of temper. Men will then be seen continually to change their track for fear of missing the shortest cut to happiness.... When all the privileges of birth and fortune are abolished, when all professions are accessible to all, and a man's own energies may place him at the top of anyone of them, an easy and unbounded career seems open to his ambition and he will readily persuade himself that he is born to no common destinies. But this is an erroneous notion, which is corrected by daily experience.... They have swept away the privileges of some of their fellow creatures which stood in their way, but they have opened the door to universal competition.... This constant strife between the inclination springing from the equality of condition and the means it supplies to satisfy them harasses and wearies the mind." (Alexis de Tocqueville, *Democracy*

An uncommonly impressive and at the same time repulsive symbol of such a race of all for everything is to be found in the spectacle that memorable day, more than half a century ago, when a part of the territory of the present state of Oklahoma (the land had been taken from the Indians) was thrown open to settlers. They were waiting at the border, and at the shot of a pistol they all rushed forward from this completely equal starting line to compete for the best plots of land. Surely it must be obvious to everyone that nothing could be more unwise or dangerous than to turn society into such a continual race. Even if the production of goods could so be maximized, it would not be worth the price. Men would be incessantly on the move; culture, happiness, and nerves would be destroyed by an unending to and fro and up and down from place to place, from profession to profession, from one social class to another, from "shirt sleeves" to a fortune of millions and back to "shirt sleeves." No, the deeper—we might say here the conservative—meaning of decentrism is that it behooves us to bethink ourselves of the indispensable conditions for a sound and happy society. These are a certain stratification of society, respect for natural developments, a modicum of variety and of horizontal and vertical social articulation, family traditions, personal inclinations, and inherited wealth. From this point of view, it is, for example, by no means foolish if a country's townships or districts try to preserve their character to some extent by not immediately granting every newcomer the same rights as are enjoyed by the original inhabitants.

---

in America, Volume II, Book II, Chapter 12, 136–38) More than thirty years ago, I found that of sixty-nine settlers in a typical agricultural district of the United States, only twenty-three had any farming experience; the others included two circus musicians, three blacksmiths, two divers, two carpenters, two butchers, three cowherds, one ship's machinist, three publicans, and three old maids. (Wilhelm Röpke, "Das Agrarproblem der Vereinigten Staaten," *Archiv für Sozialwissenschaft und Sozialpolitik*, 58, p. 492)

It is not good if all the sons of peasants and bakers should become, or wish to become, physicians, clergymen, or clerks. It is true, now as always, that it is highly desirable that men should have the happy feeling of being in the place where they belong—indeed, it is truer than ever in our age, when this feeling has become so rare because of the ideal of the race of all against all. Frédéric le Play, the nineteenth-century engineer and sociologist, was not so stupid when he discovered an important mainstay of society in the *familles-souches*, the families in which profession and economic and social position are handed down from father to son.[9] Finally, it deserves to be stressed that if equality of opportunity is to be achieved by socializing education, envy and resentment will only be acerbated. If everybody has the same chances of advancement, those left behind will lose the face-saving and acceptable excuse of social injustice and lowly birth. The weakness of mind or character of the overwhelming majority of average or below-average people will be harshly revealed as the reason for failure, and it would be a poor observer of the human soul who thought that this revelation would not prove poisonous. No more murderous attack on the sum total of human happiness can be imagined than this kind of equality of opportunity, for, given the aristocratic distribution of the higher gifts of mind and character among a few only, such equality will benefit a small minority and make the majority all the unhappier.

In order not to stray from the right path, we must always remember that the ideal of decentrism requires us to stand for variety and independence in every sphere. However, it would be equally wrong if we were to confuse decentrism with particularism or parochialism and with parish-pump politics—that is to say, with a narrow-mindedness which can't see the forest for the trees. This is not what is meant. The decentrist must in all circumstances be a convinced universalist; he must keep his eye on a larger community which is all the more genuine for

---

[9] On Frédéric le Play, see my *Civitas Humana*, 111.

being structured and articulated. His center is God, and this is why he refuses to accept human centers instead, that is, precisely that which consistent centrism, in the form of collectivism, intends to present him with. This is how he understands the inscription placed on Ignatius de Loyola's grave: "Not to be excluded from the greatest, yet to remain included in the smallest, that is divine."[10] This, no doubt, is also what Goethe had in mind when he said:

> I am a citizen of the world,
> I am a citizen of Weimar.[11]

The right spirit is one which enables us to combine an overall view with a sense of the particular. On the one hand we should cultivate a universal approach to all intellectual, political, and economic matters and reject narrow views and actions and, above all, intellectual, political, and economic regionalism and nationalism; on the other hand, we should prize variety and independence at all levels and in all spheres, on the basis of the common patrimony of mankind, which is beyond all levels and spheres.

Apart from many other insights which the centrist lacks, the decentrist also knows that it is always easier to centralize than to decentralize and to widen the powers of the state than to curtail them. There is yet another thing which the decentrist knows better, and this is that the centrist's path is bound to lead to regions where the air of freedom and humanity becomes thinner and thinner, until we end up on the icy peaks of totalitarianism, from which nations can hardly hope to escape without

---

[10] The inscription on Loyola's tomb in the Church of the Gesù in Rome is by an unknown author and reads: *Non coerceri maximo, contineri tamen a minimo, divinum est.* (I must thank Dr. Franz Seiler and Dr. Erik von Kuehnelt-Leddihn for this information.) Hölderlin used it, with a slight alteration, as a motto for his *Hyperion*.

[11] *Zahme Xenien*, V.

a fall. The trouble is that once one takes this road, it becomes increasingly difficult to turn back. Centrism is in danger of encountering no check any more, least of all in itself. The obsession of uninhibited centrism can, like so many other things, be illustrated by a story from the world's store of legends. It characterizes with exaggerated symbolism both the direction of the march and the secret wishes of its leaders. I have in mind the story of Caligula, who is reported to have expressed the wish that the people of Rome might have but a single head so that it could be decapitated with one stroke. Caligula's wish has always remained the symbol of a kind of centrism which is tyrannical because it knows no limits and also a symbol of the inevitable end to which centralization must lead.

The temptation of centrism has been great at all times, as regards both theory and political action. It is the temptation of mechanical perfection and of uniformity at the expense of freedom. Perhaps Montesquieu was right when he said (*Esprit des Lois*, XXIX, 18) that it is the small minds, above all, which succumb to this temptation. Once the mania of uniformity and centralization spreads and once the centrists begin to lay down the law of the land, then we are in the presence of one of the most serious danger signals warning us of the impending loss of freedom, humanity, and the health of society. A century ago, John Stuart Mill wrote: "If the roads, the railways, the banks, the insurance offices, the great joint-stock companies, the universities, and the public charities, were all of them branches of the government; if, in addition, the municipal corporations and local boards, with all that now devolves on them, became departments of the central administration; if the employés of all these different enterprises were appointed and paid by the government, and looked to the government for every rise in life; not all the freedom of the press and popular constitution of the legislature would make this or any other country free otherwise than in name. And the evil would be greater, the more efficiently and scientifically the administrative machinery was constructed."[12]

THE WEB OF HUMAN RELATIONS

The dangers and temptations of centrism are the more considerable because of their great variety. We must always be on guard against unwittingly making concessions to centrism or promoting it against our intentions. The world is full of centrists who neither want to be centrists nor realize what they are; these are the liberals or conservatives who reject federalism, the anti-collectivists who flirt with monopoly or government intervention in the economy, humanistic Europeans who support an economocratic organization of our continent, and many others.

In approaching the end of this book, it should hardly be necessary to point once more to the most striking and well-known symptoms of growing concentration all around us, with which, as a rule, we put up readily enough or to which we even give our blessing. But it may be useful to sharpen our awareness of the dangers of concentration and of the centrist attitude which fosters it. We shall try to do so by means of a few examples from less familiar fields.

Most important in this context is the fact that the web of human relations is growing closer as a result of the steady increase in the number of dependent wage earners. The individual is getting caught in a situation of subordination and dependence in relation to centers of decision. This process is

---

[12] John Stuart Mill, *On Liberty*, Chapter V; similarly, Gaëtano Mosca, *The Ruling Class* (New York, 1939), 143–44. The reference to Montesquieu and Mosca suggests that it would be rewarding to write a history of the concepts of centrism and decentrism, but to my knowledge this has never been done. I myself attempted an outline in my essay "Zentralisierung und Dezentralisierung als Leitlinien der Wirtschaftspolitik," in Ernest Lagler and Johannes Messner (eds.), *Wirtschaftliche Entwicklung und soziale Ordnung* (Vienna, 1952), 20ff.

part of the great upheaval which the American economist K. E. Boulding calls the organizational revolution, and it disturbs the balance of human relations. The relation between independent market parties, the buyers and sellers, is horizontal and loose, if not impersonal. As firms grow in size and the number of independent market parties diminishes, the market's more or less impersonal and loose co-ordination is replaced by the vertical, close, and personal relation of subordination and authority. Dependence upon the client or the supplier through a market wide enough to do away with rigid personal relationships is replaced by dependence upon the boss.

People used to occupy positions side by side with each other, but now they are above and below each other, and the relation is charged with the constant tension of close personal contact within a limited, fixed group. With the diminution of individual independence, this is becoming the fate of the masses, and we all know the strain it puts on human relations. Intrigues, place-hunting, informing, ill will, bootlicking, envy, jealousy, and all the other poisons of close contact spread like the plague in all large organizations and companies, as experience has shown again and again. Neurotics are in a position to make life hell for hundreds and thousands of people, and, as Boulding points out, there is a more than even chance that it will be precisely neurotics who get to the top and into a dominating position, because of their assertiveness and officiousness. A bad-tempered tax collector can let himself go with both his subordinates and with the taxpayers at his mercy; the psychologically unbalanced foreman can become the factory tyrant and intimidate all the other workers. But however irritated or worried the greengrocer may be, he has to pull himself together, without, on that account, having to feel that he is the slave of his customers.

The worst is that this organizational revolution also catches up with those who do not as yet belong to some large concern and who still have their professional independence. What, for example, has happened to the medical profession? The life of physicians—especially in highly centralized welfare states—has become utterly exhausting because they are now involved in a situation of double dependence: the old, horizontal market dependence in relation to their patients, and the new, vertical, organizational dependence in relation to the health-insurance funds. It is nothing short of a tragedy that this vice should have gripped precisely the profession upon whose calm and composure our life and health depend.

At first sight these considerations constitute a new and impressive proof of the superiority of the market economy over any kind and degree of collectivist economy. It is impossible to overstate the value of the impersonal integration of people through the market in comparison with their conglomeration in a collectivist economy, however much the former may be maligned and however much we may have had to criticize it even in this book. But it does have the merit of co-ordinating rather than subordinating people. The market and power do not go well together, and anyone who wished to use his strong position vis-à-vis some buyer or seller to establish a dominating relationship of more than transitory duration would find it difficult to do so unless he could count on government support. As long as there exists a genuine market, economic power will remain precarious, and co-ordination will not easily be transformed into subordination. On the other hand, it is one of the most damning things to be held against collectivism in any shape or form that, with the exception only of the few who hold the power to plan and direct, it presses men inescapably into vertical and personal relations of subordination and so robs them of freedom. If the socialists, incorrigible centrists as they are, demand such an economic order in the name of freedom, they afford a most depressing proof of the aberrations of which man is capable when he is blinded by political passion.

However, the medal has an obverse side which we must not overlook. In the measure in which the number of independent people shrinks and in which the large concern and mass organization become typical of our times, in that same measure the market economy loses some of its advantages over the collectivist economy. The web of human relations is impaired even within the market because of concentration within the market. It is true that as long as the market economy survives it will remain incomparably better than the collectivist economy in this respect. In the market economy there always remains some independence, and there are a thousand ways of escape and protection: change of profession or job, free trade-unions, the rule of law, and many others. And if anyone is fed up with the whole thing, as thousands are today in the oppressive air of their welfare state, then he can emigrate to some place where centrism is still kept within bounds. Nevertheless, this is a problem which is certainly becoming more and more serious.

It is only natural that the people who are caught in the hierarchy of dependence should look for some compensation. They will try to loosen the bond of subordination and to narrow down the area of arbitrariness and chance. Every step in this direction will be counted a blessing. Everything possible should, of course, be done to alleviate the human problem of large organizations and concerns. This scarcely needs stressing today, when expressions like "working climate" and "human relations" are on everybody's lips. A justified claim in this connection is that the subordinates should have a share in the responsibility and a say in the affairs or even in the management of their company or organization so that subordination may be mitigated by elements of co-ordination as far as this is at all possible in a setup based, by nature, on subordination.[13]

---

[13] It is difficult to separate the desirable from the undesirable. I tried to do so in 1950 in a report to the Adenauer government on German economic policy (*Ist die deutsche Wirtschaftspolitik richtig?*). I think that what I said there is still valid. On the one hand, every sympathy and encouragement are due the workers' and employees' wish to be taken into the management's confidence and to know about the company's affairs, which gives them a corresponding share of responsibility; the same can be said of their desire for protection against arbitrary treatment, as well as their wish to identify themselves with the company, any conflicts of interest about wage policy notwithstanding. On the

Another consequence of the process of concentration reveals the full extent of its danger to society and the economy. Suppose that a hitherto independent plumber goes to work in a factory; subordination will disturb his inner balance, and he will try to reestablish it by tending to vote for a political party which promises to make life hard for the bosses. It will depend on circumstances whether he chooses the Socialist or the Communist party. Generally, he will also join whatever union looks after his trade in order to gain at least moral support. Nowadays, when full employment or overfull employment seem to loosen dependence, he may well feel that the price of permanent inflationary pressure—which, he may or may not realize, has to be paid—is not prohibitive as long as the wage-price spiral has not become so obvious that even the trade-union leaders' sophisms cease to make any impression on our plumber's sound common sense. On the other hand, we have seen earlier that these trade-union leaders have their own particular reasons for wanting to press an expansionary wage policy at all costs.

It is understandable enough that the trade-unions should have developed as a kind of defensive reaction to the fact that subordination has become the dominant principle in human

---

other hand, it is necessary to reject firmly any attempt to do away with subordination in decisions involving the success of the enterprise or to put part of the responsibility upon people who are not qualified for it by virtue of any expert knowledge, training, or talent and who assume no corresponding risks. Such claims must be resisted all the more forcefully because they often merely conceal an attempt by the trade-unions to extend their power to the company's management. Most of all is resistance indicated when the co-management system is used as the thin end of a wedge, with the intention to upset an economic order which, being a market economy, makes the market the source of the commands which the management's decisions try to interpret correctly. By far the best and most thorough exposition of this subject is Franz Böhm, "Das wirtschaftliche Mitbestimmungsrecht der Arbeiter im Betrieb," *ORDO, Jahrbuch für die Ordnung von Wirtschaft und Gesellschaft* (1951).

relations. This situation has resulted from concentration and the increase in dependent wage earners, and the reaction is mainly moral. But a new danger threatens the dependent worker. The trade-union itself becomes one of those "organizations" which are an expression of growing concentration; it creates, in its turn, new vertical dependences and new hierarchies with an above and a below, with bosses and subordinates. This kind of dependence may become intolerable and overshadow anything that an industrial company may impose on its workers and employees, whenever trade-unions obtain the right to dictate that no one may be employed in a company or profession without belonging to the union. In Anglo-Saxon countries, this occupational monopoly is known as the union shop or the closed shop.

If the courts and the legislature are weak or injudicious enough to tolerate such a monopoly, they must take their share of the blame for a tyranny that is more brutal than any other because it can impose its will by the threat of robbing a man of any chance to earn his living. Both the British press and the American press have recorded hair-raising examples of such trade-union tyranny. Things have come to such a pass that in the United States the "right to work" has assumed an entirely new meaning and now signifies that the worker's job is to be protected from the monopoly powers of the trade-unions.[14] It is an eloquent commentary on our times that even this elementary measure is meeting with such obstinate resistance on the part of the "progressives" and that it has thus far been enacted in only nineteen of America's fifty states.

---

[14] To give some idea of the consequences of the closed shop in England, we cite the case of Mr. Bonsor, which recently did at least arouse some public interest. The unfortunate man was a musician who had fallen behind in his union dues when out of work, but who was not allowed to accept a job until he had paid up his arrears. He eventually died as a casual worker. (*Time and Tide* [July 20, 1957])

Whichever way we look at things and whatever consequences we consider, there can be no doubt that if dependent labor, which already is in an overwhelming majority in most industrial countries of the West, goes on increasing, this will create a very disturbing problem. The immense danger of the process lies in its being a process of concentration corresponding to the concentration of firms. The number of firms which transform previously independent workers into dependent workers grows, and so does the average size of firms, for a variety of reasons. At the same time, trade-union power and all of its familiar consequences are strengthened. If we take all this into account, there is every justification for asking the anxious question of whether genuine democracy and a free market economy are, in the long run, compatible with a state of affairs in which the crushing majority of the population consists of dependent wage and salary earners.

The least that can be said about it, and surely something which no one will deny, is that it is a problem whose long-term importance is second to none. It is a key problem which must be solved if democracy and the market economy are to survive. We should not despair of finding a solution, but we must not expect it to be easy and simple. For this reason we cannot discuss it here as it deserves to be discussed. But we can mention three pointers towards a solution. First, we should do everything we can to brake or even reverse the process of dwindling independence whenever and wherever this is possible without real damage to economic rationality. Secondly, we should do everything we can to mitigate the rigidity of vertical subordination as much as the structure of productive organization and the nature of the market economy permit. Thirdly, we should do everything we can to strengthen the counterweights in fields other than labor dependence, the most important of these counterweights being private property.

This program should rally all supporters of our free economic and social order. But the first point may perhaps need some amplification. It implies that if one subscribes to the view that the process which transforms our society into one of dependent labor is disastrous, then one has to face the question how to counteract a further concentration of firms. This is the test case for the decentrist. It is of no avail to look to the government for new compulsion and new legislation, which would only acerbate centrism elsewhere. The decentrist must prove his worth by his support for all the forces, whatever they be, which counteract concentration. Painstaking research would be needed to discover how, ultimately, the government itself, by means of its laws, its tax system, and its economic and social policies, continuously and injudiciously weights the scales in favor of industrial concentration and makes things difficult for small and medium firms and all others who aspire to independence. This has nothing to do with the frequently overrated technical and organizational advantages of scale. The result of such research might be surprising. We might find that a few well-aimed measures, such as the reform of purchase or sales taxes, the abolition, or at least considerable reduction, of double taxation on distributed profits, the radical revision of company law, etc., might be extraordinarily effective in strengthening the position of small and medium firms.[15]

---

[15] There is a lot more to be said about economic concentration, especially with respect to the influence of taxation and company law, than I said in my earlier works *The Social Crisis of Our Time*, *Civitas Humana*, and *Mass und Mitte*. See also Joachim Kahl, *Macht und Markt* (Berlin, 1956). The best exposition of the influence of taxation known to me is to be found in the April, 1957 issue of *Wirtschaftsberichte der Berliner Bank*, which was devoted to "the disease of the German capital market." It is rightly pointed out that the "birth rate" of industrial firms, that is, the number of new firms, has sunk alarmingly low, which suggests that there is something fundamentally wrong with the capital market and the tax system. This adds rigidity to an already concentrated economic structure. It may well be that nobody really wanted all this, and thoroughgoing reforms may therefore have good prospects. About the part played by advertising in fostering concentration, see my *Mass und Mitte*, 213ff. Meanwhile, the danger has been enhanced by television,

International Centrism

To adopt the program of decentrism has many implications. Once one has done so, it will not do to close one's eyes to the immense problem of the ever growing size of firms and of economic concentration. This problem is fraught with immeasurable dangers for a free society and economy, and the task of countering this danger with all the means appropriate to the decentrist ideal must be tackled. Yet a depressingly large number of decentrists are blind to the problem and give their blessing to the gigantesque in industry. Hardly fewer are those who thoughtlessly join up with centrism when, having done its damage on the national plane, it proceeds to the promising field of international relations.

Under the false colors of international unity, a whole apparatus of international concentration, conglomeration, uniformity, and economic planning has grown up, both within the United Nations and its specialized agencies and on a regional pattern, such as the European Coal and Steel Community.[16] These institutions are waxing in power and provide an ever growing officialdom with privileges, influence, and tax-free incomes. Apart from a few praiseworthy exceptions, the usefulness of this international centralization is fantastically out of proportion to its cost, not to mention the undoubted damage it does. Few are clear-sighted enough to detect the reality behind the semblance of high ideals, and fewer still are courageous enough

---

which should have been a touchstone by which to prove whether man dominates technology or technology man; but even Switzerland failed this test. [Television was not introduced in Switzerland until 1950 beginning with only an hour a day for five days a week.—Ed.]

[16] Ed. note: The European Coal and Steel Community was an organization of six European states formed after World War II to regulate industrial production under a central authority. Upon the expiration of the Treaty of Paris, which had established it in 1951, the organization's activities were fully absorbed by the European Economic Community (1958–1993), which was in turn absorbed by the European Union.

to speak out—and if they do, they must face a veritable conspiracy of all the *bien-pensants*.

Only a diminishing minority sees that this is centralization of a particularly insidious and dangerous kind, and since the international bureaucracy disposes of powerful means to influence public opinion, even this minority finds it difficult to gain a hearing. International organization goes by many an attractive name, such as "Europe," "supranational sovereignty," "international harmonization," or "fight against Communism," and its worst feature is that it threatens to do away with the last sound remnants of national decentralization and international variety. The shining peak in the distance is the international welfare state, our views on which have, it is hoped, already been made sufficiently clear.

The latest stage in this development is the so-called European Common Market,[17] while the further project for a free-trade area is somewhat less afflicted with centrist features. The economist has reason to be very critical of this project, but this is not our primary concern here.[18] In the present context, the decisive argument is that this project implies a considerable amount of international economic planning and the prospect of more and more concentration and organization in the European economy and is therefore bound to provide a new and powerful stimulus to international centrism. The dependence of the individual and of smaller groups upon large centers will grow enormously, the human and the personal will have fewer chances than ever—and all this in the name of Europe and the European tradition, which owes so much to freedom, variety, and personality.

---

[17] Ed. note: The European Common Market (1958–1993) was also known as the European Economic Community. See previous note.

[18] G. Haberler, "Die wirtschaftliche Integration Europas," in *Wirtschaftsfragen der freien Welt*, 521–30; Röpke, *Internationale Ordnung–heute*, 308–17; idem, *L'économie mondiale aux XIXe et XXe siècles*, 135–62.

The danger was lurking in all of the many projects and discussions and records of European economic integration, and today it faces us immediately: it is the danger of *economocracy* finally transferred from the national level to the international level. It means the yet stronger and more inescapable domination of the planners, statisticians, and econometricians, the centralizing power of an international planning bureaucracy, international economic intervention, and all the rest of it. Some few countries of Europe have thus far been able to hold the spirit of Saint-Simonism at bay within their own frontiers, but now it will invade even these, from above, in the form of an European Saint-Simonism, true to the vision of the patriarch of economic planning.[19]

I say this as a man who loves all that the word "Europe" implies in highest values and loves it with a feeling best described as European patriotism. I am second to none in my love of Europe, least of all to those who have made that word the slogan of officious meddling. To me, it is self-evident that our continent must consolidate if it is to overcome its weakness and safeguard its heritage in the face of threatening dangers; only then can Europe regain her due place in world politics, not solely in opposition to the common foe of the entire free world, but also within the great defensive front of the West and in coming to terms with the colored peoples.[20] But then I also hold the apparently old-fashioned view that this purpose cannot be achieved by the cheapest possible production of

---

[19] Ed. note: "Saint-Simonism" refers to social thought inspired by Claude Henri de Rouvroy, comte Saint-Simon (1760–1825), a French utopian socialist theorist.

[20] Ed. note: Alfred Sauvy (1898–1990) was a French demographer, anthropologist, and historian who coined the term "Third World" and introduced this distinction between the "First World" (Western capitalist nations), "Second World" (communist nations), and "Third World" (other nations, especially in Africa and Asia, not aligned with either the western capitalist or communist nations) in his August 14, 1952 *L'Observateur* article, "Trois mondes, une planète."

automobiles and radio sets but primarily by our continent's regaining its self-confidence, reviving its political and military power, and bethinking itself of the spirit and great heritage in the joint safekeeping of all Europeans.

We can be loyal to Europe only if we preserve her spirit and heritage. The political and economic consolidation of Europe must therefore be such as to embody this loyalty by preserving what is of the essence of Europe: unity in diversity, freedom in solidarity, respect for the human personality and for distinctions and particularities. No matter how far definitions may have diverged in other respects, there has always been unanimity on this capital point: in antiquity, Strabo spoke of the "many shapes" of Europe;[21] St. Stephen of Hungary, in his impressive *Monita* to his heir, warned him that "unius linguæ uniusque moris regnum imbecille et fragile est";[22] Montesquieu would speak of Europe as a "nation de nations";[23] and in our own time Christopher Dawson has stressed Europe's character of a "society of peoples."[24] *Decentrism is of the essence of the spirit of Europe.* To try to organize Europe centrally, to subject the Continent to a bureaucracy of economic planning, and to weld it into a block would be nothing less than a betrayal of Europe and the European patrimony. The betrayal would be the more perfidious for being perpetrated in the name of Europe and by an outrageous misuse of that name. We would be destroying

---

[21] Ed. note: See Duane W. Roller, *The Geography of Strabo: An English Translation, with Introduction and Notes* (Cambridge: Cambridge University Press, 2014).

[22] Ed. note: "A kingdom of one language and one custom is weak and fragile."

[23] Ed. note: "A nation of nations."

[24] Ed. note: "The unity of Christendom was no longer conceived as the unity of an imperialist aristocracy, a king of Germanic Tsardom, but as a society of free peoples under the presidency of the Roman Pope and Emperor." Christopher Dawson, *The Making of Europe: An Introduction to the History of European Unity* (New York: Meridian, 1956), 237.

what we ought to defend, what endears Europe to us and makes her indispensable to the whole free world.

It is an ominous sign that there should be any need even to argue about the fact that a certain method of European economic integration should be excluded because it is un-European, centrist, and illiberal in the broadest sense of European libertarian thought. Economic nationalism and planning on the continental scale is no progress whatever in relation to economic nationalism and planning on the national scale. Indeed, it is much worse because these tendencies would have much freer scope on the larger territory of a whole continent. If this is agreed, then it should also be clear that there are certain directions in which we should not advance, even by a few steps.

Respect for distinctions and particularities, for diversity and for the small units of life and civilization, and, at the same time, rejection of any form of mechanistic centralization—these are the general principles whose observance alone identifies us as true Europeans who take the meaning of Europe seriously. If we are of one opinion on this, then we also ought to share a certain apprehension aroused by many a misdirected excess of zeal. We should be apprehensive about the activities of the economocrats and technocrats who are busy drawing the blueprints of Europe and creating a giant European organization, all in the name of technical progress. We should be apprehensive, too, about the strange ambition of making Europe a melting pot of nations and civilizations while at the same time treating with contempt precisely that which unifies European civilization at the highest level, namely, the classical and Christian spiritual heritage. We should be apprehensive, finally, about the idea of an European industrialism, which drowns in sheer quantity everything that is qualitative, diverse, varied, immeasurable, and individual and which measures progress in terms of tons of steel, kilowatts, record speeds, and the length of airport runways.

Do we want to take as our ideal in Europe mass production and mass cities, as an ideal, moreover, which must not even be challenged? Is it an indisputable advantage for Europe, too, to follow the road of growing concentration and rationalization? Do we not have every reason to fear for all the things which may then be trampled underfoot? Can there be anyone who does not shudder at the thought of an European Detroit disgorging automobiles in such enormous numbers that the density of American traffic is reproduced on our small continent, crowded into a narrow and densely populated space? With men thinking as they do today, all of these are no doubt heretical questions, but they need to be asked all the more insistently as there are only a few who have the courage to pronounce them, for fear of being descried as old-fashioned. This kind of question ought not to be suppressed if we want to bear true witness to decentrism, which, properly understood, is the true philosophy of Europe.

Reckoning without Man

Alarming numbers of people today are prepared to yield without resistance to the centrist trend of the time or even to think that they are doing something highly commendable by promoting it as best they can. There are deep reasons for this, and they are of a spiritual nature. The same trend determines our social philosophy; we think in aggregate, mechanistic, centrist terms and are alienated from man in his concrete individuality. It is not surprising that the social sciences themselves, economics and sociology, increasingly turn to thinking in aggregate and mechanistic terms and to advocating centrism in practical policy. Ortega y Gasset wrote a famous essay on the expulsion of man from art;[25] today we might well add a study on the expulsion of man from economics. Just as, in modern art, man is sacrificed to formless abstraction because he has in reality lost

---

[25] Ed. note: José Ortega y Gasset, "The Dehumanization of Art," in *The Dehumanization of Art and Other Essays on Art, Culture, and Literature* (Princeton: Princeton University Press, 1968), 3–56.

his features and dignity, so do certain theories of the social sciences dehumanize practical policy.[26]

In deploring the centrist and mechanistic tendencies in contemporary economics, we revert to a criticism made earlier in this book. We have in mind principally a school of thought which is indissolubly linked with the name J. M. Keynes. It has the significant name of "macro-economics": the economic process is treated as an objective and mechanical movement of aggregate quantities, a movement capable of being quantitatively determined and eventually predicted by appropriate mathematical and statistical methods. The economy takes on the appearance of a giant pumping engine, and it is quite consistent that the science which treats of the economy is turning itself into a sort of engineering science. Equations proliferate, while the theory of prices all but falls into oblivion. Yet the theory of prices, we recall, is the real harvest of a century and a half of economic thought.

A number of other questionable tendencies are connected with this. Excessive specialization furthers the disintegration of the social sciences' body of knowledge; esoteric exposition, taking obvious pride in the handling of mathematics, tends to close off hermetically the separate fields of knowledge; certain intellectual acrobatics, lacking all sense of proportion, tend to lose themselves in hairsplitting arguments and in the construction of "models" without even a basis of approximation to reality; arrogant intolerance is spreading. When one tries to read an economic journal nowadays, often enough one wonders whether one has not inadvertently picked up a journal of chemistry or hydraulics.

---

[26] We may go so far as to suggest an inner kinship between Keynes and Picasso. Even if we did not know that they belong to the same era, we could guess it by the dehumanization which is characteristic of both. They also resemble each other in their alternation between the classical and the ultra-modern. Keynes greatly admired Picasso (R. Harrod, *The Life of J. M. Keynes* [London, 1951], 318), and Picasso himself, of course, is a Communist.

It is high time that we should think soberly and critically about these things. Economics is no natural science; it is a moral science and as such has to do with man as a spiritual and moral being. On the other hand, economics does occupy a special position, in so far as its subject, the market economy, objectivizes subjective matters to such an extent that we can borrow methods from the natural sciences. This special position confers upon economics all the opportunities and charms of a "borderline science"—but also all the dangers.[27] We can use mathematics for illustrating and precisely formulating functional relationships between quantities, and few contemporary economists wholly condemn such use. But this method has its dangers. Unless its user is very careful, he may be tempted into pushing the critical borderline territory—the territory between the human and the mechanical—too far into the realm of mechanics, statistics, and mathematics, and he may neglect what is left this side of the frontier, namely, the unmathematically human, spiritual, moral, and, for this reason, decidedly unquantifiable. We would be wise to use the technical methods of the natural sciences only occasionally and for purposes of illustration; the possible gain is disproportionately small in comparison with the effort and the dangers involved. *Parturiunt montes nascetur ridiculus mus*[28]—this would be a fitting motto for many a study of this kind.

It is a serious misunderstanding to wish to defend the mathematical method with the argument that economics has to do with quantities. That is true, but it is true also of strategy, and yet battles are not mathematical problems to be entrusted to an electronic computer. The crucial things in economics are about

---

[27] This idea is brilliantly developed in Daniel Villey, "Examen de conscience de l'économie politique," *Revue d'Economie Politique* (1951), 845–80.

[28] Ed. note: "The mountains are in labor, and an absurd mouse will be born." One of Aesop's Fables, the line is commonly used to refer to grand plans and efforts that have negligible results.

as mathematically intractable as a love letter or a Christmas celebration. They reside in moral and spiritual forces, psychological reactions, opinions which are beyond the reach of curves and equations. What matters ultimately in economics is incalculable and unpredictable. No more must be expected of the mathematical method than it can, at best, perform. It would be difficult to name any sound economic theory which could be discovered only by this method or, indeed, any single one which was, in fact, so discovered. There are profound reasons for this, for every economic theorem which can be demonstrated only by means of mathematics and is not evident without them deserves the greatest mistrust. In the face of such attempts, the best answer is a phrase which one of the economists of the old Vienna school used to be fond of in cases of this kind: "Rather than be surprised, I prefer not to believe it."

Voltaire's remark, which Goethe once approvingly quoted in a letter to Zelter, holds here as much as anywhere: "J'ai toujours remarqué que la géométrie laisse l'esprit où elle le trouve."[29] Only too often does mathematical economics resemble the children's game of hiding Easter eggs, great jubilation breaking out when the eggs are found precisely where they were hidden— a witty simile which we owe to the contemporary economist L. Albert Hahn.[30] The same irreverence, I am afraid, is due mathematical economics when it pretends to furnish us precise results. In a science in which the subject matter simply precludes the exactness of mathematics and the natural sciences, such a

---

[29] Ed. note: "I have always noticed that geometry leaves the mind where it finds it." Johann Goethe, "Goethe to Zelter: Weimar, 28th February, 1811," in *Goethe's Letters to Zelter,* ed. and trans. A. D. Coleridge (London: George Bell, 1892), 75. Voltaire's original phrasing is somewhat different, referring to Descartes, "He was the greatest geometrician of his age; but geometry leaves the mind as she finds it." Voltaire, *Age of Louis XIV,* trans. William F. Fleming, 2 vols. (Paris: DuMont, 1901), 2:278.

[30] Ed. note: Ludwig Albert Hahn (1889–1968) was a German banker and economist.

claim is bound to raise the gravest misgivings. We reply that it is better to be imprecisely right than to be precisely wrong.[31]

After the First World War, a French statesman said: "Un homme qui meurt—ça m'émeut. Quinze cent mille hommes—c'est de la statistique."[32] This is as true as it is bitter. Economics should not overlook the lesson. We do, of course, need a sort of technical shorthand language in our science. We speak of supply and demand, the purchasing power of money, volume of output, volume of saving, volume of investment, not to mention the hog sector, and we cannot go on repeating every time that behind these pseudo-mechanical aggregates there are individual people, with their thoughts, feelings, value judgments, collective swings of opinion, and decisions. But we ourselves should not forget it, and we should not play with aggregates as with building blocks.

Ingenious tools of analysis have been devised for the examination of the economic process, and some of them we would not want to do without. But in handling such concepts as the "elasticity" of supply and demand, the "multiplier," the "accelerator," and so on, we should always remain conscious of the narrow limits of their fruitful and harmless application. They simulate a scientific and mathematical precision which does not really exist. They are not physical constants like the acceleration due to gravity but relations dependent upon the unpredictable behavior of men.

---

[31] The problem of the use of mathematics in economics has received scant attention. We may cite a discussion in the November, 1954 issue of *The Review of Economics and Statistics*; Ludwig von Mises, *Human Action* (New Haven, 1949), 347–54; and G. I. Stigler, *Five Lectures on Economic Problems* (London, 1950).

[32] Ed. note: "One man's death affects me; fifteen thousand deaths are only a statistic." The quotation is of Phillipe Berthelot (1866–1934), a French diplomat. See Benjamin F. Martin, *France and the Après Guerre 1918–1924: Illusions and Disillusionment* (Baton Rouge: Louisiana State University Press, 1999), 17. Variants of this quotation have been misattributed to the Soviet premier Joseph Stalin.

Let us illustrate the point with an example. I recall a rather pathetic study, published many years ago by General Motors, which contained the results of years of research, in an econometric laboratory especially founded for that purpose, about the behavior of the demand for automobiles. The results were disappointing. At the end of their labors the authors had to confess that, notwithstanding a lot of mathematical symbols and figures, they were no wiser than before. It had been worked out how buyers had behaved in the past, but how they would behave in the future was as uncertain as ever. The only bright feature was that the authors frankly admitted the crying disproportion between effort and result. All that had been proved—although no proof was needed—was that while it may be interesting and even useful to discover the coefficients of the elasticity of demand for any product, such figures ultimately have only historical significance. This method is one way of research into economic history; it is an instructive method and one which facilitates the assessment of future tendencies, but this assessment always comes up against the basic uncertainty and unpredictability of the future in economic life. Any extrapolation of past facts is misuse and rests on a misconception. All the unforeseeable forces which move human history as a whole may at any moment modify supply and demand in a manner which defies econometric treatment and may continually create new and unexpected situations.

A conception which reduces the economic process to a functional relationship of aggregates susceptible of being defined in terms of mechanics and calculated by mathematical methods is, however, inevitably bound to end up in the claim that these same methods permit forecasts which are more than the mere weighing of probabilities. This claim is quite obviously unjustified. The chain of humiliating defeats which econometric prophecies have suffered in the course of decades is therefore not surprising. What is surprising is the refusal of the defeated to admit defeat and to learn greater modesty.

Is it necessary to cite examples? A few months before the beginning of the greatest economic crisis in history, in the spring of 1929, the most distinguished American economists were talking about the happily secure equilibrium of an economy running in top gear. Where are the prophets of the decline in the birth rate? Population statistics seem a firm enough ground, yet these theorists had calculated not so long ago that a rapid decline in population growth was absolutely certain and had gone on to make precise recommendations for economic and social policy. Where are the economists who had abused the Keynesian theory—not least because of the mistaken forecasts of a declining birth rate—in order to deny that our economic system had any natural growth potential? They have left behind only the theory of the "mature economy," an intellectual fossil of the Great Depression, that same Great Depression whose threatening symptoms had been misinterpreted so shortly before its outbreak. And consider the damage done by the unfortunately all too influential prophets who were Keynes's obedient disciples. They forecast another depression to follow the Second World War and put their money on the wrong horse once more. They warned governments of being too optimistic about the peace and advised them to counteract the coming depression by doing everything in their power to increase purchasing power, with the result that most governments, in fact, pursued a wholly untimely and inflationary policy of full employment. Must we still recall the prophecies of gloom with which the adversaries of the German market economy accompanied its revival and were proved wrong again and again? And what about the Swedish economists who, in 1948, predicted another American depression, which again failed to materialize, and thereby misled government and central bank into plunging a rich and prosperous economy into a disorder which it has not been possible to straighten out to this day?

It would be interesting to know how certain forecasters come to terms with contrary facts. There are those, for example, who, for more than ten years, have spoken of the "permanent dollar gap" and "structural balance-of-payments deficits," as if these were objectively determined long-period phenomena; but meanwhile, some of the structurally weakest countries, the losers in a war which devastated them, Germany and Austria (and Japan, as long as it pursued anti-inflationary policies), have resoundingly disproved these self-assured predictions and have re-established a balance-of-payments equilibrium ahead of all other countries, including the richest. Of what avail is the vast effort of mathematical speculation about import and export elasticities, terms of trade, and other props of these theories when such countries are so tactless as to prove empirically that the classical balance-of-payments theory is right?[33]

In recalling these painful memories of disproved prophecies, we do not, naturally, mean to imply that it is not a legitimate task to evaluate the effect of present trends on the future and to weigh probabilities against each other. Nothing is more natural or more necessary than this. But we should have learned to do it with a greater mistrust of deceptive mathematical and statistical calculations and alleged data—including the psychological ones with which Keynes operated. We should instead base our calculations on man, not on some fictitious man who fits into our equations, but man as he is, with his oscillation between hope and fear, with his whims and passions, with his susceptibility to mass opinions and mass tempers, his fluctuation between quiet contentment and novelty-craving boredom, his dependence upon others and upon facts, and with the imperfection of his knowledge of these "data." If we want to guard

---

[33] The discouraging experiences of Great Britain are described in detail and very frankly by Ely Devons, "Statistics as a Basis for Policy," *Lloyds Bank Review* (July, 1954). Even so conciliatory a man as D. H. Robertson says about the British planners that "the extreme inaccuracy of their forecasts ... would have had even more unfortunate consequences if the errors had not on several occasions providentially cancelled one another out." (Erik Lundberg [ed.], *The Business Cycle in the Postwar World* [London, 1955], 10) See also Ludwig von Mises, *Theory and History* (New Haven, 1957).

against errors and disappointments in the analysis of economic processes and still more in our guesses about the future, then we must bear in mind that the science which treats of these processes, economics, is a science of the behavior of man in a certain sphere and in certain circumstances. What Epictetus said of social affairs is as true as ever, namely, that the decisive matters are not facts but men's opinion about facts or even opinions about opinions, even though they are, of course, linked to the facts.[34]

We now see also why one particular form of mechanistic and centrist theory underlying economic policies deserves a very skeptical reception. I have in mind so-called national budgeting, which is a statistical exposition of the interrelationships of aggregate quantities (income, consumption, saving, investment, government receipts and expenditure, foreign trade, etc.) over a given period of time and which is intended to serve as an indication for future economic policy. In so far as this is no more than a kind of statistical economic history, setting out the estimated development of these magnitudes during the past year, there is, of course, no objection. But the very violence with which the uses of national budgeting are defended should put us on our guard: even when it is not explicitly stated, these exercises have an ulterior purpose beyond the mere satisfaction of our historical and statistical curiosity.

We are once more in the presence of economocratic aspirations to power. The obvious intention is to turn national budgeting into a tool for mastery over the circular flow of the economy, and to this end the mathematical and statistical "exactness" of the results is invoked and the claim put forward that future developments can also be calculated. A warning is in order, however. Either these calculations are just another

---

[34] Ed. note: "Men are disturbed, not by things, but by the principles and notions which they form concerning things." Epictetus, *The Moral Discourses of Epictetus*, trans. Elizabeth Carter (New York: Dutton, 1910), 257.

form of leaving man out of the accounts, that is, they are mere guesses which come to grief on the eternal uncertainties and therefore constitute a danger for any economic policy based thereon, or they are a permanent temptation to use planning and intervention in order to force the recalcitrant facts into the predicted pattern. In both cases, no good can come from national budgeting. Moreover, there is no clearly established, visible boundary between using national budgeting as a mere— even though possibly mistaken—indication for economic policy and using it for purposes of economic planning.

The enthusiasm for this fashionable product of mechanistic and centrist thought should, in any event, be damped by the sobering reflection that the countries with the soundest economic and currency policies are those which do not go in for national accounting, while the countries in which this method is at its apogee have sickly economies and unusually strong inflationary pressure (the Scandinavian countries, the Netherlands, Great Britain, France). The most charitable interpretation of this state of affairs would be that the former countries were able to do without national accounting and still make the right decisions in economic and monetary policy, while the latter were not deflected from the wrong decisions even by national accounting. In fact, it is likely that national budgeting, as an essential instrument of economocracy, is more than a little responsible for the errors.

The failures of the mechanistic and centrist approach in economic forecasting are so numerous and blatant that it is astonishing that the underlying theory seems to digest these failures without losing prestige. It is even more astonishing that the protagonists of this approach are so utterly unrepentant. This is a problem which will repay some reflection. Is the British economist Professor Ely Devons right when he says (*Lloyds Bank Review* [July, 1954]) that the role of statistics in our societies has a striking resemblance with some of the functions of magic and divination in primitive societies? "Statistical magic, like its primitive counterpart, is a mystery to the public;

and like primitive magic it can never be proved wrong.... The oracle is never wrong; a mistake merely reinforces the belief in magic. It merely demonstrates conclusively that unless you do everything the right way you will get the wrong answer. So with us, bad forecasts rarely discredit statistical magic; they merely serve to demonstrate that the basic figures were bad, that the model was wrong or the statistician mistaken in his interpretation.... Next time we shall use better figures, better models, and of course the statisticians and econometricians today would never make the silly misinterpretations made in 1944, 1945 or 1946. We are convinced, rightly or wrongly, that this is the scientific procedure and we are going to stick to it." These bitter words reveal the full measure of the disappointment in which statistical and econometric research has ended in England. We would do well to take to heart the truth they contain. But what seems even more important to me is that the true reason why this method triumphantly survives all disappointment is that it is an indispensable instrument of economocracy.

We know that the method is wrong, and, being decentrists, we are convinced that it serves a bad purpose. The purpose is bad because it is to centralize and overorganize the economy and society in a way which neglects the human element. If we manage to get away from this mechanistic and collectivist way of thinking, we shall, among other things, also see the position and function of the entrepreneur in their true light. The essentials about this can be expressed in one sentence: The entrepreneur is like a ship's captain whose principal task is continuous navigation on the sea of the market, which is unpredictable because it depends on human nature. His function, which is perennial and indispensable for the course of economic life, is to balance supply and demand and continually to adjust production to changing consumption. In discharging this function, he always has to reckon with the uncertainty and unpredictability of the market factors, and his success depends on the extent to which he achieves this adjustment in spite of extraordinary difficulties. A man is an entrepreneur to the extent that he has learned to weigh probabilities against each other and to organize production and sales accordingly; and he is a successful entrepreneur exactly to the extent that he gets the better of the uncertainty of future market situations.

To think of the entrepreneur as a navigator should make a number of things clear to us. If a firm is to be successful and, in the degree of its success, to discharge its economic functions in society, it must primarily be orientated towards the market and must continually battle with its uncertainty and unpredictability. The firm's face is turned outwards, towards the market, and competition among firms is a continuous struggle to gain a start on the others in the matter of knowing or correctly assessing or discovering new opportunities for production or sales. The firm which so gains a start obtains, for the latter's frequently very brief duration, a special, privileged position which could easily be mistaken as monopolistic if it were not at once threatened and soon removed by those hard on the heels of the leader in the field. But the possibility of temporary advantage, the dynamic character of competition, is indispensable in order to spur the entrepreneur towards the best possible fulfillment of his function. As such, it is an essential part of any genuine market economy.[35]

---

[35] Much confusion has been created by certain modern theories of "perfect" competition. Not only do these theories define competition in so perfectionist a manner that the necessary conditions can, *a priori*, hardly be expected to obtain in the economy, and not only has this theoretical toy nourished a pessimism which, as it were, suspects monopolistic radioactivity everywhere in the market economy, but this model of "perfect" competition also simply eliminates the dynamic nature of competition, which is precisely the basis of the arguments in favor of competition and the competitive market economy. The abstract mathematical model's concept of competition must be replaced with the concept of "active" or "workable" competition, as J. M. Clark calls it, which stresses the competitors' incessant struggle for the consumer's favor. Cf. J. M. Clark, "Toward a Concept of Workable Competition," *American Economic Review* (June,

The same interpretation holds if we include the many cases in which the entrepreneur does not take the market as given but influences it, or even creates it or opens it up. But no entrepreneur can influence, create, or open up a market unless there is harmony between what he, the pioneer, innovator, organizer of production, or bringer of new wares, wants to do and the latent desires and reactions of the market, that is, of the people who accept one thing and reject another. It is always the market, with all of its unknowns, which decides and which ratifies or invalidates the entrepreneur's plans. However much the entrepreneur would like to shake off or reverse this relationship, he remains the servant of the market. His compliance is rewarded and his disobedience punished as long as the market is genuine, that is, ruled by competition. Even if, like Antonio, he be a "royal merchant,"[36] he can claim this title of honor only if he is also "the greatest servant of the commonwealth," that is, the market. He can be an absolute king only to the extent that monopoly enables him to forget his subordinate position.

The entrepreneur's function of navigating unpredictable seas is also the origin and justification of profit, as it is conceived in pure theory. This has always been the most disputed and least understood form of income, largely because one usually mentions only the entrepreneur's profit, but not its twin, his loss. Since Frank H. Knight's now classical work *Risk, Profit, and Uncertainty* (1921), there ought to remain no doubt about the fact that profit and loss are linked to a basic uncertainty of the future pattern of supply and demand and that they correspond

1940); F. A. Hayek, *Individualism and Economic Order* (Chicago, 1948); Wilhelm Röpke, "Wettbewerb: Konkurrenzsystem," in *Hand-wörterbuch der Sozialwissenschaften*, which is to be published in the near future. [The sixth volume of *Handwörterbuch der Sozialwissenschaften*, in which this entry appears, was published in 1959.—Ed.]

[36] Ed. note: Antonio, the merchant in *The Merchant of Venice*, is referred to as "that royal merchant." William Shakespeare, *The Merchant of Venice*, ed. Leah S. Marcus (New York: Norton, 2006), act 3, scene 2, line 245.

to the entrepreneur's success in assessing probabilities, as it is incumbent upon him to do, and in quickly adapting himself to a changing market. In a dream world of perfect knowledge, there could be no difference between sales price and production cost (in the widest sense) and hence no profit or loss.[37]

Now there is obviously a profound and positive meaning in the fact that success in groping among uncertainties is so promptly rewarded or lack of success equally promptly punished. This specific entrepreneurial activity is not only immensely important but also extraordinarily difficult. Only in the pathological situation of an inflationary sellers' market is it degraded to a sort of amateur sport; otherwise it remains navigation which requires the experience, resourcefulness, and sound intuition of the master mariner. Neither textbooks nor training courses, neither statistics nor electronic computers, can replace these qualities. This is why we need the entrepreneur and at the same time an economic order such that the best selection of these captains of the market according to their qualifications is always ensured and such that there is always an effective inducement towards maximum performance and careful decisions on the part of the entrepreneur. Profit and loss (and, ultimately, bankruptcy) together provide this inducement, and it should be one of our major preoccupations to see to it that it does not lose its force, even in the modern large company, with all its legal and organizational complications.

---

[37] The great English writer Norman Angell provides an excellent illustration. In his autobiography (*After All, Autobiography of Norman Angell* [London, 1951], 102) he tells the story of how there was, at a certain stage, a proposal that he take over a Paris paper for which he had previously been working, and thereby become an entrepreneur. But he suddenly developed a "most appalling funk" because of the responsibility for all those whose livelihood would then depend upon him. When things went wrong for the paper, the kicks would be for him; when they went right, he would be regarded as a "capitalist exploiter."

As consumers, we all benefit from this arrangement. Yet strangely enough, we can be persuaded only with difficulty, and not always successfully, to recognize it. This is one of the things which has never been satisfactorily explained. We often behave as if the whole arrangement had been invented solely for the pleasure and the advantage of entrepreneurs, and therefore we tend to regard them as the natural advocates of the free market economy. This really is strange. It would appear natural, on the contrary, that they should consider it inconvenient and tiresome to be saddled with this inducement system of the market. At any rate, many entrepreneurs display such a feeling in their attempts to withdraw from their position as navigators on the open and uncertain sea of the market. But if we abolish the market and replace it with planning authorities, or even if we allow government intervention and monopoly to restrict the market and turn it into a stagnant pool, then we do not need the entrepreneur. If the entrepreneur, like a seasick captain, wants to escape the whims and risks of the market and to take refuge in the safe port of planning or in security guaranteed by government or cartels, he makes himself redundant.

As we said, this may be quite natural and human. The motives for such an attitude may be respectable, but they are not precisely glorious. In any case they testify to a regrettable shortsightedness. On the other hand, there is another form of discontent among entrepreneurs which deserves our full respect, even though it may be unfounded. Entrepreneurs protest when economic theory seems to attribute to them the role of mere automata which achieve the common good by simply fulfilling the function which competition assigns them, calculating their advantage without thought of any higher ethical purposes. With some slight exaggeration, this attitude may be described rather like this: Let the entrepreneur be content to produce shoes as cheaply and as well as possible and to pay the factors of production, especially labor, according to their market value; if he also happens to be a decent chap (or is clever enough to be one, as the new theory of "human relations" advises him), he can be more than satisfied.

If entrepreneurs protest against such a moral and intellectual depletion of their existence, this is not only natural, but honorable and encouraging. No man can live a full life by credit and debit entries alone, even though the honest fulfillment of a responsible task is in itself no mean thing. But it is a misunderstanding to believe that our economic order expects such emptiness of the entrepreneur. We hardly need to dwell, in the final pages of this book, on the nature of this misunderstanding and the reasons for it. We want to stress the point, however, that one can take such an empty view of the entrepreneur's activities only by starting out from the wrong concept of the economy as a mechanical process. The dehumanization of theoretical economics necessarily includes a human devaluation of the entrepreneur, as of all other economic groups. As against the physics of the economy, we have to underscore its psychology, ethics, intelligence—in short, its human elements.

The human elements in the economy also enter into the argument in a very specific sense which bars the way to all centrist and mechanistic conceptions and reveals once more, in a prosaic manner, how wrong we can go in reckoning without man. Let us leave the lofty peaks of philosophy and take the low road of sober common sense. We have already dealt with the question of what centralization means for the highest human values, for man's soul, freedom, community, and ultimate destiny. Now we ask simply: Where are the people, where, above all, are the leaders, who can take on and bear the burden of centralization? Does not centralization come up against sheer physical limits, limits which have become quite obvious by now and which make the principle of centralization not only reprehensible but downright impracticable?

Here we meet the centrists on their own plane of the tangible and practical, from which they are wont to look down upon us as dreamers romantically worrying about the fate of mankind. We, the dreamers and romantics, are unimpressed by superorganization, centralization, Gargantuan concerns, machine giants, mammoth towns, and titanic plans. Undaunted, we keep quoting Montaigne's wise words—that even on the highest stilts we still run with our own legs and even on the highest throne sit with our own rumps.[38] We humbly ask how all of these much-vaunted things are going to be done in the absence of a sufficient number of people with the required mental and physical qualities. The claims on the human mind, heart, stomach, and liver are simply more than most men can meet, since their spiritual and physical resources go only so far and no farther. Here is the weakest link in the whole chain, and we cannot but accept this weakness with humility and modesty. Neuroses, heart diseases, and stomach ulcers are the final irrefutable arguments against centrism of every kind. To disregard them is wanton *hubris*, but we may not be far wrong in interpreting our times as a concatenation of *hubris* and nemesis.

It is time to return to a thought which we touched upon in the first chapter.[39] We spoke of the excess of government intervention which vitiates the market economy, even in its model countries. We pointed to a number of tangible and measurable consequences of this hodgepodge system but left the essential thing unsaid. The essential thing, as always, lies in the realm of the immeasurable and imponderable, and this multiplies the danger in an age such as ours, which has lost the feeling for these to such an alarming extent. It is easy enough to say that, after all, we have come to quite tolerable terms with this regrettable excess of government intervention, that the Germans, or even the Norwegians and the British, are reasonably well

---

[38] Ed. note: "'Tis to much purpose to go upon stilts, for, when upon stilts, we must yet walk with our legs; and when seated upon the most elevated throne in the world, we are but seated upon our breech." Michel de Montaigne, "Of Experience," in *Life and Letters of Montaigne with Notes and Index*, trans. Charles Cotton and William Carew Hazlett, vol. 10 (New York: Edwin C. Hill, 1910), 130.

[39] Ed. note: Röpke, *Humane Economy*, 1–35.

off, that they can buy anything that may be their—not unduly immodest—heart's desire. It sounds soothing, too, if we stress the extraordinary resilience of the market economy in adjusting itself to government intervention and overcoming the resulting difficulties, its robustness, stamina, and ostrich stomach. But we know how illusory all of this is.

Let us leave aside what we have already said earlier in Chapter 1.[40] But quite apart from that, who can measure the sum of nervous tension, the time and effort wasted on the double-front war against the market and the authorities, the nights spent poring over forms, the negotiations, useless trips, the irritation and vexation due to overbearing authorities? Competition in the market economy is wearing enough, but when it is, in addition, necessary to battle constantly with officials, to take account of their commands or prohibitions, to worry how to steer the firm not only through the whirlpools of the market but between the artificially created cliffs of government intervention and financial policy—how long can anyone stand this double strain? We are all ordinary men with limited strength. The much-vaunted resilience of the market economy is, in the last resort, the resilience of the people on whom rests the responsibility; the robustness of the market economy is that of the bodies and nerves of all those who have to carry the double burden of market and officialdom; the ostrich stomach of the market economy means nothing else but the stomach, heart, and other organs of the victims of this overcentralized and overorganized system. It is in the consulting rooms of heart, stomach, and nerve specialists that the balance sheet of the system has to be drawn up. Who can measure the sum of happiness, contentment, well-being, sense of fulfillment, and elementary freedom which is destroyed every day and every hour? The more we adulterate the market economy with admixtures of intervention, the higher rises the watermark of compulsion, the narrower becomes the area of freedom. What distinguishes the

---

[40] Ed. note: Röpke, *Humane Economy*, 1–35.

centrist from the decentrist is that the former makes so much lighter of the growth of compulsion than the latter.

Our world suffers from the fatal disease of concentration, and those—the politicians, leading personalities of the economy, chief editors, and others—in whose hands the threads converge have a task which simply exceeds human nature. The constant strain is propagated through all other levels, down to the harassed foreman and his like. It is the curse of our age. It is a curse twice over because these men, who can do their duty only at the peril of angina pectoris, lack the time for calm reflection or the quiet reading of a book. This creates the utmost danger for cultural leadership. Who can imagine nowadays an age like that of the Younger Pitt,[41] when, as he relates, the Chancellor of the Exchequer in Great Britain needed no private secretary because the extent of business did not justify one? Or who can imagine the way of life of Alexander von Humboldt,[42] who could deal by himself with his annual correspondence of about three thousand letters and still remained one of the foremost thinkers of his generation and reached the age of nearly ninety years?[43]

We shall not inquire about the simple happiness which is at stake. All that is self-evident. We only have to say this: our centrist civilization, which has become more and more remote from man and the human scale, has reached the point where its own continued existence is at stake.

---

[41] Ed. note: William Pitt the Younger (1759–1806) was a British statesman who served as Prime Minister from 1783 to 1801 and again from 1804 to 1806. Pitt served as Chancellor of the Exchequer from 1782 to 1783 and served as his own Chancellor of the Exchequer for all his time as Prime Minister.

[42] Ed. note: Alexander von Humboldt (1769–1859) was a Prussian geographer, naturalist, explorer, philosopher, and scientist.

[43] The statement about Pitt is quoted from Bagehot, *Op. cit.*, 131 [see 133n73 above—Ed.], and that about Alexander von Humboldt from *Briefwechsel und Gespräche Alexander von Humboldts mit einem jungen Freunde* (Berlin, 1861), 137.

6

LIBERALISM AND CHRISTIANITY*

Ten years ago, a group of eminent men from the United States and several European countries met at Mont Pèlerin, in Switzerland, to discuss the conditions under which a society of free men can exist today.[1] They had in common a social philosophy which might be called "liberal," if this word had not become the source of many misunderstandings.

None of us there believed that a socialist economy could result in anything but misery and serfdom, and we all were convinced that collectivism in all its forms is the real danger threatening our civilization. We discussed the necessity for reestablishing a regime of active competition; and in the course of our meetings we touched upon technical questions in the spheres of economics and jurisprudence. Most of us, indeed, were

---

*Translated by Patrick M. Boarman. From *Modern Age* 1, no. 2 (Fall 1957): 128–34. Used by permission.

[1] The group included Wilhelm Röpke, William Rappard, and Hans Barth from Switzerland; Jacques Rueff and Bertrand de Jouvenel from France; Luigi Einaudi and Carlo Antoni from Italy; Walter Eucken from Germany; Friedrich Hayek, Lionel Robbins, John Jewkes, E. Eyck, Michael Polanyi, and S. R. Dennison from England; Karl Brandt, Henry Hazlitt, Ludwig von Mises, and George Stigler from the United States.

economists, familiar with the theories of supply and demand, of the prices of the factors of production, and of money. There was no one among us who was an active representative of the Catholic faith.

Then there happened something which shows strikingly the almost funereal gravity of our present hour. In this circle of technicians, the discussion turned upon the increasing conviction that if we intend to win the battle for freedom, we must pay attention not primarily to supply and demand, but to quite different things; and once the ice was broken, we "hardened liberals" spoke of what Christianity means for freedom—and, inversely, of what freedom means for Christianity. We were conscious that in speaking in the first place as Christians *or* liberals concerned for freedom and human dignity, we were on common ground: ground we did not share with the enemy.

One of us, Professor Eucken[2]—who, since then, has died before his time—spoke of the experiences of the Third Reich, where men finally were driven to ask themselves if a man might be a Christian under a totalitarian regime, since such a domination deprives him of the freedom of moral decision essential to Christianity. He added that common suffering had overthrown the old confessional barriers, and that both Protestants and Catholics worked in the same direction, or even together, to attain a common goal: the development of a political and economic order which would be the opposite of a totalist society and economy, and which would express both Christian and liberal ideals. Since then, this collaboration has culminated in Germany in the foundation of the Christian Democratic party, led by Dr. Adenauer.[3]

---

[2] Ed. note: Walter Eucken (1891–1950) was a German economist and founder of the Freiburg School of ordoliberalism.

[3] Ed. note: Konrad Adenauer (1876–1967) was a German statesman who served as the first chancellor of the Federal Republic of Germany, then commonly known as West Germany, from 1949 to 1963.

LIBERALISM AND CHRISTIANITY

In the course of our discussions at Mont Pèlerin, we entered fully into the question of the relationship between liberalism and Christianity. I believe that this question can no longer be neglected. It merits a fresh examination. In this undertaking, it is desirable to speak of liberalism in a double sense: first, in the general sense of an idea which expresses the essence of our civilization; and, on the other hand, in the narrower and more specific sense of an intellectual, economic, and political ideology, born in the nineteenth century under the influence of certain factors proper to that period. In the first sense we are, indeed, all liberals so soon as we are anti-totalitarians. But if the word is taken in its second meaning, it is doubtful if any one of us can still call himself a liberal. Liberalism in the first sense is, as I have written elsewhere,[4] a giant tree which blossomed in a respectable age: under its ample foliage we are at this moment assembled with the feeling in our hearts that we have something in common to defend, whether we be conservatives or democrats, liberals or socialists, Protestants or Catholics. In its second meaning, on the contrary, liberalism is only the newest offshoot of this tree, and more than one person is wondering if it is not a savage growth. It would be criminal to wish to cut down the tree because the newest branch does not suit us; nevertheless, a thousand hatchets are already at work to commit this crime.

He who counts as precious the essential values and ideals of our Western civilization, so precious that he would be willing to defend them to his last breath—such a man knows what we mean when we speak of this tree, that is to say, of liberalism in its large and loftier meaning. For in the shape of this tree he honors the valuable work of centuries, yes, even of millenniums, a heritage which goes back to the origins of our civilization, to the Ionian Greeks, to the men of the Stoa, to Aristotle and Cicero. He reflects on all those thinkers of antiquity who were among the first to speak of human dignity and of the

---

[4] In my book *Mass und Mitte* (Zurich, 1950).

absolute nature of the individual soul in terms that could be understood by all rational men—who discovered the kingdom of ideas, who opposed human caprice, who proclaimed the inviolability of an order beyond the State—ideals which became the guiding stars of Western thought. What the *animae naturaliter Christianae*[5] launched was completed in a grand way by Christianity and transmitted to us as Christian natural law. Christianity was necessary to wrest man, as a child of God, from the grasp of the State and to undertake (in the words of Guglielmo Ferrero) the destruction of the "Pharaonic spirit" of the State of antiquity.[6]

Most of us are still moved to wonder how it was possible for the Ancients to have had a concept of freedom so different from our own.[7] In effect, their notion of the collective freedom of the "sovereign people" did not exclude the total subjection of the individual; we find the idea of freedom in this form in the ancient *polis*, and it occurs again in Rousseau; it is at the base of the doctrinaire ideology of modern democracy. Our

---

[5] Ed. note: "[testimony] of the naturally Christian soul." The whole Latin phrase, *testimonium animae naturaliter Christianae*, was used by Tertullian to refer to the knowledge of God and certain Christian truths that even non-Christians know by nature.

[6] Ed. note: Guglielmo Ferrero (1871–1942) was an Italian historian, journalist, and novelist. He describes the "Pharaonic spirit" at work in the Roman emperor Caligula, "Caligula was an orientalizer who repudiated and wished to destroy all Roman traditions and to set up at Rome in a single day a monarchy like that of Egypt. Hence his mania for self-deification and his violent efforts to impose on the Romans and on provincials, even on the Jews who were most recalcitrant, the cult of himself and of his family." Guglielmo Ferrero and Corrado Barbagallo, *A Short History of Rome: The Empire from the Death of Caesar to the Fall of the Western Empire 44 B.C.–476 A.D.*, trans. George Chrystal (New York: Putnam's, 1919), 158.

[7] Perhaps the most noteworthy treatment of this question is the essay by Benjamin Constant: "De la liberté des Anciens Comparée à celle des modernes" (*Oeuvres Politiques*, Editions Louandre, 1874).

idea of freedom, on the other hand—the Western idea—is of a freedom which guarantees the rights of the person, limits the action of the State, and comprehends the rights of the individual, of the family, of the minority, of the opposition, of religious groups. Western man has been at pains to point out that the wall which at this point separates him from the ancients is Christianity, that Christianity to which we owe the phrase: *Render unto Caesar the things which are Caesar's, but to God the things which are God's.* If we reflect upon the whole meaning of this phrase, we recognize that it expresses, after all, what is in our minds when we speak of liberalism in its widest sense.

It is, therefore, our common inheritance from antiquity and Christianity with which we are concerned here. Both are the true ancestors of a philosophy which defines the always tenuous relationships between the individual and the State in accordance with the postulates of universal reason and of human dignity—a philosophy which conforms to the nature of man, and thus opposes personal freedom to the power of the State. A précis of liberalism could be written using only the orations of Cicero, the *Corpus Juris,* and the *Summa* of Aquinas; it would be vividly contemporary. In all of these works, we discover the venerable patrimony of the personalist philosophy, but perhaps nowhere do we find it more distinctly than in the political philosophy of the Catholic Church through all of its changes and vicissitudes.

* * *

Without bias, and excluding resolutely any ideas merely negative, we ought to examine Catholic social philosophy in all its sources, works, and documents, and in all its aspects, to find out if it is akin to our idea of universal liberalism. This is a tempting task. To those of us who are concerned with the philosophical bases of liberalism and who seek to free liberalism of the fatal errors of the nineteenth century, such a study may reveal the extent of the debt we owe to Catholic thought. It may also show that a goodly number of liberal thinkers—among whom are

Tocqueville and Acton—were good Catholics, and that even a man like G. K. Chesterton did not hesitate to call himself a liberal. Perhaps in this way we may overcome the hesitancy of more than one Catholic to make an unbiased re-examination of the case for liberalism.

For the grave problems of the modern age oblige us, regardless of our position, to examine afresh our social philosophy, that we may realize exactly where the common front lies, and thus avoid useless controversy. I may illustrate what I mean here by referring the reader to that solemn document of the Catholic Church, the Encyclical *Quadragesimo Anno*,[8] which appeared on the 15th day of May 1931. While I have space only for a brief investigation of this document, I should like to suppose that the serious reader is interested in learning of the attraction it has for a Christian and a liberal who is not a member of the Catholic Church—although one who pretends to no skill in exegesis. But such a man—and this is the essential point—who in the higher and more general sense can call himself a liberal, will not hesitate to declare that this Encyclical is one of the most impressive, profound, and noble of manifestoes, in which many things close to the hearts of all of us are expressed with a dignity, with a vigor of conviction, and with a comprehensiveness of view which are rare. Indeed, the "liberal" quintessence of this document cannot be denied, so long as we take this word in its large and eternal sense of a civilization based on man and upon a healthy balance between the individual and community; so long, in short, as we accept liberalism as the antipodes of collectivism.

I know that in making this brief observation I shall encounter the objections of those who are accustomed to see in the

---

[8] Ed. note: Röpke's citations of Pope Pius XI's encyclical *Quadragesimo Anno* (On Reconstruction of the Social Order) refer to the Latin text, which is numbered differently than the English translation. References given in the footnotes refer to the paragraph numbers in the English translation.

Encyclical an anti-liberal program of the "Corporate State," and who hold it in good or bad memory depending on their political opinion. It seems to me that this is the result of an erroneous interpretation which today might well repel the favorable opinion the Encyclical merits. He who takes the trouble of reading it with care and without bias (and, in case of doubt, refers to the Latin original) will have difficulty in seeing how the Encyclical could have been interpreted as a program of Corporatism were this interpretation not based upon a confusion of ideas to which the term "Corporatism" can certainly lead, but a confusion which cannot be excused today.[9] Let us not forget that the corporate state and the corporate economy are expressions which have meaning only if the "corporation"[10] (*ordo* in the original) becomes the structural principle of the State or of the economy. If it is made the basis of the State, it will replace the principle of existing democracy (representative, parliamentary, or direct), and will make of the corporations organs which express the general will. Likewise, if the corporation becomes the structural principle of the economy, it will replace the existing principle, notably the market, by the concord or discord of the corporations (skeptics would say by vested interests). In the first case (the case of the corporate state), corporatism is opposed to all democracy; in the second case (that of the corporate economy), it destroys the *economy of the market.*

Even with the best will, I have been unable to find any trace of such a corporatism in the Encyclical, not to speak of the disapproving way in which the Encyclical treats the corporatism of Fascist Italy of the period. In each place where the *ordines* are

---

[9] Here I refer the reader to my own books, in particular, *The Crisis of Our Time* (University of Chicago Press), and *Civitas Humana* (W. Hodge, London, 1948).

[10] "Corporation" as used in this context is a general term meaning a group of persons organized on professional lines. It must not be confounded, therefore, with the business corporation of American law.

mentioned and where their establishment is recommended, it is done simply with the social purpose of obtaining an improvement of the relations between employers and employees, that is to say, with the aim of dissipating the class struggle, and not of killing competition in the market. Even in this restricted meaning of corporation (*professional community* as we would translate the word *ordo* in our day), as an instrument of social reform (and not of economic reform), the Encyclical stresses free will before all else. One is continually under the impression that the author of the Encyclical had before his eyes the dangers arising from an imprudent recommendation of corporations, and that to avoid an anarchy of "group interests," he endeavored to restrict this organization to the sphere of social reform.

This impression is, moreover, confirmed when, in answering the question whether the structural principle ought to be collectivist or non-collectivist, the Encyclical decides in favor of the market economy (*haec oeconomiae ratio*) and against a controlled economy.[11] Such a position, obviously, does not exclude rejection of the aberrations of the market economy. I have been unable to find in the Encyclical any passage sanctioning the belief that an order based on the market economy should be replaced by another which can only be a collectivist order, exception being made for the sector in which an autonomous peasant economy prevails. The latter is given its due estimation (III.1).[12]

In my opinion, one of the very great merits of the Encyclical is that it makes a clear distinction between the principle of the market economy as such and its numerous deviations. It does this precisely in order to attack the latter and save the principle of the market, and thus rescue our economic system from an omnivorous collectivism. This is exactly what the representa-

---

[11] Ed. note: Pius XI, Encyclical Letter on Reconstruction of the Social Order, *Quadragesimo Anno* (May 15, 1931), §101.

[12] Ed. note: *Quadragesimo Anno*, §102.

tives of neo-liberalism hold, though they formulate it in a different way. This is more clearly realized when we note that the Encyclical sees the degradation of the market economy not only in the excesses of an out-dated policy of laissez-faire, but also in the progressive disfigurement of the competitive order by monopoly.[13] Doubtless, I would here emphasize certain things which the Encyclical does not, and occasionally, perhaps, I would express myself in different language to obviate misunderstanding. Thus, I hesitate to accept the Encyclical's point of view on monopolies, which it imagines to be the creations of free competition;[14] in my opinion, they are rather the result of insufficiencies in the legal framework and of a certain brand of state interventionism. But I can only acquiesce with joy when the Encyclical goes to war against monopoly (*oeconomicus potentatus*) and its disastrous economic and political consequences (in particular III.1).[15]

When it stigmatizes the "debasement of the dignity of the State which should place itself above the quarrels of special interests," it directs itself against a monopoly sclerosis of the market economy and against group anarchy—diseases which, on the one hand, paralyze the market by making impossible any just balance between what is given and what is taken in return and, on the other hand, dissolve the State by their "pluralism."[16] We cannot at the same time fight the "special interests" and recommend economic policy which would sanction and even aid their fatal growth. That, however, is what corporatism would do; only the reestablishment of real competition can provide a remedy at this point. It would impugn the perspicacity of the author of the Encyclical to understand him as meaning anything else.

---

[13] Ed. note: *Quadragesimo Anno*, §105–106.
[14] Ed. note: *Quadragesimo Anno*, §107.
[15] Ed. note: *Quadragesimo Anno*, §108.
[16] Ed. note: *Quadragesimo Anno*, §109.

If the concentration of power in the hands of private persons is a great evil, it becomes a still greater evil in the hands of an all-powerful State armored with political sanctions. This truth does not escape the Encyclical despite its emphasis on rendering to the State the things which are the State's. Thus it is led, as are all of us, to a war on two fronts: against the individualism and economic policy of laissez-faire, and against collectivism. The fact that the Encyclical should reject collectivism and individualism with equal intransigence is all the more significant in view of the omnipresent danger to see in socialism (collectivism), in its theory at least, a genuine Christian doctrine, or at least an emphasis on moral values and sentiments which are specifically Christian. The very fact that it has clearly taken a position is the great merit of the Encyclical; now that we are again hearing vague talk about a "Christian Socialism," we would do well to recall these clear and authoritative words: "... whether Socialism be considered as a doctrine or as an historical fact, or as a movement, if it really remains Socialism, it cannot be brought into harmony with the dogmas of the Catholic Church, even after it has yielded to truth and justice in the points we have mentioned; the reason being that it conceives human society in a way utterly alien to Christian truth" (III.1).[17] Even the "moderate socialists" receive a severe warning (Communism being considered as beyond discussion). If their moderation resides in the fact that they confine their activity to certain reforms which can just as well be supported by a non-socialist ideology (e.g., the struggle against monopoly concentration), "then," says the Encyclical, "they abuse the term Socialism."[18]

The Encyclical has taken up its position between two extremes so that it may seek a "third road" to avoid the "dangers both of individualism and collectivism."[19] In what direction does this third road lead us? On this point the Encyclical furnishes

---

[17] Ed. note: *Quadragesimo Anno*, §117.
[18] Ed. note: *Quadragesimo Anno*, §120.
[19] Ed. note: *Quadragesimo Anno*, §46.

some remarkable details. I shall speak first of its exposition of the problem of property. In our industrial age of huge corporate holdings, the concept of property needs redefining, if it is to withstand criticism. The Encyclical speaks of the double nature of property, of its individual and social functions; and it proves that exaggeration of the latter leads to collectivism. Though it underlines the responsibility which attaches to the possession of the means of production, a responsibility which arises out of the social function of property, the Encyclical is no less emphatic in affirming the inviolability of property.[20] In view of the recurring temptation to make of property a relative thing by appeal to the Gospels, the Encyclical takes a further stand: "Man's natural right of possessing and transmitting property by inheritance must be kept intact and cannot be taken away from man by the State. Hence, the domestic household is antecedent, as well in idea as in fact, to the gathering of men into a community."[21] The final remarks of the Encyclical may be added here: "Those who are engaged in production are not forbidden to increase their fortunes in a lawful and just manner: indeed, it is just that he who renders service to society and develops its wealth should himself have his proportionate share of the increased public riches" (III.3b).[22]

It is upon this eminent social philosophy which respects a rational natural order that the third part of the Encyclical is based (II.1).[23] This is the part which treats of social questions, and in my opinion it surpasses all the others. The high point of its argument occurs when the Encyclical, without undervaluing traditional social policy, rightly situates the real problem in a process of decomposition, a decomposition which is not essentially material but spiritual and anthropological; a process which may be summed up in the word *proletarianization*. The solution

---

[20] Ed. note: *Quadragesimo Anno*, §47.
[21] Ed. note: *Quadragesimo Anno*, §49.
[22] Ed. note: *Quadragesimo Anno*, §136.
[23] Ed. note: *Quadragesimo Anno*, §44–52

of the social problem and the solution to the problem of de-proletarianization (*redemption proletariorum*) are inseparable;[24] and the Encyclical further declares, with justice, that our civilization hangs upon the solution of these problems.[25] It is impossible here for me to give an adequate summary of the many other considerations which ought to be taken into account. I confine myself to the observation that the world would long since have done well to impregnate itself with the social doctrine and the spiritual tradition of this Christian philosophy.[26]

It would be superfluous to dilate further on the fact that such a program of de-proletarianization is at the same time a program of economic, social, and political decentralization, or better, a program of the "aerated society" (Gustave Thibon); that it is in every respect the opposite of economic collectivism and of political totalitarianism—a program, too, which has nothing in it of the romantic but is rather built on realism since it considers man in his milieu and as subject to his natural necessities, and since, finally, it puts reason above the unreal or the anti-natural of the actual world.

Behind this Encyclical we sense the able economist who does not lose himself in vague postulates, but, like the "liberal" economist, remains aware of the interdependent relationships of economics. Because he has carefully avoided viewing the social problem merely as a question of wages, the author of the Encyclical makes the legitimate observation that it will not suffice to raise wages without considering these interdependent economic relationships. He makes it plain that an arbitrary

---

[24] Ed. note: *Quadragesimo Anno*, §59.

[25] Ed. note: *Quadragesimo Anno*, §62.

[26] In addition to the writings of G. K. Chesterton (especially *Outline of Sanity*) and of H. Belloc, Goetz Briefs' *The Proletariat* must be mentioned. Also, the wholesome and refreshing works of the French Catholic peasant philosopher Gustave Thibon (*Diagnostics, Essai de Physiologie sociale, Retour au Réel*). Of Belloc, see especially: *An Essay on the Restoration of Property*.

raise in wages, indeed, is closely linked to unemployment. (II.I.3c).[27] The informed economist is once more revealed when the reform of industrial corporations is seen as an important condition for the improvement of economic life (III.3).[28]

Only now and then does the Encyclical mention the problems of the international economy. Considering the importance of this domain, this omission is regrettable. If I am not mistaken, the position of Catholic social philosophy is least definite with respect to these problems. But it seems that recently an increasing number of voices have declared that on the international level, the sociological and economic principles of the Encyclical lead to adherence to the principles of a free, "multilateral" world economy. That is precisely the kind of international economic order desired by truly liberal thinkers.[29]

Perhaps the average Catholic may balk at speaking in terms of a "liberal" world economy. It is not easy to abstract what is essential from the association of nineteenth-century ideas implied by the word "liberal"; there is an understandable hesitation to employ this word in its general meaning—that meaning which, nevertheless, expresses so well a social philosophy specifically Catholic.

In the last analysis, it may be answered that words count for little. What matters is that we recognize our entry into the decisive phase of the battle for freedom and the dignity of man and, or in this battle, the patrimony of Christian social philosophy which, increasingly, merges with all that is essential and enduring in liberalism.

---

[27] Ed. note: *Quadragesimo Anno*, §74.

[28] Ed. note: *Quadragesimo Anno*, §132.

[29] See the interesting book by the former editor-in-chief of *L'Osservatore Romano*, Guido Gonella, *Presupposti di un ordine internazionale* (Vatican City, 1942). For my own ideas, see my book *Ordnung-beube* (Zurich, 1954), and my English lecture delivered at the Academy of International Law, "Economic Order and International Law" (Leyden, 1955).

7

THE PLACE OF ECONOMICS AMONG THE SCIENCES[*]

To announce an essay on the place of economics among the sciences may seem to be short of reckless temerity. For there is hardly any subject which offers a more seductive invitation to be verbose, pedantic, and boring. Such an invitation virtually amounts to an authorization to iterate observations which have been made often enough to need no further emphasis. To be sure, it would be very malicious of me to apply to economics the characterization once levelled at philosophy which defined it as "the continuous abuse of a terminology created for that express purpose." But it must be admitted that philosophy and economics exhibit certain common features which distinguish both from most other sciences. One of these is that it can be said of each that the history of its doctrines constitutes an essential part of the science itself. Another is the highly characteristic tendency of each toward excessive and incessant preoccupation with itself, its nature, and its methods. Both sciences resemble the introvert whose gaze is ever turned inward, whose conscience, staggering under

---

[*] Translated by George D. Huncke. From *On Freedom and Free Enterprise: Essays in Honor of Ludwig von Mises*, ed. Mary Sennholz (New York: Van Nostrand, 1956), 111–27.

the load of its own sins, is forever engaging in a searching of its own soul. No science outdoes economics in this sort of "soul-searching," in puzzling at the crossroads about signposts and direction-pointers, in discussing the whence, the whither, the whereby, and the wherefor. No science is more persistent in its repetition of a query whose general formula has been made famous by Schiller in his opening lecture, "What is, and for what purpose do we study, economics?"[1]

If, despite all that, we again broach that question today, there must be some especially cogent reason to justify us. And in order to recognize that reason clearly, we should do well to consider two facts which are as conspicuous as they are important. One of them is a source of pride to the economist; the other spells humiliation for him and danger to the position accorded to his branch of knowledge among the sciences in general, and in the estimation of society at large.

For on the one hand we note that throughout the civilized world, there has been an increase in the last few decades in the technical equipment of economic science such as we older economists would not have dreamed possible when we started our career. Thirty years ago a university might have twenty to thirty students registered in courses in economics, and their existence would be regarded by a faculty of law or philosophy as a bizarre appendage to be tolerated rather than respected.[2] Each year doctorates were conferred upon a dozen or so candidates who were thereby launched on a practice that was nearly as difficult to define as their science itself. Today the enormously augmented scope which organized research, instruction, and dissemination have attained in the field of economics is no less remarkable than the corresponding increase in the student

---

[1] Ed. note: Karl Schiller (1911–1994) was a German economist and statesman. He was Federal Minister of Economic Affairs from 1966 to 1972 and Federal Minister of Finance from 1971 to 1972.

[2] The author is particularly referring to conditions as they existed in Germany.

body. In numbers that are positively unwieldy they swarm about our "chairs in economics," crowd into seminars, huddle over our library tables, and despite the immeasurably increased amount of scientific material to be mastered, including even algebra and geometry, they make heroic efforts to plumb the meaning of all of it.

That is one of the two facts that demand our consideration. In contrast to it stands the other which is no less striking but for that very reason highly disquieting. I refer to the fact that the extraordinary expansion of economics in research, organization, expert personnel, and practical effectiveness has taken place at a stage which could not conceivably be more critical in the development of a science which already has a history replete with crises and critical turning points.

The fact that our science has attained such a high rank in public esteem at the very moment when it is less sure of itself than ever before must appear striking to anyone who concerns himself with economics—a science which may truly lay claim, by reason of its maturity, experience, and methods, to a place second to none among the sciences which seek to establish the essential laws that govern society itself. Are we not here faced with a very serious contradiction which might almost move us to disapproval and gloomy foreboding? Are we not accustomed to feeling extremely uneasy whenever outward appearance does not correspond to inner solidarity? The question itself is no more than natural, yet the contradiction is only apparent. Would it not be more accurate to say that both facts are attributable to a common cause, namely, the profound crisis which confronts society itself? And that they are so attributable for the very reason that economics revolves about society, and especially about those of its problems which are most amenable to rational analysis?

In the course of the last two decades significant changes in the political, economic, and social structure of our society have taken place, and these still continue to exert marked influence. It is to these changes that we may ascribe the extraordinary increase in the importance which our times accord to economic science. But it is those same changes, too, and the profundity of the intellectual sources from which they arise and the conflicts to which they lead, that are reflected in the altered appearance of that science, in its tensions, its problems and—let us openly admit—its errors. What at first seems to be a contradiction between external appearance and inner content is in fact an inevitably indissoluble combination that lies in the very nature of the science itself. Recourse is eagerly taken to economics in the expectation that it will furnish orientation for problems arising in an era of confusion which looks upon the birth of much that is new and the death of much that is old. And there is an intensely practical justification of that expectation. It lies in the new economic structure of society with its ever-increasing organization, institutionalization, and collectivization; and it lies in the fact that those characteristics give rise to an exceptionally augmented need for trained personnel capable of handling the problems these changes bring, as well as capable of publicly representing the interests that thereby come into play.

But by the same token it need not be too astonishing that the science to which recourse is taken is itself caught in the maelstrom of this era of confusion, and that it, too, is subject to turbulation and fluctuation. Such would not necessarily have to be the case. And there is every reason for us to combat with all our power the forces that tend to sweep economic science from its moorings. There is no justification for treating as mere cause and effect the relationship between the cultural and social upheaval of our times, on the one hand, and the dubious aberrations, on the other, of which economic science has been guilty. However, it can hardly be denied that some such relationship does exist and that we are thereby put upon notice as to our obligation to establish the higher truth which must reconcile the paradox. And such denial becomes all the more out of the question when we consider the possibility of the reciprocal influence of the two members of the paradox. For attention must be called to the probability that certain tendencies exhibited by economic science, while much in accord with the spirit of our times, are themselves in no small measure responsible for some of the spasmodic manifestations exhibited by our society and our economy.

* * *

I now propose that we explore the two facts of our paradox, one after the other, in order to discover what problems they present. And I suggest that we begin with the second, the internal conditions of economic science as they affect its position in relation to its fellow sciences. A few observations respecting the first member of our paradox may constitute our concluding paragraphs.

With respect to the present situation in economics and to its position among the sciences, we may state that it is pregnant with questions to the point of crisis; but we need not linger unduly long over a number of well-known matters of a general nature. It is easy to state in general terms what economics is concerned with, even though great difficulty may be encountered in the treatment of its specific problems. The commonest point of departure for the latter is the general scarcity of goods, which can in turn be attributed to the scarcity of forces of production except, of course, for the absolutely rare goods. Thence follow those inescapable rules of all economic activity which constitute the uttermost in generality—such as the necessity for evaluation, the exercise of choice among alternatives, optimum utilization of scarce forces of production, and the like. These are the imperatives which even a collectivist economy cannot disregard with impunity. In this sense it is, of course, a mistake to think of economics as a science whose scope is limited to one definite *method* of responding to those general imperatives, that is to say, as the science of a market economy controlled by free prices and competition. Quite on the contrary, a purely collectivist economic system is better fitted than any other to place those supreme imperatives in the correct light and so progress to a better understanding of how a market economy functions. And it is so fitted, if for no other reason than that a collectivist economy is in itself a demonstration that it cannot satisfactorily control those imperatives and hence that it must necessarily result in disorder and poverty. There could hardly be anything better calculated to further contemporary science than this inordinately costly and painful "instruction by the case method" which makes whole nations the guinea pigs on which to demonstrate so utterly convincingly the *modus operandi* and the irreplaceable functions of free determination of price and of the presuppositions behind it.

However, the difference in practice between these two opposing economic systems finds its counterpart in theory. Only a market economy makes it possible for economic science to go beyond those general and platitudinous truths and to discover relationships that have the objective definitiveness and validity which a market economy actually establishes by means of the mechanism of price. Only a market economy makes of economic science an *analytical* social science rather than a science which is merely a descriptive-understanding one having a logical structure like that of historiography. In the collectivistic state the science of economics is condemned to limit the scope of its activity to two extreme positions. The first of these is the preliminary and introductory stages of instruction which do not go beyond the general truths and their imperatives; the other is the doctrine of an economy controlled for the attainment of certain political objectives, not unlike the cameralism of the old absolute and paternalistic state.

But in saying this much we have not yet told the whole truth. In fact, we shall see later that it is dangerous to exaggerate the truth of what we have found so far. But it is indisputable that economics is, in the main, a science which is rooted in our market economy. It is, to speak with Ludwig von Mises, preeminently catallactics.[3] That is the field where its actual scien-

---

[3] Ed. note: Richard Whately (1787–1863) was an English economist and theologian who coined the term "catallactics": "A. Smith, indeed,

tific discoveries have been made; and it is still true that we can forget only at our dire peril what really constitutes the content of economic theory, namely, the economic organization which functions through a system of determined and determining prices, wages, rates of interest, and other magnitudes of value. We are, of course, aware that reality differs to a greater or lesser degree from our theoretical pattern of a free price mechanism which complies in every respect with the laws of unhampered competition. Nevertheless that pattern is indispensable to us if we are to arrive at any reasoned judgment at all concerning the importance of the degree to which, in every case, reality does so differ from the pattern of free and competitive markets.

We have thus more or less determined the intellectual site of the field where actual economic thinking takes place, and which constantly serves as its point of reference for reorientation. Let us then proceed a step further in order to characterize that thinking as to its individuality, its difficulties, its pitfalls. As Keynes once observed, economics is not difficult in the same sense as, say, theoretical physics is difficult. But I believe I can hazard a judgment based on my experience at our own university, where students of international problems have the option of approaching them from the point of view of law, of economics, or of "Political Science." And within that group of the social sciences, at least, economics has the reputation of presenting heights that are particularly difficult to scale. If I charitably debar the supposition that the reason might lie in

---

has designated his work a treatise on the 'Wealth of Nations;' but this supplies a name only for the *subject-matter*, not for the *science* itself. The name I should have preferred as the most descriptive, and on the whole least objectionable, is that of CATALLACTICS, or the 'Science of Exchanges.'" Richard Whately, *Introductory Lectures on Political Economy* (London: B. Fellows, 1832), 6. The Austrian economist Ludwig von Mises (1881–1973) also adopted this terminology. See Ludwig von Mises, *Human Action: A Treatise on Economics*, ed. Bettina Bien Greaves, 4 vols. (Indianapolis: Liberty Fund, 2007), 1:3.

the professors, then we are confronted by a problem which deserves considerable reflection.

Indubitably economics demands a kind of thinking which, if not difficult, is certainly peculiar to itself and which must be the product of training as well as of intensive practice. Such must inevitably be the case since its subject, economic activity, is so prodigiously varied and complex that it eludes our best efforts to grasp it by the methods customary in scientific study generally. The same Keynes who made the remark about economics and theoretical physics told us on another occasion (*Economic Journal*, 1924) that a man like Professor Planck, the famous originator of the Quantum Theory, confessed to him that he thought of studying economics but found it too difficult. He could have mastered, says Keynes, the whole corpus of mathematical economics in a few days, but what he seems to have found so difficult was the "amalgam of logic and intuition and the wide knowledge of facts, most of which are not precise, which is required for economic interpretation in its highest form."

> Thee, boundless Nature, how make thee my own?
> Where you, ye breasts? ...[4]

The descriptive method does not advance our cause. Experimentation is ruled out by the very nature of the subject. The weaving of a fabric spun from ingeniously devised lines of thought only too often proves an escape from what is relevant and factual. When confronted by that difficulty, the mind of the untutored and the unsuspecting is prone to take refuge in the dangerous world of analogy, of metaphor, of the unwarranted transfer of what is manifest and what is observed in individual experience to economic activity of the community as a whole. But the latter field is the very place where the determining influence is exerted, not by that which is obvious, but

---

[4] Ed. note: Johann Goethe, *Faust: A Tragedy*, trans. Bayard Taylor (Boston: Houghton, Mifflin, 1900), 20.

by something that must be logically deduced, and where that which is valid in particular is not necessarily valid in general. Under these circumstances we get that dreaded "homegrown economics" which bristles with all the obvious blunders that characterize the mercantilist thinking of which David Hume and Adam Smith disposed once and for all and against which the best antidote is still that collection of essays published a century ago by Bastiat under the eloquent title *Ce qu'on voit et ce qu'on ne voit pas*.[5] That kind of thinking is the source of one of the most disastrous of economic fallacies to be designated, perhaps, as anthropomorphism, or as "realism of conception" or by Whitehead's phrase "fallacy of misplaced concreteness."[6] It is especially to be encountered where discussions treat questions of international economic relations, and unfortunately it rears its ugly head even within the ranks of the professional economists themselves.[7] Indeed, the latter have unfortunately and in no inconsiderable numbers succumbed to the blandishments of still another influence which I shall describe shortly; and they have betrayed a tendency to relapse anew into the mercantilistic thinking that antedated the attainment by economics of its scientific maturity.

The present occasion is not the one on which to describe what methods economics does employ in lieu of those erroneous

---

[5] Ed. note: "What is seen and what is not seen." See Frédéric Bastiat, "What Is Seen and What Is Not Seen, or Political Economy in One Lesson," in *The Collected Works of Frédéric Bastiat*, ed. Jacques de Guenin, trans. Jane Willems and Michel Willems, vol. 3, *Economic Sophisms and "What is Seen and What is Not Seen"* (Indianapolis: Liberty Fund, 2017), 401–52.

[6] Ed. note: "There is an error; but it is merely the accidental error of mistaking the abstract for the concrete. It is an example of what I call the 'Fallacy of Misplaced Concreteness.'" Alfred North Whitehead, *Science and the Modern World* (Cambridge: Cambridge University Press, 1926), 72.

[7] On this point cf. my *Internationale Ordnung*, new ed. 1954 (Erlenbach–Zurich), 118, 133, 241.

ones, nor to describe how our science makes use of abstraction, idealization, typification, and the creation of models, in order to make a gradual approach to reality. But it *is* in order, on this occasion, to emphasize that in this process economic science requires the constant application of supreme attentiveness and a large dose of that intuitive power which enables us to keep our eyes on all the complicated threads at once, and to emulate the juggler who never loses sight of a single one of the balls he is keeping aloft. If that power forsakes the economist, the result is that commonest of economic errors which consists in a failure to think an economic process through to its conclusion and hence to lose sight of an important part of it. Such an error arises, for instance, if we conclude that profit must have a deflationary effect because (and this is the everlasting fallacy of all underconsumption theories) demand is thereby barred from reaching the market. The truth of the matter is that we are dealing with a demand which is expressing itself in a different direction—and a direction, incidentally, which as a rule means greater economic progress. The particular intellectual effort required of us economists consists in recognizing that economic science deals essentially not with constants but with functions, with relations, with interdependent forces. The logic peculiar to economic science is the logic of relationships. As one scholar of my generation somewhat exaggeratedly puts it, "such thinking in terms of relationships ... undoubtedly" is one of "the most difficult problems the human intellect can encounter."[8]

Small wonder, then, that it is at this very point that the economic reasoning of the untrained mind most frequently comes to grief, whereas the trained economist is most clearly to be recognized by the fact that thinking in terms of relationships has become second nature with him. He knows that imports and exports, or that wages and employment are most intimately and reciprocally related. And the diagrams setting forth the mutual

---

[8] O. Morgenstern, *Die Grenzen der Wirtschaftspolitik*, Vienna, 1934, 69.

interdependence of supply, demand, and price are as much a part of the economist's mental "stock-in-trade" as, let us say, is for the jurist the distinction between claims *ad personam* and those *ad rem*. The economist will not commit the fundamental error of considering the demand for a particular good in any other light than the relative demand with respect to a certain price and with respect to the conditions which determine the demand curve itself. He does not need to be told that one cannot speak of a "shortage," of a "scarcity of dollars," or of a "deficit in the balance of payments" as something absolute. He knows that those terms apply only with respect to a definite price which is fixed in such a way as to inhibit the normal function of price, which is to equalize supply and demand. And he knows that this is so even if, in view of certain social or political postulates, it seems preferable to deprive price of that function and to assign the latter to a governmental agency, if not to such agents as the black market, political corruption, "influence," or the mere physical prowess of those who, at that price, can force their way into the market. The economist who is trained to reason along such lines must indeed wince when he reads—as it was possible for him to do in 1943, for instance, in the London *Economist*—of a "scarcity of dollars" which is destined to be permanent because the United States "needs" so little from other countries, while the latter "need" so much from the United States. Just as if this "needing" had any sense at all, except with respect to certain prices and, in this case of international economic relations, with respect to a certain rate of exchange; and as if it were not the theory of comparative costs (that incontrovertible basic law of international trade) which alone can explain the necessity, even under these unusual circumstances, of establishing an equilibrium in international trade.

To be sure, that all sounds a lot simpler than it really is. For it is another difficulty of economic science that we are ever-lastingly confronted by a painful dilemma. As Alfred Marshall once observed, all simple statements in economics are erroneous.

But when we modify them and make them conform to pertinent relationships, we soon arrive at a point where the process gets out of control and where it would be possible to reason out economic justification for any abuse that assumes the name of economic policy. To the field of economics we can perhaps apply more aptly than to any other the dictum which Leibniz applied to the entire system of human knowledge. There is no truth, said Leibniz, which does not have something erroneous commingled with it, and no error which does not contain a bit of truth. If we recognize that, we ought to be secure against all extremes and eccentricities. But it is just as important for us to shun a thoroughly debilitating relativity. And if we are to do that, it is imperative from each occasion to the next that we distinguish clearly between that which is our fundamental thesis and our general truth, and that which is a modification of the fundamental thesis. It is equally imperative that we be aware that the particular circumstances decide in each case how much practical significance attaches to the qualifying modification.

But that demands of the economist a further special virtue. He must possess judgment, sound common sense, a feeling of proportion and perspective—in a word, qualities that are the exact opposite of those which so often characterize the average type of modern intellectual.[9] In the words of Solomon,[10] "To everything there is a season, and a time to every purpose under the heaven." That which is ordinarily folly may by exception be wisdom, and vice versa. In a desperate situation, such as the depression of 1930–1933, it may be correct to place every

---

[9] Cf. my *Mass und Mitte* (Erlenbach-Zurich, 1950), 54 et seq. "Celui qui regarde naturellement les choses a le bon sens" [The one who looks at things naturally has common sense—Ed.], says Vauvenargues (*Introduction à la connaissance de l'esprit humain*, 1746, VII). Then he adds, "Pour avoir beaucoup de bon sens il faut être fait de manière que la raison domine sur le sentiment, l'expérience sur le raisonnement" [To have a lot of common sense, one must be made in such a way that reason dominates over feeling, experience over reasoning—Ed.].

[10] Ecclesiastes 3:1.

emphasis on a policy of "spending" and not on saving. But the economist must possess sufficient judgment not to make that into an article of faith, but must promptly recall the general truth, only temporarily modified, which teaches the exact opposite. Or let us choose a different example. It is, of course, quite correct that a "passive balance of payments" can be brought about not only, as Ricardo taught, through the internal financial and money policy of a state, but also, as his opponent Malthus emphasized, by "real" factors which lie completely outside the sphere of things for which such a policy is responsible. But the more stubborn and more pronounced this passivity is, the more does the monetary policy operate causatively, and the more importance is to be attributed to the responsibility borne by the state and its central bank. In the long run, Ricardo's position is right and Malthus's wrong; and this is all the more true the more violent the departure from the norm. In the period of the German inflation which followed World War I, the most primitive conception of the quantity theory laying the entire blame for the soaring prices and the disruption of foreign exchange on the increase in the issue of currency was a thousand times superior to the most ingeniously worked out theory that looked for the trouble elsewhere, e.g., in the "passive" balance of payments. And even today time is running out for those countries in Europe that want to excuse the stubbornly continuing "dollar scarcity" on the ground that it is an effect of the war or the result of other "real" factors.

* * *

These things, unfortunately, require emphasis, even among professional economists. For it cannot be denied that these very qualities—the ability to exercise judgment, of *bon sens*, and of a sense of reality—have suffered diminution. They have tended to cede their position to a formalistic facility in the manipulation of methods which have been unwarrantably adopted from the natural sciences and used in economics. That brings me to the painful subject of a revolution in the field of economics which, on the whole, invites severe criticism, and which has led to an undeniable crisis in the status of economic science. I need not do more than mention the name of Lord Keynes to indicate the origin and character of that revolution. It is a broad subject, and as any adequate treatment of it would go far beyond the limits of my present observations, I shall therefore restrict myself to a few remarks which shall serve to bring out what is important for us in this connection.[11]

Keynes, more than any other one person, became responsible for a certain lamentable development in the economic science of our day. It is probable that he did so contrary to his own basic intention, but that is at this point irrelevant. That development takes on the high-sounding name of "the new economics" or "macroëconomics" and consists of a tendency to regard the whole economic process as something purely objective and mechanical. Hence purely mathematical and statistical methods, it seems, can be applied and the whole economic process can therefore be quantitatively determined and even pre-determined. Under those circumstances an economic system readily takes on the appearance of a sort of huge waterworks, and the science which treats of that economic system quite logically assumes the appearance of a kind of engineering science, which teems with equations in ever-increasing profusion. And so oblivion threatens to engulf what, as I see it, is the actual fruit of a century and a half of intellectual effort in the field of economics, namely, the doctrine of the movement of individual prices.

That brings in its train a number of other tendencies well calculated to arouse anxiety. One of these is an ever-increasing specialization in research which promotes a sort of fragmentation process throughout the field of the social sciences. Another

---

[11] For a fuller treatment I refer the reader to my essay "Alte und neue Oekonomie" which appeared as a contribution to a symposium entitled *Wirtschaft ohne Wunder* (Engen Rentsch, Erlenbach-Zurich, 1953). [See ch. 8 in this volume.—Ed.]

phenomenon, inevitably consequent to the first, is an occultism which at times positively glories in the esoteric incomprehensibility of its presentation and proudly points to its use of mathematics as something which raises the "new economics" almost to the dazzling heights of physics itself. We encounter, too, a species of intellectualism or scholasticism which is bereft of all sense of proportion, loses itself in a maze of hair-splitting, and sets up "models" or "patterns" which abandon any possible approach to reality. And that leads, finally, to a stiff-necked intolerance which can justly be termed a *rabies economica* since it is no whit less intransigently bigoted than the comparable *rabies theologica*. It has come to the point where we must often ask ourselves, as we open the pages of one of the technical publications of our science, whether we have not inadvertantly gotten hold of a technical journal on chemistry or hydraulics.

There is pressing need, then, for calm reflection and critical deliberation.[12] Their starting point must be the self-evident fact that economics belongs to the estimable family of the *Geisteswissenschaften* and that it is a "moral science" in the sense that it deals with man as an intellectual and moral being. But our reflection and deliberation must also not lose sight of the point previously established, that economics occupies a special position in that it deals with that institution which we call a market economy. Now that is an institution which goes so far in translating subjective feelings into objective actions that we economists are able to employ methods which are foreign to other moral sciences. And this special position makes economics truly a "border science" with all the attractive possibilities the term implies, but also subject to all the great dangers inherent therein. Economics does, in actual fact, permit of recourse to mathematics to illustrate and to formulate with precision causal relationships of a quantitative character. And there are indeed few modem economists who would reject all utilization of mathematics. But

---

[12] The reader hardly needs to be told how much the author is indebted to the writings of Ludwig von Mises for much of what follows.

this very method is open to question because it will lure the unwary into pushing forward unduly the frontier that delimits the border territory, the zone between what is human and what is mechanical. They will thus advance too far into the region of the mechanical, the statistical, the mathematical, and they will be prone to neglect that which lies on the hither side of the boundary, that which is human and unmathematical, that which is intellectual and moral and hence not quantitatively measurable. There should be a readiness to forgo the technique and methods of the natural sciences except occasionally and for illustrative purposes, particularly in view of the fact that the possible gain from their employment involves disproportionate danger of gross error. *Parturient montes—nascetur ridiculus mus*[13] is truly an apothegm that should be borne in mind by those who engage in studies of this kind.

And it is an error to attempt to defend mathematical economics by pointing out that our science does, after all, deal with quantities. That statement is true. But it is true in even greater measure of strategy, and yet battles are no mere mathematical problem of computation that can be consigned to the care of an electronic calculating machine. The determining factor in economic activity is furnished by things that are as downright unmathematical as a love letter or a Christmas festival, by forces that are moral and intellectual, by reactions and opinions that simply have no place in curves and equations, but lie in the domain of the everlastingly incalculable and unpredictable. We must not, in our "border science," demand more from the mathematical method than it can accomplish. I know of no really effectual economic theory that could be discovered by that method alone, nor indeed any that has actually been so discovered. There are profound reasons for this, for any economic doctrine deserves the jaundiced eye of suspicion if it can be demonstrated only mathematically without being at the same time unmathematically comprehensible. Wherever any

---

[13] Ed. note: On this phrase, see 169n28 above.

attempt is made to advance such a doctrine, it would be well to apply the wise principle laid down by a brilliant Viennese economist who used to say in such cases, "Before I marvel, I'd rather disbelieve."

I find equally sound that remark of Voltaire's which Goethe once quoted in the course of a letter to Zelter, "J'ai toujours remarqué que la géometrie laisse l'esprit où elle le trouve."[14] As one of our contemporary economists, L. A. Hahn, wittily remarks, mathematical economics all too often resembles the game of egg-hiding that children play at Easter. How they shout for joy when they find the eggs in the very place where they hid them! But even that is one of the most innocent objections that can be raised against this method. Its worst feature is that it deludes us into a dehumanization of economic science. To rediscover hidden Easter eggs is an innocent pleasure that we need not, after all, begrudge anyone. But it becomes a serious matter when the game exposes us to the danger of sticking our hands into a rattlesnake's nest.[15]

The French statesman Philippe Berthelot once said, after the First World War, "Un homme qui meurt—ç'a m'émeut. Quinze-cent mille hommes—c'est de la statistique."[16] It is an observation as bitter as it is true, and the economist is the last person who should be deaf to the warning it contains. Of course, we economists cannot avoid the use of a species of technical shorthand. We speak of supply and demand, of the purchasing power of money, of the amount of production, the volume of savings, the volume of investment, not to mention a pork sector, and we cannot forever be emphasizing that behind all these pseudo-mechanical concepts there stand individual human beings with their feelings, their deliberations, their appraisals of value, their collective suggestions and decisions.

---

[14] Ed. note: On this phrase, see 170n29 above.

[15] On the limitations of the mathematical method cf. G. F. Stigler, *Five Lectures on Economic Problems* (London, 1950).

[16] Ed. note: On this quotation, see 171n32 above.

But neither should we ever forget those things ourselves, nor play heedlessly with these collective symbols as children do with building blocks. Certain economists today speak of "coefficients of elasticity," "marginal propensities," "multipliers," "accelerators," and other ingenious devices, just as if it were a question of physical constants, so to speak, with which they were going through mathematical procedures. Then the moment has come when we have to express our disapproval in no uncertain terms.

Those are aberrations which make it very clear why the word "crisis" is hardly too strong a term to describe the present situation in economic science. But we have now arrived at the point where we must revert to a remark I made earlier in these pages. This tendency toward a quantitative and mechanical conception of our branch of the moral sciences is, of course, merely a reflection of a general inclination in the same direction in all the thinking of our era. It expresses itself with especial clarity in all questions bearing on our social life and in this respect runs parallel to developments in the practical politics of our day. The tendencies I deplore in economics are merely one particular case exemplifying the general tendency toward impersonalization, toward collectivization, toward mechanization, toward dehumanization. The spirit of our times is in very fact predominantly collectivistic, predominantly hostile to the human being, the human soul, the human personality. Anyone who perceives in that spirit a threat to human destiny must needs watch vigilantly for every manifestation whereby that spirit expresses itself. And that applies to economic theory just as truly! I make bold to aver that basically Keynes and Picasso both demonstrate that they belong to the same era, and that even in their alternation between classicism and ultramodernism they are remarkably alike. Ortega y Gasset has written a famous essay on "The Banishment of the Human Being from Art."[17]

---

[17] Ed. note: José Ortega y Gasset, "The Dehumanization of Art," in *The Dehumanization of Art and Other Essays on Art, Culture, and Literature* (Princeton: Princeton University Press, 1968), 3–56.

We economists can well supplement it by making some observations on "The Banishment of the Human Being from Economic Science." And unfortunately here, too, developments in the field of theory parallel those in the field of its practical application.

* * *

That brings us back to the original point of departure for these observations. After we have attempted to explain and appraise the place of economics as a science, it still remains for us to say a concluding word on its place in modern society. What is it accomplishing here? What are its specific functions, and how can it fulfill them?

Let us not linger over the trivial truth that it is the function of economics to provide governments, organized groups, and public opinion with orientation and guidance in all decisions concerning economic policy, and to supply a training ground for the forces that specialize in these pursuits. There still remain two important observations to record.

The first of these is the need for repeating emphatically an old complaint. It is to the effect that hardly any other science has to struggle as hard as does economics against the layman's stubborn proclivity to adhere to the "homegrown economics" I mentioned earlier. Despite a complete lack of training and in naive reliance on the obvious evidence of his senses, he opposes his own economies to two centuries of not entirely fruitless reflection and research by the economist. For economics is the one field where every layman feels able to render a competent opinion because it is the field where his interests are involved and his sentiments are aroused. And as Frank H. Knight, then president of the American Economics Association, somewhat bitterly remarked a few years ago, that is all the more remarkable because it is just the more essential economic truths which are of such a nature that people would be bound to understand them without any elucidation by the economist, if they only wanted to. But they *will* not see "that imports are either paid for by exports, as a method of producing the imported goods more efficiently, or else are received for nothing. Can there be any use in explaining, if it is needful to explain, that fixing a price below the free market level will create a shortage and one above it a surplus?" And Knight adds the further remark, "Let me observe that rent freezing, for example, occurs not at all merely because tenants have more votes than landlords. It reflects a state of mind, a mode of reasoning, even more discouraging than blindness through self-interest."[18]

The second point that I feel requires to be recorded is that the task which confronts economic science, difficult enough in itself, becomes virtually impossible of accomplishment if that science itself betrays in its answers the uncertainty that is evident in the critical situation that obtains today. That seems even more emphatically true if economics enrolls under the Keynesian banner and bestows the blessings of mathematical science on the pronouncements of unlettered laymen. It is to be expected that the overwhelming majority of laymen will look upon the "passive balance of payments" as an Act of God. We may further take for granted that in the eyes of those same laymen the only cure for this affliction is an economy that relies on forcible control of exchange rates plus American subsidies. But what are we to think of a science of economics that confirms an ingenious version of that lay theory—a theory already exploded back in the days of David Hume and David Ricardo? Much of what goes today under the name of "new economics" has virtually deprived humanity of every last bit of firm ground on which to stand and combat such things, and there should be no divided opinion as to the crying need for something to heal the rupture they have caused in the body structure of our science as a whole. Fortunately, indications are increasingly numerous that granulation of the wound is progressing apace.

In the meantime economic science has other social functions which far transcend the aforementioned orientation and guid-

---

[18] Frank H. Knight, "The Role of Principles in Economics and Politics," *American Economic Review*, March 1951, 4.

ance in matters of economic policy. Thus, it is unquestionable that economics has become indispensable to modern man as a component element of his "culture." By "culture" I mean here the system of concepts which comprise his universe. In that sense it is the function of economics to provide the individual with that orientation—so supremely important for the genuine inner life—which instructs him concerning the structure and functioning of society and the place which he himself occupies within it.[19] It is necessary to add that orientation of that kind is vitally necessary to the existence of society and to economic order itself. For as Lucien Romier justly observed some twenty years ago,[20] no cultural system can long survive if the great mass of people who are its bearers no longer understand its inner laws and its essential structure. And it is that very understanding of our economic system which has gradually become lost in the ever-increasing complexity of its own bustling activity.[21] One of the primary tasks confronting present-day economic science is to make that system transparently intelligible, to explain its functioning with elementary clarity to every man, and thus to indicate beyond question the place he occupies in his world. But such a task presupposes that the economic scientist is wholeheartedly convinced of the compelling necessity for so presenting economics that it should be clearly intelligible, well synthesized, and universal in scope—in short, so that it shall be a living part of the body of our era's cultural

---

[19] This characterization of economics gives it its proper place in the total program developed by Ortega y Gasset in his book, *Schuld und Schuldigkeit der Universität*, Munich, 1952.

[20] Lucien Romier, *Si le capitalisme disparaissait,* Paris 1933, "Aucune société, aucune humanité n'a pu vivre longtemps sans savoir pourquoi elle vivait et comment elle devait vivre, sans philosophie et sans moral" [No society, no humanity could live long without knowing why she lived and how she had to live, without philosophy and without morals—Ed.] (156–57).

[21] Cf. Walter Eucken, *Grundsätze der Wirtschaftspolitik* (Bern-Tübingen, 1952), 194.

knowledge. And that task imposes on economic science (and here we echo another demand by Ortega y Gasset) the further requirement that it emerge from its esoteric seclusion and recognize the necessity for making such intimate contact with society's organs of public opinion as to become a vital factor in its intellectual life.

And as if that were not enough, economics has, besides, a very specific function to perform in the modern democracy. It has an humble but all the more useful mission. Amidst the passions and self-interest of politics, it must assert the logic of things, it must bring to light all the inconvenient facts and relationships, must put them in their proper place with dispassionate justice, must prick all the soap bubbles, must unmask illusion and confusion, and must defend before all the world the proposition that two and two make four. It should be the one science *par excellence* which disillusions, which is anti-visionary, anti-utopian, and anti-ideological. Thus it can render society the priceless service of cooling off political passion, of combating mass superstition, of making life hard for all demagogues, financial wizards, and economic prestidigitators. At the same time it must avoid becoming the willing handmaiden of that social emotionalism of which Solomon says in the 13th canto of *Il Paradiso*, "E poi l'affetto l'intelletto lega."[22]

That does not by any means imply that we economists may or can retreat to the ivory tower of an economic neutrality. We, beyond all others, are representatives of the social sciences and under the duty to make up our minds at the great cross-roads of our civilization. It is not enough for us merely to decipher the roadmarkers; we must know whether we are sending society along the road to freedom, to humane living, to unalterable truth, or in the opposite direction and toward slavery, the prostitution of man, and crassest falsehood. To evade that decision would just as assuredly be a *trahison des clercs*[23] as if we were

---

[22] Ed. note: On this phrase, see 134n74 above.

[23] Ed. note: On this phrase, see 135n76 above.

to betray the sanctity that lies in the truth of science to the political passions and the social emotionalism of our era. The performance of that duty means no less than the erection of the most important possible "guide-post" for determining the place of economics among the sciences of today.

8

KEYNES AND THE REVOLUTION IN ECONOMICS: ECONOMICS OLD, NEW, AND TRUE*

With the possible exception of Protestant theology, there is hardly a branch of learning today that, like economics, is split into two almost irreconcilable camps with almost no dialogue passing between them anymore. This split has its origin in an exceedingly bold revolution in economic thought dating back fifteen years and, perhaps by an unjust simplification, associated with the name of the late Lord Keynes, who died in 1946.

THE REVOLUTION IN ECONOMICS

Radical rethinking is not alien to other disciplines. To take theoretical physics as an example, we all know how far quantum mechanics and the theory of relativity have deflected that science from Newton's classical tradition. But this revolution in the physical concept of the universe has not created a rift between the "old" and the "new" schools. As and when the new theories asserted themselves by irrefutable proof or empirical probability, they became the common property of science,

---

*Chapter 11 of Wilhelm Röpke, *Against the Tide*, trans. Elizabeth Henderson (Chicago: Regnery, 1969).

and there was no sound of venomous dispute, all the less so as the practical applications of physics in everyday life were not affected by this palace revolution in theory. The revolution in economics, on the other hand, has so far essentially done nothing but shock and divide. It originated in a theory that combines provocative radicalism with far from fully convincing argumentation, with a precision that proves to be apparent rather than real and throws up problems of the most confusing kind. Furthermore, thanks to its influence on actual economic policy in our time, it has become a force that has a decisive bearing on the life and interests of every individual, indeed of whole nations and classes and, with the mere term "full employment," has furnished both one of the most seductive and one of the most dangerous slogans to the political life of the mid-twentieth century. As a result, economics is today split into two camps apparently without prospect of reconciliation, and it would be hard to find a parallel to this split in the whole history of the science.

Healing the Rift

The adherents of the Keynesian School, or of the "new economics," as it is widely called, are, like all revolutionary leaders, inclined to regard the victory of their doctrine as complete. The idea of so serious and genuine a rift offends their sense of domination. But if the rift is to be healed—and to do so is a task that is gaining in urgency but perhaps steadily losing in difficulty—the first step must be to acknowledge its existence and full implications.

It is probably still not generally realized just how deep is the rift and how critical, therefore, the inner predicament of economics. One of the most distinguished of contemporary economists, whom I met again recently after many years, said to me that he was not prepared to enter into a discussion of the last ten years' literature, which, because it was essentially inspired by Keynes, he regarded as useless, not worth reading, and stultifying, and I frankly confess that while I would not make this temperamental judgment my own, I would far sooner see him in charge of a central bank or an economic government department than any of the authors of the literature he condemns. As eminent a mind as Professor F. H. Knight, of Chicago, not long ago described the "new economics" of Keynesian origin as the worst of the fashion crazes that from time to time afflict our science and as a return to the dark Middle Ages, and Schumpeter, to name another master, remained to his dying day in hardly less vehement opposition, no matter how politely elegant the style in which he couched it.

Rigid Fronts

The revolutionaries' answer to these legitimists of economics is vehement self-assertion and barely veiled contempt, such as are habitual to the "enlightened" in dealing with those who remain in the dark. They seem to regard themselves as all the more superior in that they can point with obvious pride to the difficulty of their literature and to the use of mathematics, which lifts the "new economics" almost to the lofty heights of physics. A leading Keynesian in the United States, to give an example, recently dismissed one of Hayek's books with the contemptuous remark that there was no breath of the "new economics" in it and that the author had thus behaved like an astronomer who failed to take account of the Copernican revolution. The columns of this very publication were recently the scene of the tragi-comic spectacle of a reviewer's (V. Muthesius) thinking he was lavishing special praise upon an English book by stating with relief that the author had not fallen victim to the Keynesian School, which remark, in turn, called forth the protests of adherents of the "new economics," who clearly felt the object of the reviewer's praise needed to be defended against such an insult. They seemed anxious to counter any impression that there might be a dissenter among England's ranking economists by suggesting that, at any rate in that country, the "new economics" had permeated everywhere—not reflecting, perhaps, that if the theory's domination really were as absolute as all that, the chronic crisis of the British economy is not much of a recommendation for it. Conversely, if the Germans compare the economic developments of their beaten country with those of the victor's, they have reason to note with some satisfaction that at any rate they victoriously withstood the onslaught of the Keynesians.

But enough of this description of a conflict and opinions and theories that is so sharp that one cannot but agree with Professor J. M. Clark, of Columbia, when he declares that the Keynesian revolution has split economics into two spheres of logic, where the sense of one is nonsense in the other. It can easily be imagined what disastrous consequences this disintegration of traditional economic theory has had for economic policy in practice. The remarkable advances of economics, in research, organization, and external influence alike cannot obscure the cracks that have appeared in its foundations and that certainly signify an extremely serious retrogression in comparison with the "old economics." There can surely be no doubt that the disintegrating and confusing influence of the "new economics" must be taken into account by anyone wishing to gain a serious and unbiased understanding of the agonizing economic history of the last ten years, with its "repressed inflation," its *ad hoc* experiments, and the Sisyphus labor of international reconstruction failing over and over again.

EXPEDIENT INTO DOGMA

This is a depressing state of affairs, a clear view of which is continually obstructed by the fact that it is not easy to say just what is the essence of Keynesian economics and what constitutes the revolution it brought about. What did Keynes want, and what have his disciples—typically overzealous like all adepts—learned from him?

To put it in a nutshell and, hence, inevitably in simplified terms: Quite rightly, the Great Depression of the 1930s had appeared to Keynes as a gigantic circulatory disturbance marked by a series of deficiencies of income and demand, which, regardless of their original cause, kept entailing others; he considered it as basically due to a breakdown in the mechanism that should ensure that the decision of some individuals to save, and thereby forgo spending their income, finds its normal compensation in the decision of others to invest. Whereas the "old economics" had focused attention on the ordering and guiding mechanism of the system of individual prices and wages and had viewed the economic process mainly as one of continuous readjustment of production and of redistribution of factors of production in response to this guiding mechanism, the world was now faced with a situation that could not be interpreted in terms of that theory. It was a disturbance to be explained no longer as the result of wrong prices or wages, as an expression of a wrong distribution of factors of production; rather, it was to be explained only as a disproportion between the economic aggregates of the circular flow (saving and investment, income and expenditure, decline and renewed creation of purchasing power), and the cure lay in removing that disproportion. In other words, it was a case where a deficiency of "effective demand" was the true cause of mass unemployment and as such had to be removed by a policy that, in bold reversal of sound economic thought, put the main emphasis on "spending," on boosting "effective demand," and, in taking this course, on neither being frightened by the danger of inflation nor waiting for prior savings.

Had Keynes stopped there, he would have done no more than the rest of us, who at that time advised a policy beginning with the "spending" end. He would have secured for himself only a modest little nook in the Valhalla of economics, but, on the other hand, no one could have said of him that he did more harm than good. But the crucial point is that he did not stop at calling for extraordinary means in an extraordinary situation.

He went much further. He declared the method of thinking in aggregates to be the only valid one, now and in the long run. And together with the method, he elaborated its results—his diagnosis of an extraordinary situation and the treatment accordingly prescribed—into a general theory in which "deficiency of demand" is always around the corner, and economic policy must always be poised to close this "gap" in order to ensure eternal "full employment." It is only with this that he really brought into economic thought a revolution that thrusts aside the previously ruling method and puts an opposite one in its place, literally standing on its head most of what theory and sound common sense have so far considered right and proven. That is the calamity, and that is the reason that the adherents of the "old economics" cannot be reconciled with those of the "new economics" so long as this torrent of exuberant destruction has not been forced back into its bed.

A Biased Approach

This is not the place to demonstrate in detail why, for all its seductive brilliance and elegance, the chain of thought that led Keynes to these bold conclusions does not hold. Our main concern on this occasion is with the result of this revolution for economic theory and policy. A whole generation of economists (especially in the Anglo-Saxon countries, but likewise wherever else it is thought important to be in the swim) was so one-sidedly brought up to operate with economic aggregates that it forgot the things that until then were the real content of economic theory and that never should be forgotten: namely, that the economic order is a system of moving and moved prices, wages, interests, and other magnitudes. Keynes's aggregative functions made the plain mechanism of prices look outdated and uninteresting, and we witnessed the development of a sort of economic engineering with a proliferation of mathematical equations.

This new method was one part of the training of the new generation of economists and economic policy makers; another was the idea that saving is, at best, unnecessary (since investment takes care of saving afterward *via* the multiplier and the marginal propensity to save) and, at worst, harmful. It follows that a policy measure is good when it increases effective demand and bad when it threatens to diminish effective demand.

THE DANGER OF INFLATION UNDERESTIMATED

The danger of inflation was reduced to a remote theoretical possibility; the thing to be feared constantly was what was described as deflation. Budgetary deficits, leveling taxes that diminish both the ability and the willingness to save, "cheap money policy," a combination of growing popular consumption and investment stimulation, expenditure and credits on all sides, mercantilist foreign-trade policies with the twin purposes of mitigating the effects of those other policies on the balance of trade and of creating export surpluses as a further stimulant for the domestic money flow—all of these practices now received the blessing of economic science.

NOT WITH IMPUNITY ...

Years ago, in an obituary of Keynes in the *Neue Zürcher Zeitung*,[1] I wrote that while it is legitimate to think that there exist times when a resolute increase in the money supply averts trouble, it is not with impunity that a man of outstanding intelligence may give the blessing of his authority to the inflationary inclinations of government, which are strong enough as it is. It is legitimate to think that in certain circumstances the growth of the public debt is the lesser evil, but not with impunity may this be turned into a maxim. It may happen that mass unemployment cannot

---

[1] Ed. note: Wilhelm Röpke, "Keynes und unsere zeit," *Neue Zürcher Zeitung*, May 5, 1946.

be quickly removed by any means other than an increase in effective demand by means of credit expansion, but not with impunity may the proven rules and institutions be flouted with barely veiled contempt, lest, without these long-run guardians of an orderly economic process, the economy become subject to permanent inflationary pressure. There may be some previously overlooked problem to discover in the process of saving, but not with impunity may people be deprived of the feeling that they are doing the right thing by saving and setting aside from their income a reserve for themselves and their children instead of spending as long as the money lasts, and then, when there is none left, relying on help from the state, which is accumulating debt upon debt. Just as a ship in distress may have to cut away its masts and jettison its cargo, so there may be hurricanes in economic life that force us temporarily to neglect the principles of sound economic and monetary policy, but not with impunity may these principles be declared as outdated just because they are inconvenient for the full employment policy rigidly pursued after the shock of the Great Depression.

"To the Tropics with the Equipment for a Polar Expedition"

We ought not to forget that this is the seed that Keynes has sown. No honest person can overlook how abundantly it is bearing fruit. There is no other explanation for the utterly wrong postwar orientation of the Western world, which, taught only to fear and combat deflation, followed the banner of "full employment" right into permanent inflation. In spite of all the warnings of the old-style economists, the danger was recognized too late, so that it has become exceedingly difficult to face about and abandon the wrong position. As I wrote some years ago, it was like a man going to the tropics with the equipment for a polar expedition, and I was pleased to see in a recent article by

Professor Erich Schneider, of Kiel,[2] that he took up the simile with a slight variant.

It is time to admit honestly and openly that such is the nature and such are the effects of the Keynesian approach, the last manifestation of which was the United Nations Experts' Report of December, 1949, soon thereafter recognized as untimely and quietly shelved.

There is not much to be gained by pointing out that Keynes was a man of genius to whom we owe remarkable and fruitful stimulation. There are few who would deny it, and I myself in my above-mentioned obituary have compared him with Adam Smith, albeit with strong reservations. Nor is it much help that Keynes himself at the end of his life was troubled and tried to restrain the excessive zeal of his followers, and that, flexibly open-minded as he was, he himself, had he lived to do so, might well have written the most effective correction of Keynesian economics. What for him was intellectual working capital with a rapid turnover has been turned by the less agile into fixed investment capital, the productivity of which is defended by all means, including monopolistic protection. Keynes cannot be absolved from the reproach that in the exuberant vitality of his mind he did not make sufficient allowance for this.

KEYNES AND THE MARKET ECONOMY

Finally, it is cold comfort that Keynes himself always regarded himself as a liberal, professing his belief in the freedoms of the bourgeois world and meaning to serve them after his own—in our view, strange—fashion. The desire to reconcile his theory with the market economy is laudable, but practical experience has proved that this theory has instead become one of the supporting pillars of an opposite economic policy of the collectivist and inflationary kind. It can be shown that there are profound reasons why one could hardly expect it to be otherwise.

---

[2] *Frankfurter Allgemeine Zeitung*, September 4.

And has not Keynes himself in his magnum opus outlined this development clearly enough, as proof of how little he was in earnest about the market economy? If the countries of Europe are today grouped according to the style of their economic policy, there are those with a market economy on one side, and those with a collectivist, inflationary, full-employment policy on the other. It is the latter that cause most concern, even to the more impartial representatives of the "new economics." It really seems grotesque that recently a French author, J. Cros, in a study entitled "Le Néo-Libéralisme,"[3] contrasted Keynes as "le véritable néo-libéral" with such muddle-headed writers as Lippmann and Röpke.

Ideology and Analytical Technique Combined

The developments of the last ten years have in fact so compromised the Keynesian approach, and compromised it so openly, that it is easy enough to understand the attempt to water it down and present it as a mere analytical technique, which can now, with disinterested impartiality, be switched from the struggle against deflation to that against inflation. When, however, this attempt is combined with the claim to illuminate us with the pure light of Keynesian theory, then the legitimists among the rest of us economists will be forgiven for displaying some surprise at such agility. After we have spent years warning the adherents of the "new economics" of precisely those dangers that have materialized, we have some difficulty in getting used to their now stealing our thunder in the name of the selfsame "new economics." At the very least we shall, no doubt, be permitted a few words on the subject.

First of all, we have to admit that the use of the Keynesian analytical technique in combating today's inflation in the full-employment countries is in a way quite legitimate. We do,

---

[3] Ed. note: Jaques Cros, *Le Néo-libéralisme: Etude positive et critique* (Paris: Librairie de Médicis, 1950).

after all, use it ourselves when we say that these countries "live beyond their means," in the sense that the sum of consumption and investment releases more purchasing power upon the economy's goods than can be satisfied at current prices, so that inflationary pressure develops and with it a deficit in the balance of payments. We could, of course, have learned that from the "old economics" as well, but we do not deny that the technique of thinking in flow aggregates has been refined by the "new economics."

But if we concede that much and thus make a step toward reconciliation, it would not be unfair to expect that the adherents of the "new economics" in their turn should frankly admit two things: first, that in fact a passionate ideology has been turned into a mere analytical technique, and second, that if this technique has now to be applied to a situation exactly opposite to Keynes's assumptions, this has not happened, to put it mildly, entirely without the help of the Keynesian ideology. They might even be expected to admit that the fact that it is so desperately hard to deflect the full-employment countries from their inflationary course is not least to be ascribed to the firm hold gained in the meantime upon public opinion in those countries by the Keynesian ideology, with its sole emphasis on the fear of deflation, full employment at any price, expansion and reckless spending—so much so that some pessimists doubt whether the task can be achieved without grave social and political upheavals.

A Brake against Inflation, but ...

This alone throws light on the great difficulty of applying the analytical technique of the "new economics" with fine impartiality to inflation or deflation in turn, according to the situation. A number of serious objections may be raised against the possibility of such symmetry. It is bound to be heavily lopsided insofar as the Keynesian approach at best always remains latent inflationism. This inflationism at once becomes virulent in the presence of any disturbances, including those which, because they are accompanied by unemployment and a shrinking volume of business activity, look like "deflation," even though they are to be interpreted, not according to the "new economics" as a disproportion of the economic aggregates, but according to the "old economics" as a result of wrong values (prices or wages) and a wrong distribution of the factors of production. What happens then? What happens when excessive wage increases cause unemployment? And, above all, how about the difficulty that disinflation in a full-employment situation tends to be associated with such pseudo-deflationary symptoms?

The point is that even though the "new economics" is reduced to a mere analytical method of a neutral kind and in the present situation agrees in its conclusions with those of the "old economics," the desired synthesis will be a good deal more difficult than meets the eye. It will hardly be possible at all unless the exponents of the "new economics" make up their minds to surrender their method's and their theory's claim to domination and to evacuate a good many more positions than they have already given up.

The idea of continuous manipulation of aggregates with a view to counteracting now an inflationary, now a deflationary, tendency, as the case may be, is indeed most seductive. It is not, of course, the sole privilege of the "new economics" but has always been a guideline of sensible economic policy. But it remains a dangerous idea so long as it is not purged of all Keynesian vestiges far more radically than has been done so far. Keynesian analysis will always look at the danger of inflation through a diminishing glass and at the danger of deflation through a magnifying glass, and in matters of economic policy, to change the metaphor, will always limp with the inflation leg. So long as the analysis remains spellbound by the "new economics" to the extent of working only with aggregates, its underlying models are bound to misrepresent the nature of inflation and even more so of "deflation." Nothing could be better proof of the inner bias of the whole approach than the fact that it took so much time and persuasion, and the present inflationary tendencies had to grow to such massive proportions, before at least the more circumspect among the champions of the "new economics" bowed to the evidence and changed over from an anti-deflationary to an anti-inflationary course. The analytical machine worked out with so much ingenuity by Keynes and his disciples does indeed possess a brake against inflation. But the machine is so constructed that this brake comes into play only at breakneck speed and, moreover, has the awkward habit of cutting out again immediately after the first effect.

A Highly Unmathematical Circumstance

This is one of the main reasons why the Keynes-inspired theory of continuous anti-deflationary and anti-inflationary compensation, brought about chiefly by means of what is known as compensatory fiscal policy, has not so far proved its worth in practice. Expansion causes no trouble, but when it comes to the contraction demanded in the boom, which, in compensatory fiscal policy, implies swinging the budget from deficit to surplus, it has never worked, not in the United States, nor in Switzerland, nor anywhere else. "Under the 'compensatory' theory," we read in the Guaranty Trust Company's *Guaranty Survey* of September, 1952, "the last twelve years should have witnessed an unbroken series of substantial budgetary surpluses. The contrast between this and the actual record would be amusing if it were not so tragic. Experience so far indicates that what is in theory a two-sided influence actually operates on one side only—the inflationary side—and that the inflationary effects tend to be strongest at times when they are least desired." The reason lies not only in the lopsided character of the philosophy underlying this compensatory theory. It lies also in the damnably unmathematical circumstance that one cannot talk Parliament and public opinion into saving and economical management, by exceptionally praising them as virtues, if all the rest of the time they are reviled as folly and sin, not to speak of modern mass democracy's built-in obstacles. This is something that has not been accorded the attention it deserves, thus giving away the theory as a typically intellectual construction that forgets the social reality behind the integral calculus.

9

A Value Judgment on Value Judgments*

Science sans conscience n'est que ruine de l'âme.

—Rabelais, *Pantagruel*

I

Economics is full of problems which seem to find no rest. They are being turned over again and again and seen now in this light, now in another. Problems of this sort are such which do not admit of any dogmatic answer in one sense or another. Instead, they seem to demand solutions which follow some "reasonable middle course" and which are embroidered by a number of variable qualifications and reserves.

To this group of problems belongs the question of *the scientific legitimacy of judgments of value*. It has so long and so feverishly been discussed that it appears tedious to make any attempt to stir up the discussion again. Recent personal experiences, however, suggest that a fairly general consensus on a dangerously *dogmatic* answer has become crystallized in our academic

---

*From *Journal of Markets & Morality* 18, no. 2 (Fall 2015): 497–514. Originally published in *Revue de la Faculté des Sciences Économiques de l'Université d'Instanbul* 3, nos. 1–2 (October 1941–January 1942): 1–19.

world, a dogmatism which is not far from being a real impediment in our academic activities.[1] To a great number of social scientists it seems to be beyond any possible dispute that every judgment on what ought to be in economic life must be scientifically illegitimate. For them the question appears to be settled once and for all while in our view it is and will remain an extremely delicate and intricate problem.

It seems, therefore, useful to reconsider this methodological problem and to give some idea of the state of mind of those who thoroughly disagree with what appears to be the prevailing attitude today, i.e. the positivist puritanism with regard to value judgments and the reproachful insistence on so-called scientific "Objectivity."[2] This task is deemed all the more necessary as the dogmatic attitude in question is closely connected with the present unsatisfactory state of social sciences in general, to which more and more fellow economists are growing alive.[3] This attitude, moreover, is one of the grave symptoms

---

[1] The personal experience to which I allude is particularly the criticism which has been directed by some friends against a report on "International Economic Disintegration" which I prepared as part of a research programme sponsored by the Rockefeller Foundation. Some critics to whom this report has been sent in mimeographed form have raised a warning finger against my way of calling bad things bad and good things good. In fairness to these critics it must be added that this happened before the outbreak of the war. In the final form of the report, which will shortly be published (by Hodge & Co., London), I have tried to meet these criticisms as far as possible, without bothering, however, about the deeper methodological questions involved.

[2] The word "positivism" is being used here in its narrower anti-axiological, not in its wider anti-metaphysical meaning. Though the use has become quite common in Anglo-Saxon literature, it may lead to regrettable misunderstandings. Therefore, it should be replaced by other terms like "axiological relativism." Cf. Herbert Spiegelberg, *Antirelativismus, Kritik des Relativismus und Skeptizismus der Werte und des Sollens* (Zürich, 1935).

[3] See e.g., E. F. M. Durbin, "Methods of Research—A Plea for Co-operation in the Social Sciences," *Economic Journal* (June 1938).

of the general intellectual and moral disorientation and of the decadence of "liberalism" from which our civilization is manifestly suffering.[4] Relativism appears, in fact, to reflect the deliquescence of the "liberal" bourgeois world, the growing spiritual emptiness of our civilization, and the vanishing of absolute values and compelling convictions. If seen in this large perspective, an attempt at restating the problem of value judgments seems tantamount to struggling with the solution of the spiritual crisis of the Western world.

The question of value judgments in social sciences is, unfortunately, also an example of the melancholy tendency of man to swing from one extreme to another without coming to rest at the "reasonable middle course"—an example of the "loi de double frénésie,"[5] as Henri Bergson has called it.[6] There was a time when many economists had assumed the habit of muddling economics naively with hygiene, politics, or theology, demanding for their personal views the authority and dignity of science, a time when one had really to remind economists of the absurdity to construct a system of economics e.g. from the point of view of the non-smoker. It was against this indiscriminate use of value judgments that men like Max Weber raised their voice, but then the reaction went much further until it reached the opposite extreme of stigmatizing as "unscientific" to express any definite views on values, ends, and "oughts." It is probable that not even the leading advocates of axiological relativism are quite happy under this austere régime, but very few seem to know how to answer the seemingly irrefutable argument that the scientific measure of truth cannot be applied to values and ends.

---

[4] This view has been forcefully expressed by President Harry D. Gideonse (Brooklyn College) in his Inaugural Address, October 19, 1939 (printed by the Brooklyn College) with which I find myself in cordial agreement.

[5] Ed. note: "the law of double frenzy."

[6] H. Bergson, *Les deux sources de la Morale* (Paris, 1934), 319–20.

II

The argument of axiological relativism appears so plausible that there will hardly be any economist who, in the course of his intellectual development, has not felt compelled to accept it at least for some time. Therefore, even those who are past this almost inevitable stage cannot fail to have sympathy with the honorable scruples of the relativists. They know that the problem is a complex one, and they also appreciate some of the reasons prompting the positivists.

First of all, it seems impossible to refute the argument that there is something peculiar about value judgments which separates them from other scientific statements. Of these there are three classes which can be ranged according to the degree of stringency appertaining to each of them. The first on the list are the strictly logical and logically cogent conclusions of the type "A cannot be non-A." Next in order come the statements on facts the truth of which can only be established by empirical ascertainment with all its sources of possible errors. The last group is that of judgments of value. It is not only indisputable that these different kinds of statements have a different logical structure, but also that the degree of stringency is least in the last group. Moreover, it is obvious that it is the last group which passes into the sphere of unscientific statements. So much is undebatable. The only question is where to draw the line; whether between group two and three as the relativist demands or *within* group three. The latter seems to be the right answer.

Furthermore, if by strict elimination of value judgments the relativists want to free scientific discussion of disputes which cannot be settled by rational arguments and to bridge irreconcilable disharmonies of opinions, one is bound largely to agree with this sort of scientific pacifism. The question remains, however, whether this "appeasement" is not bought at a high price without ultimately securing the peace. For either the disagreement concerns highly subjective views on ends and values merely of subordinate importance, whereas there is agreement on ultimate ends and values—then the dispute ought to be capable of being settled with a view to these common valuations. Or the disagreement concerns really ultimate ends and values, in which case (a) either party may still have a chance of convincing the other by rational arguments, or (b) any hope of restricting the discussion to a peaceful exchange of views on technicalities may easily prove an illusion, or (c) there may be no point in any discussion at all. The present state of the world certainly suggests the previously forgotten truth that no really fruitful and worthwhile discussion is possible in the absence of a common scale of ultimate values. If this fundamental agreement is lacking, scientific intercourse is impossible. If it exists, however, all disputes on ends and values appear to be those on intermediate (not ultimate) ends and values which can be judged by the common measure of the ultimate ones. In other words, if scientific intercourse is possible at all because there is a tacit agreement on the ultimate values, rational discussions and judgments on intermediate values are possible too and, being rational, perfectly legitimate from the strictly scientific point of view.

So much on the pacifist intentions of the Relativists—intentions which, by the way, are based on a rather dubious value judgment on "peace at any price." Equally polite must be our attitude with regard to the argument that we must not abuse the authority of science for expressing purely political convictions which, if not clearly marked as such, may be smuggled into science. Everybody will whole-heartedly agree with this demand which is nothing else than that for intellectual probity, but it is hard to see what it has to do with the question of the scientific legitimacy of value judgments. Nobody has questioned and ever will question the fact that, truth and honesty being the prime conditions of science, the least cheating, even if it be subconscious, is a deadly sin in this "game."[7] If nobody can

---

[7] On this important aspect see J. Huizinga, *Homo Ludens, Versuch einer Bestimmung des Spielelementes der Kultur* (Amsterdam, 1939), 171–191, 327–329.

be called a true scientist who is not most ruthlessly criticizing himself; if, in other words, every scientist *must* be honest and sincere with himself, it goes without saying that he must also be so with others. All these are commonplaces on which there is universal agreement precisely because we all feel the value judgments implied by them to be unshakably true.

On this occasion it seems necessary to unravel a confusion which has become very common today, i.e. the indiscriminate use of the term "ideology" which, under the influence of Marxist philosophy and its modern version of the "sociology of knowledge," has assumed a dangerously wide significance. It is a useful and even indispensable term to denote the pseudological character of phrases and conceptions masking behind respectable and high-sounding words much less respectable ends, and therefore a term making us deeply suspicious against pompous declarations covering crude political aims or sectional interests.[8] If such ideological phrases creep into science—and, unfortunately, they do very frequently—they must be exposed and eliminated with utmost vigour, and it can surely be doubted whether so far we have been vigorous enough in this respect. In this sense, nothing could be more welcome than "pure economics" or "pure law." It is, however, only another case of the "loi de double frénésie" if this discovery of "ideologies" leads us to the extreme conclusion that all ideas and value concepts are mere ideologies which, being highly subjective and deceptive fancies, must be ousted from science.[9] Such

---

[8] In order to show that I tried to do my part in demolishing "ideologies," I may be permitted to refer to my forthcoming book on "International Economic Disintegration" (part III) and to my paper on "International Economics in a Changing World," *The World Crisis*, ed. the Graduate Institute of International Studies (London, 1938), 275–92.

[9] As a well-known example of the sweeping conclusion referred to in the text, Professor Kelsen's "pure theory of law" may be mentioned (cf. Hans Kelsen, "The Pure Theory of Law: Its Method and Fundamental Concepts," *The Law Quarterly Review*, vol. 50 and 51). In a somewhat less rigorous sense, Professor Robbins' forceful *Essay on the Nature and*

a conclusion, which would let us end in total skepticism and complete nihilism, seems wholly unwarranted. Everybody, for instance, is familiar with monopolistic ideologies appealing to the "common interest," "justice," or "patriotism," and we can hardly do enough to fight them. But that does not mean that "common interest," "justice," or "patriotism" are ideologies themselves. They are value concepts the essence of which will be approved by all normal men; they contain, therefore, that degree of objectivity which makes them presentable at the court of science. That is exactly an additional reason why we grow so indignant at the sight of "ideologies" sneaking into this court under false pretences. There is another motive of the relativists which, though highly respectable in itself, seems to rest on a misunderstanding, i.e. the fear of the "politicalization" of science after the example of the totalitarian countries. True science as we understand it was born when the early Ionian philosophers established the principle that science must be autonomous in the sense that in the search for truth, the conscience of the scholar is to be the ultimate authority, independent of the heteronomous authority of the worldly or ecclesiastical rulers. Galilei's "eppur si muove" will remain for ever one of the noblest expressions of this principle with which science indeed stands or falls. To bow to authorities other than that of truth itself is a disgrace to science; it is the "trahison des clercs" of which Jules Benda is speaking in his famous book bearing this title,[10] and heaven knows how many today are committing this treason. Heteronomy and science are forever incompatible with each other, and no fine-spun sophistry or thunderous bullying can make them compatible. No iota can be taken away from this evident truth. But here is a snare in which the advocates of scientific heteronomy might hope to catch some inattentive

---

Significance of Economic Science, 2nd ed. (London, 1935) may be called a treatise on "pure economics."

[10] Ed. note: Julien Benda, *The Betrayal of the Intellectuals (La trahison de clercs)*, trans. Richard Aldington (Boston: Beacon, 1955).

birds: It is obvious that the autonomy of science can never mean that scientific work is a creation *ex nihilo* depending on no subjective conditions whatever. *Voraussetzungslosigkeit*[11] in this strict sense is, of course, an illusion or even an absurdity which no fairly modern philosophy of science will defend any longer. Every scientist has his personal equation, his perspective determined by place and time, his inner experience, his peculiar milieu, his valuations some of which he is sharing with others while some are more or less his own. He is pursuing his researches as a child of his age and as a member of his community, and all we must ask for is that he is honestly conscious of all these pre-scientific determinants and weighing the degree of subjectivity which they give to his researches.

Now, the advocates of heteronomy might be tempted to claim this "concession" as a proof of their assertion that there can never be such a thing as an autonomous science. On the other hand, the relativist—in his laudable effort to forestall this retreat to pre-Ionian archaism—might become all the more determined in his endeavours to purify science of all pre-scientific determinants and to make social sciences as exact as he believes (probably without justification) natural sciences to be.[12] Both, however, are wrong, the Heteronomist as well as the Relativist. They are drawing opposite conclusions from a common misconception of the "autonomy" of science: the Heteronomist throwing out the child with the bath-water, the Relativist bathing no child at all in spite of a vast expense of soap and perfume. The latter course is perhaps a shade better than the former and, at all events, of a different moral calibre, but we still think a middle course would be the best. This middle course consists in recognizing that *Voraussetzungslosigkeit*

---

[11] Ed. note: "being free from presuppositions."

[12] "Exactness" in moral sciences, which have to do with man as a moral and intellectual being, is a dubious ideal betraying an inferiority complex towards the natural sciences; it must be bought at the price of emptiness and lack of vital significance.

and autonomy of science are entirely different things so that the absurdity of the former does not disprove either the feasibility or the necessity of the latter, and vice versa.[13] I may, on perfectly scientific grounds, defend e.g. the proposition that a large number of family farms is essential for the health of a society, and in doing so I am, of course, under the influence of certain valuations and pre-scientific determinants; my proposition is certainly not *voraussetzungslos*. It is quite another thing, however, if in one country (Russia) the scientist will lose his chair by defending my proposition while in another like Germany he will likewise suffer for denying it. Then the autonomy of science is lost and therewith its prime condition. If it is a "trahison des clercs" to submit to heteronomous pressure, it is hardly less a betrayal of science to interpret its autonomy as a duty to behave as if the scientist had no valuations at all. It is more than likely that the self-castration of science as practiced by axiological relativism will create a vacuum which will be filled by the demagogues and dilettanti and sooner or later engender the wild reaction of the "politicalization" of science.[14] Relativism and Heteronomism are not only based on a common misconception of autonomy, they are playing hand in hand like all opposite extremes.

Let us develop a little further what has been said on the "determinants" of science. Relativism, like any other philosophy, is not a bus which can be stopped at any intermediate station. It must be pursued to its ultimate consequences, but

---

[13] Cf. Ludwig von Mises, *Nationalökonomie. Theorie des Handelns und Wirtschaftens* (Geneva, 1940), 745–46.

[14] "The masses ... have just reached the point where the ancestors of today's scientists were standing two generations back. They are convinced that the scientific picture of an arbitrary abstraction from reality is a picture of reality as a whole and that therefore the world is without meaning or value. But nobody likes living in such a world. To satisfy their hunger for meaning and value, they turn to such doctrines as Nationalism, Fascism and revolutionary Communism": Aldous Huxley, *Ends and Means* (London, 1938), 269.

these appear logically untenable. Relativism has that in common with the materialistic conception of history that it is a negative statement which "comprises itself," and that as such a statement it is self-defeating. As it is the obvious objection to the Marxist interpretation of history that, if all philosophies are merely an "ideological superstructure" and therefore only of relative value, Marxist philosophy is bound to fall under this same verdict of relativity, so axiological relativism must be judged also by its proper philosophy and gracefully accept the result.[15] Evidently, there is no getting away from the fact that a scientific methodology condemning value judgments contains itself a value judgment while intolerantly forbidding all others as unscientific.

This is only a striking example of the fact that science in its very foundations rests on value judgments. That men pursue science at all, that the science of economics has been developed as a special branch, that we select worthwhile subjects of research from the endless number of possible ones, that we economists decided to devote ourselves to this science, that we regard truth as an inviolable scientific principle—all this implies judgments of value. We do not discuss them because no sane person is questioning them, and we do not care for the small minority of those suffering from moral insanity, just as medicine starts from the value judgment that life is better than death and health better than sickness without regard to suiciding neurotics or nosophile hysterics. If the Relativist is not satisfied with this, let us ask him whether he is seriously prepared to devote his life to discovering the means for impoverishing a nation in the quickest possible way or for improving the much neglected "fine art of murder."[16]

---

[15] Cf. Johan Akerman, *Das Problem der sozialökonomischen Synthese*, Publications of the New Society of Letters at Lund, no. 21 (Lund, 1938), 57–58.

[16] In order not to be accused of oversimplifying the problem, let us admit that those ultimate "value relations" (H. Rickert) underlying all

Science—above all, moral sciences of which economics is a part—is indeed inseparably mixed up with value judgments, and our efforts to eliminate them will only end in absurdity. If we look properly, it is not difficult in economics to discover a value judgment lurking behind theories and propositions which give the outward appearance of innocent neutrality.[17] Every time that such a discovery is made many economists seem to be thoroughly shocked, but instead of recognizing the value judgment involved and examining it on its proper merits, they seem to hesitate between two courses which are equally dubious. Either they abandon hastily the contaminated proposition, or they go out of their way to prove that there is no value judgment involved (or that the proposition can be restated without a value judgment). It has been always obvious, for instance, that all theories working with an optimum concept belong to this class of propositions whose neutrality is spurious. But it has also long since been discovered that terms like "inflation" or "deflation" can hardly be used without an implicit reference to a value judgment about what should be regarded as "normal" in the monetary sphere.[18]

---

scientific activities are somewhat different in structure from the value judgments proper. The difference, however, is not such as to deprive our argument of its force.

[17] Cf. J. Akerman, *Das Problem*; G. Myrdal, *Das politische Element in der nationalökonomischen Doktrinbildung* (Berlin, 1932); Harvey W. Peck, *Economic Thought and Its Institutional Background* (New York, 1935). The last-named two books evidently start from the curious assumption that the reader will be shocked to learn that economic doctrines have always been "impure" from the relativist point of view. After what has been said above, it would be more surprising if they were not.

[18] It is not difficult to show that all moral and to some extent even natural sciences abound with concepts and terms which, at closer analysis, reveal an axiological and volitional element. We cannot define "law," "state," "art," "big cities," etc. without thinking at the same time of some preferences, values, and wishes. The Austrian philosopher K. Roretz has made the commendable suggestion to call these terms

A further good illustration is the recent discussion about the scientific legitimacy of interpersonal comparisons of utility. After the concept of marginal utility had been indiscriminately used for proving "scientifically" the advantage of a more equal distribution of incomes or of progressive tax rates, it was later discovered that it is an illusion to believe that such a proof is possible without recourse to the value judgments which every interpersonal comparison of utility implies. Individual and interpersonal comparisons of utility are indeed on entirely different levels, and those who reminded us of this irrefutable truth did a great service to our science. The new situation which ensued, however, is highly unsatisfactory. Some reject sternly the whole proposition of "welfare economics" as political and therefore unscientific[19] while others are racking their brains to find some way of reconciling it with the relativist ban on value judgments.[20] It seems, however, a logical impossibility to defend the scientific legitimacy of interpersonal comparisons of utility on the ground set by relativism; in such a dispute one is bound to take sides with the relativists. The only possible way is to refuse to meet relativism on its own grounds. The same applies to all efforts to defend free trade on purely "economic" grounds and, in fact, to all "inherently economic" value judgments, i.e. those based on criteria which are taken from economics itself.

"vital concepts" ("Ueber Vitalbegriffe"). See *An den Quellen unseres Denkens, Studien zur Morphologie der Erkenntnis und Forschung* (Vienna, 1937), 95–103.

[19] That is the position taken by Professor Robbins and probably by most members of the Austrian school.

[20] That is what Professor Hicks tried to do in his interesting article on "The Foundations of Welfare Economics," *Economic Journal* (December 1939). One has the definite impression that, in spite of his ingenuity, he has been compelled to let in new value judgments at the backdoor. It could hardly be otherwise.

III

It seems that the Positivist is being torn between his intellectual honesty and the moral and intellectual difficulties which his position involves. He is uneasily and restlessly shifting on the uncomfortable chair he has chosen. We would have the highest respect for his martyrdom if he would not interfere with our own scientific work and if we did not believe his position to be scientifically untenable. Enough, it is hoped, has been said now to suggest that the whole problem of value judgments has been wrongly stated. The question is not whether we are to have value judgments at all, for to dispense with all of them would lead us to sheer absurdity. The real question, instead, seems to be *what kinds of value judgments are scientifically legitimate* and *on what grounds.* In other words, the relativist is deceiving himself if he believes himself to be above the normative sphere, and it makes it all the worse if he is not even aware of it. He is in the unsatisfactory position of a man who draws the line somewhere without telling us on what principle. *There can be no dispute about the necessity of drawing a line, but it must be done on the basis of a rational principle, not in a subconscious or arbitrary fashion.* The real task is to find this principle and then draw a new line. By stating the problem in this manner we realize that, like so many debatable questions, the dispute about relativism is capable of being settled on a higher level.

The popular indignation of scientists at value judgments seems to suggest that it were more or less like a matter of the taste in neckties. In the case of neckties our judgments—perhaps very fortunately so—will be highly various, arbitrary, and subject to individual fancies.[21] Here the degree of subjectivity

---

[21] The example sounds ludicrous, but it has also its serious side. In fact, aesthetic values are not mere subjective fancies which we can always dismiss with the adage *de gustibus non est disputandum* [in matters of taste there can be no dispute—Ed.]. The beautiful is certainly an objective quality of thing though always related to the apprehending subject. The same applies to the "Numinous" which, according to

in the judgment of value is particularly high, and all the higher the more it is a question of details in colour combinations and designs. But taking all possible value judgments together we observe that the degree of subjectivity may range from anything like zero to 100 percent. In a great number of cases, i.e. in that of the more vital and comprehensive judgments of value, the degree of subjectivity becomes so negligible as to give them an objective character.[22] Save again for the "idiotic fringe," we all agree on them because they are part of the normal make-up of man. It is these ultimate values (like truth, justice, peace, social coherence, etc.) which are guiding us also in our judgments on the desirability of this or that form of society or on the pathological character of a certain economic or social development. The fact that we cannot state the "health" of a society by simply inspecting its tongue cannot do away with the other fact that there *are* healthy and unhealthy societies. The great difficulty, to be sure, is the question of *criteria*. Since this is a serious obstacle in social nosology as compared with the medical nosology of individuals, we get a much larger margin of indeterminateness, subjectivity, and arbitrariness than exists in medicine, though a good amount of this may be found there too.

Now the important point is that the difficulty of social nosology varies with the degree of abnormality which we encounter. The margin of indeterminateness in social pathology will be large under microscopic and negligible under macroscopic conditions. It is, for instance, difficult to determine whether a small increase in the monetary circulation may be inflationary and even more difficult to decide whether something ought to be done about it; there is the largest scope for disputes on

---

Rudolf Otto's terminology, denotes the religious value. See R. Otto, *Das Heilige* (Munich, 1917). Cf. A. N. Whitehead, *Science and the Modern World* (New York, 1926), 285–93; Alexander Rüstow, *Zur geistesgeschichtlichen Ortsbestimmung der Gegenwart* (manuscript).

[22] Cf. also Felix Kaufmann, "The Significance of Methodology for the Social Sciences," *Social Research* (November, 1939).

index numbers, on niceties of monetary theory, and on the right balance of advantages and disadvantages. This margin of indeterminateness, of qualifications, of reserves, and of agnosticism grows smaller and smaller the more we are approaching macroscopic conditions until we come to the case of the colossal German inflation when it was absurd to deny the existence of inflation in the most disparaging sense of this term and the indisputable necessity of combating it. Then the crudest index numbers and the most sweeping formulations of the quantity theory did their service, and all discussions about possible qualifications (e.g. the influence of an adverse balance of payments, the possibility of "self-inflammatory" price movements, etc.) sank into insignificance.[23] Those who overlook this difference are rightly blamed for their lack of the sense of proportion which is so essential in any science and above all in economics.

What is true with regard to monetary phenomena applies also to other fields of economic and social life. So it would be a value judgment with a high degree of subjectivity to say that the distribution of incomes, the commercial policy, or the tax system ought to be such and such, but it is quite otherwise if such postulates can be related to a wider conception of economic policy which is based on more ultimate and "objective" judgments of value. The latter are final "points of relation" which give orientation to the more subjective postulates. It would surely be defensible to suppose an agreement between all morally sane men on the conviction that a society is in a pathological state if, let us say, 90 percent of its surface belongs to a few feudal estates, or if 20 percent of its members are unvoluntarily unemployed for a long time, or if 70 percent are proletarianized job-hunters, or if suicide and divorces become mass phenomena,

---

[23] It should be added that in medicine it is hardly otherwise. Doctors might quarrel whether a slight cold or a small fever are really diseases which ought to be cured, and it is well known that in this respect there exist different schools. But there is no disagreement in the case of pneumonia and of a temperature of 40° [104° F—Ed.].

or if there is a hyper-inflation like the German one, or if the family is in complete dissolution. It can also be safely assumed that it is not a wild fancy of the present author to believe that a healthy society is characterized by a "normal" degree of integration (as the human body is best adapted to a certain range of the outside temperature) so that the "sub-integration" of France during the last decade appears just as pathological as the "super-integration" of totalitarian countries.[24]

Let me explain my meaning still further by the example of *autarky*. Some Relativists may be surprised or even shocked if I make no secret of my belief that to say indiscriminately that autarky is condemnable implies a highly subjective judgment of value which, personally, I would not dare to make. Under certain circumstances, I confess, I would be very much in sympathy with it while under others I would condemn it. The point is that autarky as such cannot be judged without reference to a wider system of ultimate values. It may be either the indispensable means of defending a healthy society of primitives against the deadly contagion of Western civilization or the symptom of an utterly pathological state of a civilized society. I for one have no scientific scruples whatever in saying that the latter is that case with which we have to do today. Autarky in our time is only a part and a manifestation of the universal process of economic and social international disintegration. How to judge this process? Is it possible to suggest that international disintegration may be after all a wholesome readjustment to new conditions and the forerunner of a new arrangement in international economics and politics? It is not; for the evident reason that the international disintegration of our time is linked up with the wider process of general social disintegration which implies the destruction of the ultimate foundations of our society. It is a social catastrophe which has now culminated in a world war

---

[24] Cf. Professor Rüstow's paper on the reasons of the decline of liberalism in "Compte-Rendu des séances du Colloque Lippmann," (Paris: International Institute of Intellectual Cooperation, 1939), 77–83.

as its logical end, a war which, in its confusion and brutality, appears the true expression of this age of moral dissolution and of social disintegration.

IV

The long and short of it is that *value judgments are to be classified according to their degree of subjectivity* which is tantamount to classifying them according to their vital and ultimate character. It is this classification which determines the degree of their scientific legitimacy and therefore the amount of reservation or peremptoriness with which they may be pronounced in science. This is not a new and bold proposition but precisely what we are doing all the time (the relativists included, as we saw), only with more or less consistency and consciousness.

Moreover, this classification implies the *reason* for the scientific legitimacy of the higher orders of value judgments. They are simply *anthropological facts* which science has to respect just as it has to respect the meaning of words in the human language. This reference to the language seems useful in order to indicate the real structure of the problem and to answer the obvious question of how to ascertain and to prove those anthropological facts. The meaning of the word "jealousy," for instance, cannot be ascertained and proved like the behavior of stock exchange prices; we find it in ourselves where it has been formed by social contact from childhood on; our statement that the word "ought" to mean this or that is simply one about a fact. Without this tacit convention on the meaning of words, no social intercourse is possible. It is hardly otherwise with our elementary normative concepts regarding the forms and ends of social and economic life. They are *anthropological constants* which, after careful examination, we are bound to accept as facts. Even the sternest relativist knows quite well that there are "right" and "wrong" relations to property, to the other sex, to one's children, to work and leisure, to nature, to time and death, to youth and age, to the sequence of generations, to the pleasures of life, to the holy and unworldly, to the beautiful, the true and the just, to reason and sentiment, to society as a whole, to war and peace. We also know that in our disjointed world of today, most of these relations are dangerously wrong. The individual who lost his sense of the "normal" in all these respects will be found sooner or later in the consulting-room of the nerve specialist or even in an asylum while a society made up of too many of such individuals will end in war and revolution.[25] Such is the terrible penalty for disregarding those anthropological constants which the relativist believes to be scientifically unascertainable. The neurologist and psychiatrist,[26] the ethnologist[27] or the sociologist[28] know better, and the econ-

---

[25] "We are living in a crazy world, and we know it. Nobody would be surprised if one day the madness suddenly broke out in a frenzy from which this pitiful European mankind would sink back, stunned and demented, while the engines are still humming and the flags still fluttering though the spirit has gone." J. Huizinga, *Im Schatten von morgen* (Bern, 1935), 9. (The English translation entitled "In the Shadow of Tomorrow" has not been accessible to me.)

[26] Out of the vast literature on psychopathology, special mention may be made of C. von Monakow Mourgue, *Biologische Einführung in das Studium der Neurologie und Psychopathologie*, trans. E. Katzenstein (Stuttgart, 1930) (the French original was not at my disposal). The relativists would do well to consult this book of a leading neurologist of our age. Cf. also W. Riese and A. Réquet, *L'idée de l'homme dans la neurologie contemporaine* (Paris, 1938); G. Villey, *La psychiatrie et les sciences de l'homme* (Paris, 1939). Dr. Carrel's popular book on "Man—The Unknown" is based on the same trend of thought.

[27] As an example I mention the researches of the so-called Viennese school of ethnology on the concept of the "normal" with regard to property. See Wilhelm Schmidt, *Das Eigentum in den Urkulturen* (Münster, 1937).

[28] See especially C. Bouglé, *Leçons de sociologie sur l'évolution des valeurs* (Paris, 1922), as well as M. Halbwachs and other French sociologists.

In this connection, the family as the normal nursery and the most natural community of men should be mentioned as a good example of the anthropological constants. Throughout the ages and under all

omist can hardly afford to ignore what they know. The demand that things ought to be *à la taille de l'homme*[29] is imperative. The famous dictum of the Digest, "hominum causa omne ius constitutum est,"[30] applies to all institutions of society. Ours is the world of man; we cannot go beyond it, and it is this which gives us measure and norm. If we keep this in mind, we shall know how to find our way between relativism on the one hand and the abuse of value judgments on the other. In doing so, we shall follow that "reasonable middle course" which itself corresponds to human nature.

In order to prevent a possible misunderstanding, let us add that it would, of course, be too much to expect that all value judgments which are anthropologically "valid" must always be such that they are generally accepted by the overwhelming majority. The optimist belief that you cannot fool all the people all the time may be justified in the end, but it is obvious that at least temporarily large discrepancies between what is anthropologically true and what is commonly accepted are possible. Common opinion in a society may, for instance, be completely wrong in what ought to be the right place of women because it is blind to some anthropological—or, specifically, to some gynaecological—facts and to the subtle sociological functions of women which follow from their unalterable natural functions. We must squarely face such a divergence in order to see quite clearly that it can be scientifically settled by a last appeal to

---

latitudes, the institution of the family can be considered as such a constant, in spite of the miserable experiment of Sparta and of the modern totalitarian countries. It is highly significant that in Soviet Russia today the indispensability of the family seems again to be recognized (cf. a leader in the *Izvestia* of September 21, 1940).

[29] Ed. note: "to the height of humanity."

[30] Ed. note: "every law has been created for the sake of human beings." See *Corpus Iuris Civilis*, vol. 1, *Digesta*, ed. Theodore Mommsen (Berlin: Weidmann, 1893), 1.5.2.

anthropological facts. Hence the "validity" of value judgments must not ultimately be based on current acceptance alone.

Finally, a possibility of supplementing the anthropological interpretation of value judgments must at least be mentioned, though it is here that we feel especially the urgent necessity of getting beyond the field of mere tentative suggestions. What we have in mind is the *morphological interpretation* and justification of value judgments. As everybody fairly familiar with the *Gestaltphilosophie*[31] and its general drift (which is not without its pitfalls) will readily understand, the morphological approach could be based on the assumption that values may be capable of being interpreted in terms of *forms* and *functions* which give everything its significant and appraisable place as part of a definite social structure. In this way we arrive, in the social sphere, at *morphological judgments* as they are known as perfectly legitimate in other sciences like history, botany, crystallography, etc. As it were, we are reducing the higher plane of values to the lower one of forms, just as a logarithmical operation enables us to reduce a multiplication to a mere addition.

V

This suggested solution of the intricate problem of the scientific legitimacy of value judgments seems so obvious that, as I said, not the slightest originality can be claimed for it. Moreover, it is in accord with a line of thought which can be traced through the centuries despite the recurrent waves of relativism. The germs may already be found in scholastic rationalism as represented especially by St. Thomas Aquinas. It is beyond my own competence and the scope of this article to give a correct and detailed picture of the complicated way in which rationalism and the doctrine of the *jus naturale* develop, secularize, or contradict,

---

[31] Ed. note: Gestalt psychology is a philosophy of mind that originated in the Berlin School of Experimental Psychology headed by Carl Stumpf (1848–1936), a German philosopher and psychologist.

during the seventeenth and eighteenth century, the early scholastic rationalism. To do this would involve a discussion of the difficult problem of rationalism in general and an account of the excesses of rationalism and antirationalism which are again a melancholy example of the "loi de double frénésie." It is indeed in an excess of rationalism that Relativism is rooted: in one of the aberrations which, unfortunately, have deprived the age of Enlightenment of some of its best fruits and which have given to rationalism the pejorative sense it has today. From the seventeenth century onward, rationalism shows the tendency to become unbridled analytical criticism which, by disregarding the vital data of thinking, is bound to end in futility and self-destruction.[32] In a description of this development, even such venerable names as Descartes and Kant must not be left unmentioned.[33] It is in this world of uncontrolled criticism, of Pyrrhonic skepticism, of solipsism that our relativism has been born.

It seems, however, that there was never a time when this sort of rationalism completely held the field. It is impossible to overlook the highly normative character of the doctrine of the *jus naturale*. In fact, during the eighteenth century, rationalism slowly seems to make efforts to find its compass again. When Montesquieu says in the preface of his *Esprit des Lois*: "I have not drawn my principles from my prejudices but from the nature of things," he gives evidence of a philosophy of social

---

[32] See the beautiful book by Paul Hazard, *La crise de la conscience européenne, 1680–1715* (Paris, 1936).

[33] Descartes' role in this process has been properly stressed by A. N. Whitehead, *Science and the Modern World*, 280–89. He rightly remarks: "A selfsatisfied rationalism is in effect a form of anti-relationalism. It means an arbitrary halt at a particular set of abstractions" (289). As far as Kant is concerned, we know that in his later years he became deeply dissatisfied with "pure science." A fruit of this dissatisfaction is his famous tract entitled "Zum ewigen Frieden" (1795). There is a touching (undated) letter where he confesses to have been deeply influenced by Rousseau.

science which, one hundred years later, we find fully developed in its anthropological meaning in Tocqueville's essay on "Politics as Science" (1852).

During these hundred years between Montesquieu and Tocqueville, the spiritual climate of the West underwent changes which, decisive as they were, can hardly be characterized with a few words. It is safe to say, however, that men like Rousseau, Herder, the Scottish School of philosophy (Reid and others), and later Romanticism did much to forge arms against relativism and to reestablish the factual character of the vital and anthropological data.[34] It is again a complicated story how, during the nineteenth century and under the influence of Hegel, Comte, the natural sciences, the theoretical and practical materialism, the historicism and other factors, relativism reached a new zenith. Suffice it to say that this zenith has long since been passed until today we have reached a situation which perhaps has been best described by Professor Whitehead in his well-known book on *Science and the Modern World* and by Ortega y Gasset in his important essay entitled "El tema de nuestro tiempo."[35] It is impossible here to tell the story of this latest development, but let us say at least that the names of Jacob Burckhardt and Friedrich Nietzsche ought to find in it a prominent place.[36]

---

[34] Of particular interest in this respect is the post-Kantian philosopher Jacob F. Fries whose book on *Neue oder anthropologische Kritik der Vernunft* (1807) contains the new programme already in its title.

[35] (Madrid, 1923). It is accessible in a German translation: *Die Aufgabe unserer Zeit* (Stuttgart, 1923).

[36] See especially the chapter "We scholars" in *Beyond Good and Evil* (ch. 6). That it is possible to name in the same vein catholic writers (e.g. Theodor Haecker or Christopher Dawson) shows how broad the front of modern anti-relativism has become.

VI

On the present occasion, the subject of value judgments cannot be pursued any further without overtaxing the patience of the reader who may already have asked himself what all this has to do with economics as it is understood today or even with what justification an article like this finds its place in an economic review. It is to be hoped, however, that this article itself will be accepted as a sufficient answer to these questions, for its main purpose is to broaden the scope and field of economics in our time. Refuting that sort of scientific prohibition which relativism wants to impose on us means to push open the door to those wider fields of research where the real roots of the present crisis of Western civilization are to be found. It would be an insult to the relativists to insinuate that they are less aware of the extent to which the foundations of our economic and social system are being undermined and of the necessity of thoroughly exploring the reasons of the disaster and of building up a new substructure. But, unfortunately for them, these problems—which are so gigantic as to require all the available talent and energy—are lying in fields to which the relativists are "painstakingly refusing themselves admission" (Nietzsche). Hence the widespread prudery in looking the wider but decisive problems in the face, the reluctance to establish contact with sociology, ethics or political science, the tendency to look askance at demands for "synthesis" and "scientific cooperation," and the insistence on fiddling while Rome is burning. But the last phrase is perhaps somewhat unkind if the fiddler is honestly and to his own distress convinced that it is sin to help put out the fire. It seems kinder to shake his conviction.

Appendix 1

A Glance at Economic History*

It is universally agreed that the division of labor in modern times has been extended and refined to a degree unknown in previous history. Completely self-sufficient economies of the Robinson Crusoe type are practically unknown today. Indeed, it is doubtful whether a wholly exchangeless economy of this kind, ambiguously termed *natural economy* (ambiguous because the term is also applicable to a moneyless exchange economy), could have existed at any period in history in pure form and on a large scale. The contention that, for instance, the early Middle Ages were characterized by such natural economies has been refuted by contemporary historical investigation. See A. Dopsch, *Naturalwirtschaft und Geldwirtschaft in der Weltgeschichte* (1930).

Economic historians have attempted to trace through the course of economic history the red thread of a principle labeled "development." This has produced the so-called *theories of economic stages*, the earliest of which we owe to Friedrich List in his *National System of Political Economy* (1841; Eng. Trans. by Lloyd, 1885). More scientifically accoutered statements of the same theory appear in Bruno Hildebrand's *Die Nationalökonomie*

---

*This appendix originally appeared as a footnote in "The Problem." See 21n1 above.

der Gegenwart und Zukunft (1848). Hildebrand distinguished three stages of development: the natural economy, the money economy, and the credit economy. K. Bücher's *Die Entstehung der Volkswirtschaft* (tr. under the title of *Industrial Evolution* by S. Morley Wickett from the 3rd German ed., New York, 1901) distinguishes the stages of (1) the search for food by individuals, (2) the closed household economy (isolated economy without exchange), (3) the urban economy of the Middle Ages (with its emphasis on production for individual consumers of "custom-made" goods), and (4) the modern market economy (production of goods which are supplied by middlemen to an anonymous circle of buyers). G. Schmoller and many others have enriched the literature devoted to this theme, and it remains the object of intensive study by economic historians. As it turns out, the idea that economic history can be reduced to a series of developmental stages was much too arbitrary and required doing more or less violence to the facts. The basic error was to conceive of this "evolution" as progressing in a straight line—an echo of the eighteenth century's faith in linear progress. Recent researches have shown that the ancient world, and in particular the Roman Empire, reached an astonishing degree of economic development. The ancient world too, it appears, had its capitalism and its world economy. For information on this point, the reader is referred to M. I. Rostovtzeff's magnificent work *Social and Economic History of the Roman Empire* (New York, 1926).

A theory which has enjoyed a considerably longer life is the one made popular by Bücher, viz., that from the Middle Ages onward, economic life evolved directly from more primitive to more complex forms, up to the present worldwide division of labor. To this theory are joined more or less romantic and idealized notions of the idyllic characteristics of medieval economic life and medieval economic thought. The writings of Sombart, especially his voluminous work *Der Moderne Kapitalismus* (three volumes: I, II—1902; III—1928, Berlin), have given currency to these ideas among a wide circle of readers. Here too, recent investigation demonstrates the need for thorough revision of received opinion. We know now that even in the Middle Ages there was an intense degree of economic activity and that it is legitimate to speak of a "world economy of the Middle Ages," an economy which was not by any means confined to the exchange of luxury-type goods. We have evidence also that the individuals engaged in this economic activity—and this should not surprise—exhibited a pronounced propensity for business enterprise. What is particularly significant is that this highly developed economic system of the Middle Ages crumbled at the beginning of the modern era, to be succeeded by a less differentiated type of economy in the period which saw the rise of mercantilism and of national territorial states. Like the world economy of antiquity, the world economy of the Middle Ages fell in ruins, together with the political system which supported it. It is a story with special relevance to our own age. See F. Rörig, *Mittelalterliche Weltwirtschaft, Blüte und Ende einer Weltwirtschaftsperiode* (Jena, 1933). In his *Die Grundlagen der Nationalökonomie* (6th ed., 1950, tr. into English as *Foundations of Economics*, London, 1950), Walter Eucken offers a fundamental criticism of the evolutionary interpretation of economic history and a convincing analysis of the relations between economic history and economic theory. See also: Ludwig von Mises, *Theory and History, An Interpretation of Social and Economic Evolution* (New Haven, 1957).

Appendix 2

MARGINAL UTILITY: FOUNDATION OF MODERN ECONOMIC THEORY[*]

The significance of the marginal utility principle was recognized quite early, for example, by Gossen in 1854. Later, it was further developed and established as the foundation of modern theory by three scholars working simultaneously but independently: the Austrian Carl Menger (1871), the Englishman W. Stanley Jevons (1871), and Leon Walras, a Frenchman who was then teaching in Switzerland (1874). The most important stages in later development of the principle are indicated by the following works: Friedrich von Wieser, *Theorie der gesellschaftlichen Wirtschaft* (1914; English tr. *Theory of Social Economics* by A. F. Hinrichs, New York, 1927); E. von Böhm-Bawerk, *Positive Theorie des Kapitals* (1889; there are several versions in English, the earliest being that of William A. Smart in 1891 and the most recent being that of George D. Huncke and Hans F. Sennholz, *Capital and Interest,* South Holland, Illinois, 1959); Alfred Marshall, *The Principles of Economics* (London, 1890); V. Pareto, *Cours d'économie politique* (Lausanne, 1896/97); M. Pantaleoni, *Principii di economia pura* (Florence, 1889; English tr. *Pure Economics,* London, 1898); J. B. Clark, *The Distribution of Wealth* (New

---

[*] This appendix originally appeared as a footnote in "The Problem." See 33n5 above.

Appendix 2

York, 1899); Philip H. Wicksteed, *The Common Sense of Political Economy* (London, 1910; newly edited by L. Robbins, 1933); K. Wicksell, *Lectures on Political Economy* (2 vols.; London, 1934; published originally in Swedish in 1901); G. Cassel, *Theoretische Sozialökonomie* (1918; English ed. *The Theory of Social Economy*, 1923); Ludwig von Mises, *Nationalökonomie, Theorie des Handelns und Wirtschaftens* (Geneva, 1940; an amplified version of this work in English is Mises' *Human Action*, New Haven, 1949). These works are truly the pillars upon which reposes all of modern theory. In spite of their differences of perspective and of opinion on many individual matters, they form a unified body of thought which the serious student of economics cannot afford to neglect.

In some quarters, the marginal principle is contemptuously dismissed as a *plaisanterie viennoise*[1] and nothing more. But it cannot be too strongly emphasized that the whole of present-day economic thought is inconceivable outside the framework of this fundamental concept. Even those economists who expressly deny the usefulness of the marginal utility theory are heavily dependent upon it, nevertheless. An especially typical example of this is supplied in the book cited above by the Swede Gustav Cassel. Cassel, if the truth be known, is largely in debt to Walras and his school, though he never once refers to this source. By putting Walras' involved theories into intelligible form and by enriching them with his own valuable ideas, Cassel performed a most useful service and contributed greatly to the advancement of economic science, especially in Germany after World War I. But there is no doubt that he is a product of the general tradition of modern economics.

Pantaleoni's observation (1897) that there are really only two schools of economists, those who understand economics and those who don't, is worth recalling. If limited to pure theory, the statement is by no means the joking exaggeration it might appear to be. This is evident in the theoretical developments of

---

[1] Ed. note: "a Viennese joke."

recent decades. Thus, the three schools which simultaneously discovered the principle of marginal utility (the Austrian school of Menger and Wieser, the Lausanne school of Walras and Pareto, and the Anglo-American school of Jevons, Marshall and Clark) have shown a convergent evolution. The Austrian and Anglo-American movements agree much more than they disagree (especially as a result of the strong emphasis on and persistent investigation of objective cost factors by the Anglo-American school). The Lausanne school, however, is distinguished from the others, firstly, by its emphasis on synthesis rather than analysis. With but brief attention to the motives underlying individual economic behavior, it attempts by means of mathematical formulae to arrive at a method for determining when a state of *total* economic equilibrium exists. Secondly, the Lausanne theory is more a functional theory (one, that is, which *describes* mutual dependencies in a state of equilibrium) than a genetic-causal one (which explains *how* and *why* the factors work toward a given equilibrium).

The Lausanne school teaches a general and doubtless more comprehensive truth, but this is of little help in solving individual problems. Granted the necessity of dwelling, even at some length, on the more general and more comprehensive truth, the Lausanne theories are too abstract for significant practical application, entirely apart from the forbidding and not altogether necessary mathematical formulae in which the theories are expressed. In spite of the respect which it rightly inspires, the work of the Lausanne school seems somewhat like a mathematical castle in Spain. Its divorcement from reality gives it a patently static character, and this is precisely what renders it of little use in solving the most important concrete problems of the economic system, viz., those arising from *disturbances* of economic equilibrium. On this subject, the reader should consult Hans Mayer, "Der Erkenntniswert der funktionellen Preistheorien," in *Wirtschaftstheorie de Gegenwart* (vol. 2, 1932; in this memorial to Friedrich von Wieser is to be found perhaps the most comprehensive survey of modern economic theory;

Appendix 2

an excellent supplement is the anthology published under the auspices of the American Economic Association entitled *A Survey of Contemporary Economics*, ed. H. S. Ellis, Philadelphia, 1948; a critical review of the most recent trends in economic thought is furnished in the essay by Murray N. Rothbard, "Toward a Reconstruction of Utility and Welfare Economics" in the "Festschrift" for Ludwig von Mises, *On Freedom and Free Enterprise*, New York, 1956). It is clear from the foregoing that the differences among the schools are not differences between true and false but differences of presentation and emphasis, and even these have lessened with the passage of time.

Modern marginalist theory must be understood against the background of the so-called classical theory which it overthrew. The fathers of classical theory were Adam Smith (*An Inquiry into the Nature and Causes of the Wealth of Nations*, 1776), David Ricardo (*The Principles of Political Economy and Taxation*, 1817), and Thomas Malthus (*Essay on the Principle of Population*, 1798). Classical theory was further refined by J. B. Say, J. H. von Thünen, N. W. Senior, Hermann, J. S. Mill, and others. One of its last representatives was J. E. Cairnes, whose book *Some Leading Principles of Political Economy* (London, 1874) still makes enjoyable reading and was published, piquantly enough, in the same year which saw the birth of modern theory.

A fact which, of course, did not escape the classical theorists was that utility is somehow connected with value. Obviously, a thing which is good for nothing can have no value, but does utility determine value? For the classicists, the case of water and diamonds seemed to prove that utility might well be one of the conditions, but not the cause of the value of a good. Because they had not grasped the *specific* character of utility (marginal utility), they reasoned that so soon as a thing possessed any utility whatsoever, its value (price) was determined by quite other factors. Unfortunately, the classical economists, in spite of their acumen, did not succeed in reducing these value factors to a homogeneous formula. In fact, from their early gropings, *three distinctly different theories* emerged. They began by distinguishing two kinds of goods: scarce goods, whose quantity could not be increased by production, and goods which could be "produced at will." The value of the first would be determined solely by the degree of their scarcity; the value of the second by their costs of production, thus by something objective. Onto this classification, the classicists grafted a distinction between a normal price (natural price) and a market price which oscillates around the normal. The normal price was supposed to be determined by the costs of production, whereas the market price was determined by supply and demand.

The existence of three different explanations of the same phenomenon was unsatisfactory enough. But the classicists, in addition, became ever more entangled in the internal inconsistencies of their concepts the more they sought to get to the bottom of things. Of what do the "costs of production" consist? How can cost factors be reduced to a common denominator? Up to the very end, the classical school struggled vainly to find an answer to these questions. (See A. Amonn, *Ricardo als Begründer der theoretischen Nationalökonomie*, 1924). It became increasingly clear, too, that a cost-of-production theory was of no help at all in explaining a variety of important phenomena (monopoly price, prices of jointly produced goods, international price formation).

The labored disputes of the classical economists were brought to an end with the simple discovery that their too hasty examination of the utility concept had led them to confuse *general* with *specific* utility. From this time on, the objective-technical explanation of value was supplanted by the subjective-economic emphases of modern theory. It is to be noted also that the marginal utility concept makes the labor theory of value, which constitutes the theoretical base of Marxism, wholly untenable. In fact, the purely economic basis of Marxism must be regarded today as merely an intellectual anachronism. Specifically, a suit is not eight times as valuable as a hat because it requires eight times as much labor as a hat to produce. It is because the *finished suit* will be eight times as valuable as the finished hat that society is willing to employ eight times as much labor for the suit as for the hat (Wicksteed). It is upon this discovery that the remaining parts of Marxist theory (surplus value, capitalist disintegration) have foundered. This certainly does not mean that socialism can be dismissed as mere foolishness, but simply that it cannot be scientifically established upon a Marxist base.

Notwithstanding, it would be an error to believe that classical theory is a collection of sterile fallacies. On the contrary, modern theory itself remains heavily in debt to the spadework of the classical school. There is no difference in the approaches of the classicists and the moderns to the fundamental issues of economics, a fact which, as the *Methodenstreit* (conflict over methods) has demonstrated, flows from the internal logic of things. Moreover, there is no great difference in the conclusions arrived at by the two schools, even though their underlying premises are, in part, quite different (e.g., with respect to the law which causes prices, under competition, to fall towards the costs of production). In several instances, indeed, classical theory anticipated the basic notions of modern theory (e.g., in international trade theory). The acumen which enabled the classical school, in spite of its false foundation and its tortured constructions, to come to useful conclusions deserves admiration. Where modern theory showed the greatest advance over the classical school was in the practical sphere. The stiff classical machinery of "natural laws" has been made so much more flexible that economics has gotten closer to reality, become more capable of adaptation, and more largely human. Purified of the premature economic policy conclusions professed by the classical school (laissez-faire liberalism), modern theory has not only become less partisan politically, but in virtue of that very fact has developed into an indispensable instrument in the solving of current problems of economic policy. Classical theory was philosophical in character while modern theory is primarily instrumental in character.

An extended analysis of the principle of marginal utility will raise difficulties too numerous to be dealt with here. Then too, the process of analysis in this instance is itself subject to the law of diminishing marginal utility, that is, as economic analyses are increasingly refined, they tend to produce less and less interesting results. Much of the criticism of the marginal utility principle is, upon closer inquiry, seen to be aimed at such exaggeratedly long and psychological marking of time at the point of departure. The same impression, indeed, is created by the true but otherwise not very helpful intellectual architectonics found at the other extreme in the mathematical equilibrium models of the Lausanne school. At all events, these are difficulties which must one day be resolved.

A good survey of the relevant discussion on these matters may be found in the article "Value" in the *Encyclopedia of the Social Sciences* and in D. H. Robertson, *Utility and All That* (London, 1952). To bewail such clarification would be just as unintelligent as to let ourselves be irritated by the footnotes in a book. (Though he who believes he can skip the footnotes is quite at liberty to do so). On the other hand, a book should consist of something else besides footnotes. If this point of view were more widely adopted, many a sterile dispute over the principle of marginal utility would be avoided.

Appendix 3

ECONOMICS AND ETHICS*

Though the business method is in itself ethically neutral, business income may be used for ethically positive (altruistic) ends. The concept "individual increase of well-being" must, therefore, be understood in a broad sense, one which embraces all the possible objectives which the individual fixes for himself, including altruistic objectives. Certain Western peoples are noted as much for their charity and generosity as for their shrewd business insight. Money as an end in itself holds less attraction for them than it does for many Orientals who, while despising Western "business methods," take a miser's joy in accumulating treasure for its own sake.[1] Experience shows that business is only a method of acquiring means which may be then employed for every imaginable object. Even charitable institutions find it necessary to use purely commercial methods to raise needed funds. Heinrich Schliemann, the

---

*This appendix originally appeared as a footnote in "The Basic Data of Economics." See 40n2 above.

[1] Ed. note: Röpke was free of neither the language nor the prejudice of his time and place. It is hoped that this statement will not be an obstacle to the reader's appreciation of what is timeless in his writings presented here.

Appendix 3

ingenious discoverer of ancient Troy, amassed a fortune in business with the sole object of paying for the costs of his excavations. On this and related questions, see the comprehensive study by P. Hennipman, *Economisch Motief en Economisch Principe* (Amsterdam, 1945). Other significant contributions to the literature on this subject include L. von Wiese, *Ethik in der Schauweise der Wissenschaften vom Menschen und von der Gesellschaft* (Berne, 1947); F. H. Knight, *The Ethics of Competition and other Essays* (London, 1935); F. H. Knight, *Freedom and Reform* (New York, 1947). The role of ethics in economics is considered in detail in my own book *A Humane Economy* (Chicago, 1960).

Appendix 4

COSTS AS A RENUNCIATION OF ALTERNATIVE UTILITIES[*]

The interpretation of costs as a loss of utility ("opportunity cost") sheds light on what has long been one of the most baffling problems of economics. What are the "real" costs behind the money costs which we encounter initially in the market economy? One of the most important and least contested contributions of modern marginal theory was its discovery of the answer to this question. Prior to the application of the marginal analysis—and Marshall himself had held to this view—costs had been regarded as primarily the expression of and the compensation for the pain and sacrifice entailed in production ("pain cost"). This was a conception which found in Marx's labor theory of value its purest and most radical formulation. There is some evidence that this interpretation of costs reflects the moral climate in which the English bourgeoisie of the eighteenth and nineteenth centuries lived, a climate in which every honest gain was thought to require a corresponding sacrifice. This tendency, and the economic errors which developed from it, are especially evident in N. W. Senior's (1790–1864) attempt to describe and to justify the price of capital

---

[*]This appendix originally appeared as a footnote in "The Basic Data of Economics." See 46n5 above.

(interest) as an appropriate reward made to the saver for his sacrifice ("abstinence"). Doubtless, it was this attempt which inspired Ferdinand Lassalle to utter the well-known jest: "The profit from capital is the reward for privation! Admirable maxim, worth its weight in gold! The European millionaires, the ascetics, the penitent Hindus, the stylites perched on one leg on the tops of their pillars, arms outstretched, the body bent over, the face pale, proffering their cups to the faithful in order to collect the reward for their privations! In the midst of them, and overshadowing all the penitents, the penitent of penitents, the House of Rothschild!" The thought expressed here is indeed a disquieting one, for it is obvious that the so-called "sacrifice" of the saver (lender) diminishes with increasing wealth, to the point where saving among millionaires takes place in a quasi-automatic fashion. In due course, we shall see why interest must be detached completely from notions such as "sacrifice" and "reward." The phenomenon of interest is independent of the concept of saving as a sacrifice or a pleasure, just as an author's income from a novel is independent of the pleasure or lack of it the writing of the novel gave him. An author's income is in reality contingent on his writing a good novel and on the fact that good novels are rare. Likewise, interest results from the fact that capital is at once useful and rare. There is simply not enough capital to supply the demands of all those who should like to use it. In the level of the interest rate, which must be entered on the ledger along with the other costs as the "cost of capital," is reflected the utility of an alternative but rejected use of capital. What is true for capital costs is true, also, for all other costs. Costs, as reflected in prices, do not represent a compensation we are compelled to pay for a sacrifice someone has incurred, for often it is precisely the most laborious work and the dirtiest which is the least well paid. The function of costs is to compel us to compare the utility of *our* use of productive factors with the utility of some other alternative use of the same factors.

The interpretation of costs as a renunciation of alternative utilities involves a number of difficulties which we cannot deal with here. But it may be observed in passing that this interpretation is valid only when a means of production can be used in more than one way ("general" as opposed to "specific" means of production in Wieser's terminology). These and other aspects of cost theory are the subject of lively discussion by present-day economists. See F. von Wieser, *Theorie der gesellschaftlichen Wirtschaft* (2nd ed. 1924, 61ff.; published in English as *Social Economics*, trans. by A. Ford, London, 1927); O. Morgenstern, "Offene Probleme der Kosten- und Ertragstheorie," *Zeitschrift für Nationalökonomie* (Vol. 2, 1934), 481–522; F. H. Knight, "Cost of Production and Price over Long and Short Periods," *Journal of Political Economy* (Vol. XXIV, 1921), reprinted, together with other pertinent material, in Knight's *The Ethics of Competition* (London, 1935); G. J. Stigler, *The Theory of Price* (2nd ed., New York, 1953); and finally the extended discussion of these matters in *The Economic Journal*, beginning in 1926 (by Sraffa, Pigou, Shove, Robertson, Robbins, *et al.*).

Subject Index

Acton, Lord, xi, 16, 97, 192
Adams, John, 111n53, 114
advertising, 85, 107–8, 119–20
aggregates, 228–30, 235, 236–37
altruism, 38–39, 40, 43–44, 275
anarchy, 19–23, 61
   liberal, 101–2, 195
Aquinas, Thomas, 97n42, 191, 258
aristocrats, moral, xxxii, 110–14, 151
   economists, 116–18
   scientists, 114–18
Aristotle, 14, 189
Austrian economists, xxvi–xxvii, xxviii–xxix, 250n19, 269
   Viennese, xxviii, 170, 217
autarky, 254–55

Bentham, Jeremy, Benthamite, 83n23, 103n46
Bismarck, Otto von, xxxiii, 4
Boulding, Kenneth E., 155
bourgeois, 70–75, 85–86, 96–97, 105, 241
Burckhardt, Jacob, 16, 144n4, 260
business principle, 37–44

Caligula, 153, 190n6
Calvinism, 41n3, 97n42
capital, 31–32, 277–78
capitalism, 22–23, 41n3, 56, 91–92
   Marxism and, 42–43n4
   moral choice, 98–99
   socialism and, 4–5, 9
Cassel, Gustav, 268
Catholic Church, Catholicism, 18, 188
   liberalism, 191–93, 199
   Quadragesimo Anno, xi, 192–99
   social philosophy, xxxiii, 191–93, 194, 198
central bank, 138, 141–43, 173, 213
centralization, centrism, 15, 142n3, 147
   freedom, 153–54
   international, 162–67
   leaders, 182–85

281

Subject Index

power and, 155–56
social philosophy, 145–48
totalitarianism, 152–54
Chateaubriand, François-René de, 134
China, 86
Christianity, x–xi, 17–18, 196
  of Europe, 11, 165n24, 166
  liberalism and, 189–9
  morality, 41, 96–97
  Protestants, 18, 41n3, 97n42, 188
  totalitarianism, 188, 198
  See also Catholic Church, Catholicism
classical economic theory, 270–73
Cold War, 10, 76, 85–88, 121–24, 164
collectivism, 11–12, 57, 61, 128, 144, 148
  Catholic social philosophy, 196–97
  competition, 68–69, 101
  economic equilibrium, 12, 57–60, 205–6
  freedom, 6–8
  tyranny, 98–99
collectivist economic system, 12, 57–60, 101, 148
  competition, 67–69
  economic order, 78–79
  market economy and, 156–57, 194, 205–6
  morality, 98–99
Colloque Walter Lippmann, xx, xxviii
commercialism, 42, 44, 89, 92, 107–9, 119–20
Communism, 50, 57, 66, 71, 76, 79, 106
  collective needs, 59–60
  competition, 67–68

East-West trade, 121–24
  ideology, 74, 145n4, 242, 248
  New England, 97n42
  social disintegration, 85–87, 88
  standard of living, 85–88
compensatory fiscal policy, 237–38
competition, 109–10, 148, 178
  collectivism, 67–69, 101
  in Communism, 67–68
  dual nature, 67–69
  ethics, 14, 44, 100–101, 102–6
  free, 44, 149
  market economy, 67–69
conservatives, conservatism, xxx–xxxi, 16, 140–44
consumer credit, 72–74, 76n12, 120–21
consumption, 73–75, 85, 231
corporatism, corporations, 193–95
Croce, Benedetto, 77–79
culture, xxx–xxxi, 221–22

debt, 72, 231–32
  consumer credit, installment buying, 72–74, 76n12, 120–21
decentralization, xxxii–xxxiii, 15–16, 128, 198
  freedom, 152–53
  human nature, 146–48
  independence, 143, 151–52
  social philosophy, 145–48, 150–51
  universalism, 151–52
deception, 85, 95, 98
deflation, 138–40, 210, 231, 232, 235–37
dehumanization, 167–68, 182, 217–19
demand, 27–29, 30–33, 50

282

democracy, xxxiv, xxxv, 4, 141–43, 190–91
economics, 124–25, 133–35, 222–23
mass, 16, 124–25, 129–31, 133–35, 138, 238
dependent wage earners, 155–61, 163
Descartes, René, 170n29, 259
Devons, Ely, 176–77
division of labor, 20–21, 56–57, 263–64

East-West trade, 121–24
economic development, 202–4, 263–65, 272
Westernization, 86–88
economic equilibrium systems
collectivist, 12, 57–60, 205–6
mixed, 51–55
price, 49–50, 51–53, 55–57, 58–59
queue, 49–50, 51–52
rationing, 40, 51–52, 53–54
economic goods. *See* goods, economic
economic policy, 133–35
interest, pressure groups, 124–29
laissez-faire, 56, 195, 196, 272
mass democracy, 124–25, 133–35
mass opinions, 129–31
national budgeting, 175–76
political, xii, 48
economics
classical theory, 270–73
definition, 205–6
growth of, development, 86–88, 202–4, 263–65, 272
homegrown, 208–9, 219–20
humans and, 167–68, 181–83

methods, 205–6
modern theory, 271–73
as moral science, 169–71, 215–19, 248–49
morals, ethics and, vii–viii, 14–15, 37–44, 64n2, 77, 275–76
political policy, xii, 48
relationships, 209–12
religion and, viii, xxxii–xxxiii, 14, 17
as science, xii, 201–2, 203–5, 206–7
society and, 76–79, 203–5
studying, 202–3, 207–10
theory, 33, 133n73, 170, 181–82, 206–8, 216
traditional, old, 229–30
economism, 80–83
economists, 63–65, 66–67, 72
American, xx, xxiv, xxviii, xxxi, 137–38, 173, 187, 270
aristocrats, moral, 116–18
Austrian, xxvi–xxviii, xxviii–xxix, 170, 217, 250n19, 269
economic policy and, 133–35
free economic order, 77–80
judgment, 212–14
Lausanne school, theory, 269–70, 273
orientating, 221–23
relationships, identifying, 210–12
schools, 268–70
economize, 26–29, 33–35
economocracy, 133, 164, 175–77
employment, full, 141, 158, 173, 226, 230, 232
England, British, 174–75, 176–77, 227–28, 277–78
National Health Service, 50
Enlightenment, the, 41n3, 259

283

Subject Index

entrepreneurs, 32, 177–82
Erhard, Ludwig, xxi, xxiii
ethics, 103–4
   competition, 14, 44, 100–101, 102–6
   economics and, vii–viii, 14–15, 37–44, 64n2, 77, 275–76
   market economy, 88–90, 93–99, 101–4
   See also morals, morality
Eucken, Walter, xxii, xxv, xxvii
   Freiburg School, xxix–xxx
   interventionism, xxxi–xxxii
Europe, xv, 144, 234
   Christianity, 11, 165n24, 166
   heritage, 164–67
   intellectuals, 91–92
   liberalism, 144–45n4, 166
European integration, xxi–xxiii, xxxiii, 162–64, 165–67
European Union, xxxiii
expansionism, 140–41
exploitation, 39–40, 41, 42–43

families, 16, 41, 151, 247
   destruction of, 73, 86–87, 142, 254, 257n28
   support of, 12–13, 96, 100
Ferrero, Guglielmo, 190
forecasting, economic, 172–77
foreign trade, 48, 105, 131, 231
forgotten men, 70, 131
France, xxiii, 130, 254
   French Revolution, 16, 141–43, 145n5
Frankfurt School, xxix
freedom, liberty, xxix, 66–67, 121–23
   centrism and, 153–54
   Christianity and, xi, 188, 189–90

collectivism, 6–8
competition, 44, 149
decentralization, 152–53
economic order, 78–79
moral aristocrats, 110–11
political, 78–79
private ownership, 66–67, 68–69
socialism, 11–13, 155–56
spiritual, 78–79
standard of living and, 84–85
state and, 190–91
subordination, 155–56
Western ideal, 190–91
free market, economy, 10–12
law and, 13–14, 53, 102
Freiburg School, xvii, xxix–xxx, 188n2
French Revolution, 16, 141–43, 145n5
Freud, Sigmund, 84
full employment, 141, 158, 173, 226, 230, 232

Galbraith, John Kenneth, 109
Geneva, xx–xxi, xxii
German Historical School, xxvi, xviii–xix, xxv
Germany, xv, 8, 120, 144n4
   Bismarck, Otto von, xxxiii, 4
   Christian Democratic party, 144n4, 188
   economy, 63–64, 67, 103n43, 138, 157, 173–74, 213, 228
   Federal Republic, xxii–xxiii
   National Socialism, xix, xxi, xxiii, xxviii, 57
   Nazis, Third Reich, 8, 188
   Weimar Republic, xix, xxv–xxvii, xxxii–xxxiii

Subject Index

Goethe, Johann, 110, 148, 152, 170, 217
Faust, 19, 39, 99–100n45, 102, 140, 208
goods, economic, 19–23, 27–28
  free, 27–30
  luxury, 21, 31–32, 33, 265
  scarcity, 27–28, 33–34, 37–39, 271
  value, 270–72
Great Britain. *See* England
Great Depression, the, xix, xxvii–xxvii, 10, 52, 173, 229, 232
  secondary, xxvi–xxviii
Greeks, ancient, 95–96, 189–91, 245

Hayekians, xxxiv, xxxv
Hayek, Friedrich, vii, xx, xxi, xxiv, xxviii–xxix, 227
  interventionism, xxvi–xxvii, xxxi
  Road to Serfdom, xxi, xxviii–xxix
  Röpke, Wilhelm and, xxvi, xxvii, xxix–xxx, xxxi–xxxii, xxxv
  social philosophy, xxix–xxx
Heine, Heinrich, 94, 95
heteronomy, 245–47
Hildebrand, Bruno, 263–64
human dignity, xi, 6, 84, 108, 188, 189–90
  materialism and, 72–73, 83–84
  work, 89–91
humanism, 11–12, 17, 41
human nature, 12–14, 62–63, 64n2, 174–75, 177–78
  consumption, 73–75, 85
  self-interest, 12–14, 219–20
  social philosophy, 146–47

human relations, 154–55
  dependent wage earners, 155–61, 163
  subordination, 143, 154–58, 160
Hume, David, 209, 220

ideologies, 244–45
  Marxist, Communist, 74, 145n4, 242, 248
  socialism, 11–13
immanentism, liberal, 101, 103n46, 105
imperial exploitation, 42–43
income, distribution of, 31–32, 56
  money, 74–75, 81, 129
  wealth, redistribution of, 31–32
independence, 21, 68–69, 105, 122
  decentralization, 143, 151–52
  individuals, 155–58, 160–61
  institutions, 132–33, 141–43
India, 87
individualism, 61, 103n46, 132, 144, 196–97
inflation, 103n46, 129, 130–32, 137–38, 231–33
  anti-inflationism, 140–41
  deflation and, 138–40
  employment, full, 158, 173, 234–35
  German, xxvi, 213, 253, 254
  hyperinflation, xxv–xxvi, 254
  Keynesian theory, 234–38
installment buying, 72–74, 76n12, 120–21
intellectuals, 91–92
interest, 24, 277–78
interest, pressure groups, 124–29

Subject Index

international economy, 5, 19–23, 163, 199, 211, 220, 264–65
   centralization, 162–67
   disintegration, 254–55
   ethics, 103–4
   foreign trade, 48, 105, 131, 231
   international order, 9–10
   interventionism, xxv–xxviii, 182–85
   market economy and, xxxi–xxxii, 195
Islam, Muslim world, 86, 87
Istanbul, xix
Italy, 144n4, 193

Jacobins, 16, 141–43, 145n5
Japan, 86, 87, 174
Jefferson, Thomas, 111n53
Johnson, Samuel, 89, 114–15, 118
judgments, value, xxix, 248–49, 251–52
   anthropological facts, 255–58
   classes, 242–43, 255

Kant, Immanuel, 259
Keynes, John Maynard, xix, 72, 83n23, 131, 140, 207, 208, 218
   aggregates, 228–30
   dehumanization, 168n26, 218
   interventionism, xxvi–xxviii
Keynesian theory, 173, 214, 220, 225–28, 230–34
   inflation, 234–38
   macroeconomics, new economics, 168, 174, 214–15, 220–21, 225–28
Knight, Frank H., 179–80, 219, 220, 226–27

laissez-faire, 56, 195, 196, 272
Lausanne school, theory, 269–70, 273
law, xxx, 13–14, 53, 102
League of Nations, 10
Leibniz, Gottfried Wilhelm, 212
Lenin, Vladimir, 123
liberalism, xxxiii, 5, 10–11, 63, 144, 148–49, 240–41
   American, xxiv, 144–45
   Catholic, 191–93, 199
   Christianity and, 189–91
   classical, xi, 56
   double sense, 189–91
   European, 144–45n4, 166
   immanentism, 101, 103n46, 105
   neo-liberalism, xx, 63, 194–95
   ordoliberalism, xv–xviii, xxii, xxvii, xxx, xxxii–xxxiii, xxxv
   progressivism, 16–17
   social philosophy, xxx–xxxii, 187–88
   universal, 191–92
   utilitarianism, 101–2
Lichtenberg, Georg Christoph, 63
Lippmann, Walter, xxviii, 131, 234
Lutheran, Lutheranism, xxxiii
luxury goods, 21, 31–32, 33, 265

Macaulay, Lord Thomas Babington, 82–83
Malthus, Thomas Robert, 213, 270
marginal utility, 26–33, 34–35, 250, 267–73
   costs, 277–79
   diminishing, 29–30

Subject Index

market economy, x, xxxiv, 14, 148
  asymmetry, 118–24
  bourgeois, 70–73
  collectivism and, 156–57, 194–95, 205–6
  competition, 67–69
  costs, 277–79
  ethical foundations, 88–90, 93–99, 101–4
  freedom, 66–67
  interventionism, xxxi–xxxii, 195
  socialist market economy, xxii–xxiii, 65–66, 67
  social order and, 61–63, 65–66, 194
Marx, Karl, Marxism, 59, 70, 89, 103n46, 146n5, 271–72
  capitalism and, 42–43n4
  labor theory, 271, 277
  philosophy, ideology, 244, 248
mass democracy, 16, 124–25, 129–31, 133–35, 138, 238
mass opinions, 129–31
mass society, 15–16, 71–72, 111
materialism, 73–75, 80, 81–85, 87, 89–90, 248
  human dignity, 72–73, 83–84
mathematics, economic, 168–72, 214–18, 230–31
  forecasting, 172–77
  models, 168, 177–78, 215, 236–37, 273, 269–70
  statistics, 130, 146, 168, 171, 173, 175, 176–77
medical profession, 40, 50, 106–7, 155–56
merchants, 40, 90–91, 97, 179
Middle Ages, 30, 41, 227, 263–65
militarism, 6–7
Mill, John Stuart, 153–54

Mises, Ludwig von, xx, xxv–xxvi, xxxi, 206, 215n12, 268
models, 168, 177–78, 215, 236–37, 269–70, 273
money, monetary, 24–25, 141, 252–53
  earning, 89–90
  income, 74–75, 81, 129
  purchasing power, 22, 56, 173
  value of, 71, 131, 275
monopolies, 39–40, 81, 107, 148, 195, 245
  occupational, 158–59
Montesquieu, Baron de, Charles Louis de Secondat, 94–95, 126–27, 142, 153–54, 165, 259–60
Mont Pèlerin Society, xi, xxii, xxiv, 187–89
moralism, 77, 98, 102, 106, 147
morals, morality, vii–viii, 14–15, 37–44, 64n2, 77, 275–76
  aristocrats, moral, xxxii, 110–14, 116–18, 151
  capitalism, 98–99
  choice, 98–99
  Christianity, 41, 96–97
  collectivist economy, 98–99
  socialism, 12–13
  traditions, 110, 112
  See also ethics
moral science, economics as, 169–71, 215–19, 248–49

nationalism, 4–5, 8
National Socialism, xix, xxi, xxiii, xxviii, 57
natural sciences, 63n1, 169–70, 213–14, 216, 246, 249–50n18
Nazis, Third Reich, 8, 188
neo-liberalism, xx, 63, 194–95

287

Nietzsche, Friedrich, 260, 261
nobilitas naturalis, xxxii, 110–14
  scientists, 114–18
  See also aristocrats, moral
nosology, social, 252–53

opportunity, equality of, 148–51
order, 9–10, 19–23, 180
  economic, 63–64, 77–80
  international, 9–10
  social, 61–63, 65–66, 194
ordoliberalism, xv–xviii, xxii, xxvii, xxx, xxxv
  religion and, xxxii–xxxiii
Ortega y Gasset, José, 167, 218–19, 221n19, 222, 260

Pascal, Blaise, 83–84, 93, 98
pathology, of society, 252–55, 256–57
patronage, 113–14
philosophy, economics and, 201–2
  Catholic social, 196–97
  Marxist, 244, 248
  social, xxxiii, 145–48, 150–51, 191–93, 194, 198
physics, 207, 208, 215, 225–26, 227
Picasso, Pablo, 168n26, 218
Pius XI, Pope, xi
pluralism, 121–23, 125–28
political economy, xxiv–xxviii, 8
Popper, Karl, xxviii–xxix
population growth, 80, 140, 173
positivism, 240, 242, 251
power, 81, 130–33
  centralization, 155–56
  purchasing, 22, 56, 173
  state, 7–8, 195–96

prices, 25–26, 28, 30, 168, 211, 271–72
  controls, fixed, 25–26, 51–52, 54–55
  economic equilibrium, 49–50, 51–53, 55–57, 58–59
  mechanism, 65, 206, 214
private ownership, 68–70, 75, 76n12, 105
  freedom and, 66–67, 68–69
  property, 13, 16
privilege, 39, 112–14, 115, 130, 133n73, 149n8, 178
production, 54
  costs of, 45–48, 55–56, 270–72, 277
  productivity, cult of, 83–85
profit, 81, 132, 210, 278
  and loss, 100–101, 179–80
  as motivation, 94, 99, 122–23
progressivism, 16–17, 61, 140–44, 166
proletarianism, proletarianization, 71–72, 73, 75, 85, 197–98
property, 13, 16, 197. *See also* private ownership
Protestants, 18, 188
  Calvinism, 41n3, 97n42
Prussia, Prussian, xxxiii, 4, 30, 185n42
purchasing power, 22, 56, 173

Quadragesimo Anno, xi, 192–99

radicalism, 17, 89, 112, 226
rationalism, 258–60
  scholastic, 258–59
  social, 65–66, 69–70, 74–76, 80–83, 146–47

Subject Index

rationing, 40, 50, 51–52, 53–54
reciprocity, 38–39, 43–44
relationships, 209–12
relativism, 240–43, 245, 246–49, 250, 251, 254, 255–61
  axiological, 242–43, 247–48
religion, viii, xxxii–xxxiii, 14, 17
rent controls, 52, 76n12, 129–30, 220
Ricardo, David, Ricardians, xxv, 213, 220, 270
rich, the, wealth, 31–32, 112–14
Röpke, Wilhelm, vii–ix, xi–xiii, xvii–xxiv, xxxiii–xxxv
  ordoliberalism, xvi–xviii
  political economy, xxiv–xxviii
  social philosophy, xxviii–xxxiii
Rousseau, Jean-Jacques, 145n5, 190, 259n33, 260
Russia, xxxii, 6. *See also* Communism; Soviet Union

saving, 31–32, 72, 229, 231, 232, 278
Say, Jean-Baptiste, 103n46, 104, 270
scarcity, 27–28, 33–34
  of goods, 27–28, 33–34, 37–39, 271
  production, costs of, 45–48
  struggle against, 37–39
Schliemann, Heinrich, 99, 275–76
scholastic rationalism, 258–59
science, sciences, 246–47
  economics as, xii, 201–2, 203–5, 206–7
  economics as moral, 169–71, 215–19, 248–49
  heteronomy, 245–47
  natural, 63n1, 169–70, 213–14, 216, 246, 249–50n18
  objectivity, autonomy, 240, 246–47
  politicalization, 243–44, 245–46, 247–48
  truth and, 243–44, 245
  value judgments, 248–49, 251–52
self-interest, 93–94, 96, 97–100, 101–2, 116
human nature, 12–14, 219–20
Shakespeare, William, 28, 97, 113, 145, 179
Siegfried, André, 83–84
Small Is Beautiful, xxxii, xxxiv–xxxv. *See also* decentralization
small communities (*Gemeinschaft*), xxxv, 15–16
large societies (*Gesellschaft*), xxxv
Smith, Adam, 63, 97, 118, 206–7n3, 209, 233, 270
socialism, 4–5, 144
  capitalism and, 4–5, 9
  Christianity and, 196–97
  collectivism, 6–8
  freedom, 11–13, 155–56
  historical liberalism, 10–11
  ideology, 11–13
  immorality, 12–13
  market economy, xxii–xxiii, 65–66, 67
  national, 5–6
  National Socialism, xix, xxi, xxiii, xxviii, 57
  state power, 7–8
social justice, 54, 59, 76n12, 113, 147

289

Subject Index

social philosophy, xxviii–xxxiii
  Catholic, xxxiii, 191–93, 194, 198
  centralization, 145–48
  conservatism, 140–44
  decentralization, 145–48, 150–51
  Hayek, Friedrich, xxix–xxx
  Jacobins, 141–43
  liberal, 187–88
  progressivism, 140–44
  socialism, 11–13
social rationalism, 65–66, 69–70, 74–75, 76
  centrists, 146–47
  economism, 80–83
society, 76–79, 203–5
  disintegration, 85–87, 88, 254–55
  mass, 15–16, 71–72, 111
  pathology, 252–55, 256–57
soldiers, 6–7, 34, 41
Solomon, 212, 222
Soviet Union, 10n3, 52, 56, 105
  queue system, 49–50
  See also Communism; Russia
special interests, pressure groups, 124–29, 195
spirit of the age, economic, 40–41, 42–44
standard of living, 31–33, 74–75, 76, 82–85
  Communism, 85–88
state, the, 190
  collective needs, 57–59
  freedom and, 190–91
  pharaonic spirit, 190–91
  power of, 7–8, 195–96
  welfare, 13, 100, 113–14, 157, 163, 250
statistics, 130, 146, 168, 171, 173, 175, 176–77

subordination, 143, 154–58, 160
Switzerland, xxiii, 8–9, 144n4, 162n15

taxation, 47, 146n5, 161
  public finance, 57–59
  technology, 161–62n15
Tito, Josip Broz, 65, 67
Tocqueville, Alexis de, 112n54, 133n73, 149–50, 191–92, 260
totalitarianism, 10, 16, 85–86, 122, 245
  centralization and, 152–54
  Christianity and, 188, 198
  trade unions, 159, 102–3, 129, 158–60
traditions, 16, 61, 71, 87–88
  moral, 110, 112
truth, 212
  dignity of, 115–17
  science and, 243–44, 245
tyranny, 98–99, 155

underdeveloped countries, 86–88, 96
United Nations, 162, 233
  League of Nations, 10
United States, 31, 53, 149–50n8, 159, 173, 227, 237
  business, 44, 53, 91, 167
  capitalism, 91–92
  economists, xx, xxiv, xxviii, xxxi, 137–38, 173, 187, 270
  intellectuals, 91–92
  international economics, 211, 220
  Keynesian economics, 227–28
  liberals, liberalism, xxiv, 144–45n4
  opportunity, equality of, 149–51
  Tocqueville, Alexis de, 149–50

290

Subject Index

universalism, 151–52, 191–92
utilitarianism, 82–84, 101–2, 103n46, 132–33
utility, 28–29
  marginal, 26–33, 34–35, 250, 267–73

Voltaire, 170, 217

wealth, 31–32, 112–14
Weber, Max, xxix, 41n3, 241
welfare state, 13, 100, 113–14, 157, 163, 250
Westernization, 88, 96
West, Western civilization, xxxiv, 75, 275
  Cold War, 10, 85–87, 164
  conservatism, 140–41
  culture, values, xxx–xxxi, 12, 189–91, 260
  dependent labor, 159–60
  East-West trade, 121–24
  economic order, 63–64
  inflation, 129, 131
  threats to, xvii–xviii, xix, xxvi, xxviii
World War I, 1–3, 6–8
  impact of, vii–viii, 3–5, 213
World War II, 9, 173
  price controls, 51, 52
  rationing, 53–54

Yugoslavia, 65, 67

291

Printed in the USA
CPSIA information can be obtained
at www.ICGtesting.com
LVHW012025210923
758371LV00005B/24